Brothers, Sing On!

Brothers, Sing On!

My Half-Century Around the World with the Penn Glee Club

BRUCE MONTGOMERY

University of Pennsylvania Press
Philadelphia

10   9   8   7   6   5   4   3   2   1

PUBLISHED BY
University of Pennsylvania Press
Philadelphia, Pennsylvania 19104-4011

Text design and composition by Ellen Beeler

LIBRARY OF CONGRESS CATALOGING-IN-PUBLICATION DATA

Montgomery, Bruce, 1927–
    Brothers, sing on! : my half-century around the world with the Penn Glee Club /
Bruce Montgomery.
        p. cm.
    ISBN-13: 978-0-8122-3856-3 (alk. paper)
    ISBN-10: 0-8122-3856-7 (alk. paper)
    1. Montgomery, Bruce, 1927–. 2. University of Pennsylvania. Glee club—History.
3. Men's choral societies—Pennsylvania—Philadelphia—History. I. Title.
ML28.P5 U94 2005
782.8'06—dc22   2005041828

to

THE UNIVERSITY OF PENNSYLVANIA

its Administrators

its Faculty

its Staff

its Alumni

its Students

and most particularly to

THE PENN GLEE CLUB

all of whom afforded me the

fifty happiest years imaginable

1950–2000

Contents

Prelude

I'm reasonably assured of about seventeen people who will buy this book if they are told it's my autobiography. The number does not include my large and loyal family. They assume I'll give them complimentary inscribed copies for Christmas.

But the truth, of course, is that this is *not* my autobiography. The fact that virtually every event described is one in which I played a major role would lend some credence to the rumor. But if it is a biography at all, it is that of a group: the saga of the nearly fifty years that it was my amazing good fortune to direct the University of Pennsylvania Glee Club through thirty countries on five continents.

It is very possible that I would have decided to set down these many experiences somewhere along the way. I have threatened to do so for some time. But, after hearing me recount some of them in an informal lecture at Germantown Friends School on Alumni Day 2000, my GFS classmate Edward Rosen has prodded me into taking action and actually doing it. Thanks, Ed. It's been a rewarding excursion into years of fabulous memories with marvelous companions.

Many of those companions know well and participated actively in some of these recollections. But college students, for the most part, have a four-year limit to their undergraduate journeys. For forty-four years I was the lone constant who went the distance with the Penn Glee Club, and there were so many marvelous experiences and fabulous people crisscrossing during that time that they simply had to be put down in one place before they were lost. This, then, is that place. The Penn Glee Club has existed for nearly half the life of the university; I was its director for nearly one-third of that time.

Through good portions of the five decades I worked at Penn, it was my great joy to direct and work with numerous other student groups as well—particularly the Penn Singers, the Penn Players, the Marching Band, the Concert Band, the Penn Pipers, the Mask & Wig Club, the short-lived Apollo Club (for those who didn't quite make the Glee Club), the Pennguinettes (a fine women's synchro-swimming team), and the University Symphony Orchestra, among others, to say nothing of the legions of students with whom I worked individually.

This volume is the story of the fabulous students with whom I spent my fifty years at Penn—and a little beyond. But that experience did not just spring full-blown like the legendary birth of Venus. Many steps of learning, hard work, instruction, and interrelationships along the road contributed to and prepared the way for those years.

This book, therefore, must include some of the early stepping stones that led me to the life I have so enjoyed. And so, I apologize ahead of time for so many personal references that are required to begin and fill out the story.

I'm certain that the first four years of my life contained numerous marvelous and colorful experiences, but since I don't remember any of them you are spared the details. I must launch directly to the age of five and *Trial by Jury* and "The Sea" and *The King of Arabia*. So, intrepid readers, press on.

OK, confess now. Isn't this your idea of what a college glee club looks like?
Well, it's the University of Pennsylvania Glee Club in 1966 singing the
wonderful Welsh song "Men of Harlech." But in addition to stand-up
singing, the Penn men put on a real show with plots, many costume
changes, dialogue, and a lot of athletic dancing.

A sailor's hornpipe was danced in several glee club shows. This one was in 1977.

Rich Gusick and Marvin Lyon dueled before their astonished onlookers in *Jack Bean Nimble* in 1989.

Sporting huge pink satin bow ties and vests, in 1974 the club performed an intricate minstrel show routine to a medley of Stephen Foster songs.

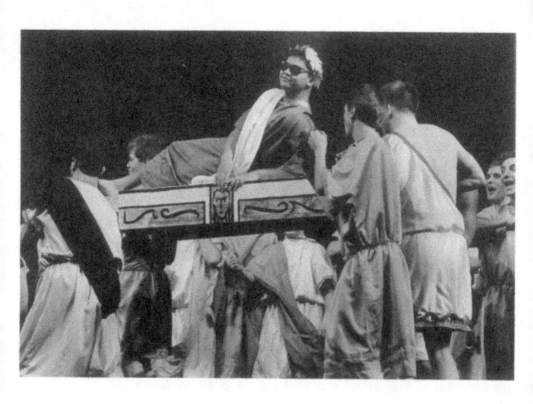

Joey Sayson, a fast-talking, mod Julius Caesar, was carried in on a gold litter in *Roman in the Gloamin'* in 1989.

We spared little expense in costuming the club for our shows—
this time in 1981's *Double Take*. Did you ever price forty white cutaways?

Some costumes, of course, were less expensive. Here Jack Weiss, Stu Morse, Mark Rubino, Mike Drosner, and Bob Smith hammed it up in "King Tut" in *The Magus* in 1979. Photo by Kenneth Kirshenbaum.

In a song from *Casino* in 1979, we donned striped blazers and straw hats for a song from the "Gay '90s." Photo by Kenneth Kirshenbaum.

David Goldberg rallied his Arthurian troops in *Extravagancelot* in 1977.

Phil Schroeder as Dr. Watson and George Pologeorgis as Sherlock Holmes made a fine duo in *Holmes Sweet Holmes (or Watson a Name?)* in 1986.

Pete McLaughlin, Mike Fradkin, Mark Rubino, Tom Fosnocht, and Stu Morse
were the poster boys for *Extravagancelot* in 1977.

The big tap-dance is a finale staple of the club's performances.
This one was in 1979. Photo by Kenneth Kirshenbaum.

Bob Holt, Peter Berg, Larry Turns, Brian Percival, Bill Tost, and Ken Nichols displayed their beefcake on the beach at San Juan, Puerto Rico, in 1959.

One of the first television shows we did was for the popular Philadelphia personality Marciarose in 1957. In this, we traced the history of collegiate singing from the students of Heidelberg to the present. Here some of the guys are in traditional Heidelberg uniforms to sing an old drinking song. Jules Schick Photography.

Members of the Penn Glee Club posed with Pablo Casals in 1959 after he invited us to his home in San Juan to make music together.

Bob Taylor posed at Cape May Point, New Jersey, for the signature
photograph that appeared on the program cover and many ads
for the world premiere of *Spindrift* in 1963.

Famed Broadway producer-director Harold Prince discussed *Spindrift*
with me in 1963. Hal, in town with one of his own shows, came to
each of our performances. Jules Schick Photography.

Each season used to begin with the Club as the guests of the Inn at Buck Hill Falls in the Pocono Mountains. In addition to rehearsing and putting on a full show in the Inn's fine theater, we always found time to relax around the swimming pool. Jules Schick Photography.

But let's start at the beginning:

My sister Connie and I waited in the wings for a second act entrance in Gilbert and Sullivan's *The Gondoliers* in 1939. Photo by Herbert Gehr for *Life*.

The Bethany Oratorio Society played a major role in the festive 1945 celebration
of the Salvation Army's 80th anniversary. Here we're positioned to sing,
accompanied by the Kansas City Philharmonic.

Wayne Holmstrom led the company in "Candy Store" from *If This Is New York* in 1950—my first full-length musical.

The PitchPipers as we appeared on the Arthur Godfrey show. Left to right: Carol Anderson, Bruce Montgomery, Wayne Holmstrom, and LaRue Olson. Talk about your clean-cut all-American boys!

Brothers, Sing On!

Words after the Swedish original by
Herbert Dalmas

Music by
Edvard Grieg

Come and let our swelling song
Mount like the whirling wind
As it meets our singing throng
So blithe of heart and mind.
Care and sorrow now be gone,
Brothers in song, sing on!
Brothers, sing on,
Sing on!

Youth is a wand'ring troubador
Sailing the singing breeze,
Wooing a maid on a distant shore
Over the tossing seas;
Steering by the stars above.
His vessel a song of love,
Brothers, sing on,
Sing on!

Errant minstrels, thus we greet you,
List' to our voices strong;
With glad and open hearts we meet you
In our festival of song.
Care and sorrow now be gone,
Brothers in song, sing on!
Brothers, sing on,
Sing on!

Do You Care Where You Go?

E VERY BOOK must begin somewhere, and I suppose my grand debut on the stage of Philadelphia's great opera house, the Academy of Music, is as good a place to start as any. It probably seems bizarre to most people that a five-year-old should be offered—and accept—a role in an opera by Sir William S. Gilbert and Sir Arthur Sullivan, but that's how it all began with me. Gilbert & Sullivan will be a recurring theme throughout this book, as I have continued to pursue my interest, fascination, and love of their works throughout my life.

It should be mentioned at the outset that my father, James Montgomery, was an opera singer by profession. Along with his other roles, to my knowledge he was the only singer of his day to have performed the tenor lead in all thirteen extant G&S operas. Many were the times that I had stood at his elbow in his dressing room in one theater or another and watched him make up to do a handsome young Nanki-Poo in *The Mikado* or an amorous Alfredo in *La Traviata* or an ancient Spalanzani in *The Tales of Hoffmann* or a dashing Don José in *Carmen* or a freckled simpleton Wenzel in *The Bartered Bride*. And my mother, Constance, would have been an opera singer had she not elected instead to raise a family. Some of my earliest recollections are of my mother and father singing opera's great soprano-tenor duets. Little wonder, then, that with burnt-match-drawn eyebrows this stagestruck second son went about play-acting much of the time to impress others or simply to amuse himself.

The Savoy Company was going to present a Gilbert & Sullivan double bill of *Trial By Jury* and *The Sorcerer*, directed by Pacie Ripple, a talented Englishman well versed in these immortal works. He was the only person I have ever known who actually knew and worked with and was directed by Gilbert himself. Pacie remembered that in the first revival of *Trial by Jury*, Gilbert had added the character of a small boy to interrupt the proceedings in the courtroom by throwing a large ball from the stage left spectators' chorus and then chasing after it. My father would be singing the role of Edwin in *Trial* and guess who was signed to play the part of the kid. The run went without a hitch and this young lad was bitten by the theater bug for life. I never really did determine if this brat was considered typecasting.

At that time my grandparents, the Winfield Scott Peirsols, had a year-round home on Swarthmore Avenue in Ventnor, a southern suburb of Atlantic City. Granddaddy, whom I idolized, had been secretary-treasurer of the Bell Telephone Company and had known Alexander Graham Bell personally. We often went to visit them for a few days or a week. On one such visit, my brother Jimmie, my sister Connie, and I had spent a full day playing on the beach and reveling in the sea air. Upon returning to the house, I promptly sat down at the piano and played my first musical composition "The Sea." I had begun piano lessons at the age of four so the task at hand was relieved of the tensions and frustrations that would have developed had I not already been familiar with the instrument. This first composition was age five. Mozart it wasn't. But just for fun, I quoted "The Sea" in its entirety two times in shows that I wrote in the 1960s and '70s.

We also had a cottage at the shore. In the 1930s, 129 East Myrtle Road in Wildwood Crest, New Jersey, was on the second block from the beach to the east and the third-from-the-last street to the south. From there on, it was an unbroken stretch of dunes and tall grass all the way to the channel over to Cape May. Jimmie and I often would steal away, with no danger to civilization, and challenge each other to target practice with our .22 caliber rifle. Today that same stretch is a succession of homes, motels, nightclubs, and restaurants. I rather think I liked it better the old way.

Our house was blessed with a huge open porch that went all the way across the front and halfway up the east side. My unsuspecting mother and father stepped out for a pleasant afternoon of sitting on the porch one July day in 1934, only to find it crowded with total strangers who had seen a flyer and paid a penny apiece to see the world premiere of the latest musical extravaganza, *The King of Arabia*. The show naturally boasted book, lyrics, and music by me. It also starred and was produced and directed by the author. My career of self-aggrandizement had begun.

The show boasted at least three deathless lines that are still quoted quite regularly in our family. My sister Connie played the role of a Japanese servant—she owned a little pink kimono—whose entire part consisted of entering from down right, crossing the stage, and exiting down left as the King sang, "Here she comes and there she goes. I hope she will be back an-o-o-o-ther day." The extended vowel was to accommodate a highly dramatic vocal trill.

Marie Louise Vanneman, playing the part of a mail carrier, delivered a message from a rival king that read, in part: "You are invited to a war. If you do not accept you will become lame." After an impassioned speech proclaiming his odium of war, the King emphatically refused the invitation and, in one of the most ostentatious pratfalls in the history of theater, promptly collapsed to the floor, thoroughly incapacitated. He then dragged himself over to the throne and delivered what proved to be a highly successful prayer. The prayer was silent. The audience was privy only to an unobstructed view of the King's rear end. Following the prayer, the King rose slowly, tested his legs for whatever maneuverability had been restored, and walked unencumbered while delivering the breathless line "Golly! That was quick work!" In our family, that line ranks right up there with "To be or not to be." Mother and Dad remained on the porch to see the entire performance. I probably had the gall to charge them admission. *The King of Arabia* continued to play all summer and even enjoyed a revival the following year.

All this detailed description is not from a remarkable memory. My mother taught me to write so that I could give a complete libretto to my father for Christmas. And he in turn made a sixteen-millimeter film of the entire show. I still own both. So there it is, fully documented to haunt me for the rest of my life.

In 1935, the Philadelphia Orchestra Opera Company staged a lavish production of Gilbert & Sullivan's *The Mikado* at the Robin Hood Dell, the large open-air theater in Fairmount Park, which was then their summer home. My father was hired to play Nanki-Poo, and they sought a young boy to play the swordbearer for Ko-Ko. Following my legendary stellar performances in *Trial by Jury* and *The King of Arabia*, it was only natural that I should be hired for the run.

It was the first paycheck I ever received, and I am reasonably certain that I was told to bank the major portion of it, but I also was permitted the childish joy of blowing some of it on Necco Wafers and a blue Kodak Brownie box camera. In the several moves during my long life, I have thrown out tons of the objects one accumulates. But I simply couldn't bring myself to dispose of my first professional purchase. The Kodak Brownie has survived all moves and now resides in a drawer of the desk on which I wrote this manuscript.

After *The Mikado*, my theatrical life continued with a 1936 production of Gilbert & Sullivan's penultimate opera, *Utopia, Limited*. My sister Connie and I were cast as pages to the royal princesses. This may not sound terribly challenging, but for Connie it was a substantial increase over her walk-across in *The King of Arabia*. For me, this was followed by a triumphant stint as the Drummer Boy in *The Gondoliers*. The most memorable facet of this production for me was that it was the first time I appeared in a photo in *Life* magazine. So did Connie—a page once again.

The greatest event of 1938 was the birth of another sister, Elizabeth. Liz was a ham from the very start and would become a marvelous soprano, lively companion, and treasured costar for me, sharing my musical and theatrical passions to the point of our performing in parallel for life.

Appearing in *Life* gave new impetus to my journalistic bent. My all-time best friend, Herb Middleton, and I began a highly successful venture into publishing in 1939. We both lived on Wellesley Road in Mount Airy, and the *Wellesley Road News* was a monthly that we would write, lay out, and mimeograph downtown at Herbie's dad's office, the John Middleton Tobacco Company. Mr. Middleton was given the generous option of either receiving a free ad in the paper or being paid five dollars for the use of his equipment and materials—a bargain for us even in 1936! But we also gained a modicum of business sense from it. The *Wellesley Road News* became such a hot item that my mother had to make some shoulder-strap cloth bags (they were green), and we hired our sisters Connie and Anne and neighbors Eddie Koch and Bobby Bast to help deliver the issues each month. Our subscription list extended far beyond Wellesley Road to Durham Street, Mount Airy Avenue, Glen Echo Road, and even a few customers on Lincoln Drive. We were overnight tycoons.

The Gondoliers proved to be the last time that I could handle the "little boy" roles in G&S, as I had grown too tall for them. Therefore, my theatrical and musical activities lay fallow for a while. Until high school, to be precise. I attended Germantown Friends School from kindergarten on and was active in music and even a grammar school play or two. But any real concentration came about in ninth grade. For it was then, in September 1941, that I met Mary Brewer and my life would never be the same again.

Mary Brewer had recently been hired to be the head of the GFS music department and early in her first semester she hosted an assembly program during which she was determined to learn what the students knew of music. The initial portion of her program took the form of a quiz. She led off with a tough question.

"What symphony begins with a bassoon solo?"

My right elbow rose very slightly, very tentatively. As a ninth-grader I was sitting all the way at the rear of the hall. Such esoteric questions were intended, of course, for seniors. Not one stirred. Coleman Webster, a classmate sitting next to me, put his palm under my quivering elbow and shot my hand into the air. Miss Brewer was so relieved to see a response that she called out an order to the rear of the hall.

"Stand up, young man."

I stood and ventured my answer. "I believe it's Tchaikovsky's Sixth," I said.

"Young man, I want to see you immediately after this program," she said with a broad, toothy grin.

I introduced myself at the end of the assembly and thus began a friendship that continued until the day she died in 1998.

I was becoming more and more interested in composing and wanted to begin serious study of composition, harmony, and counterpoint. There were several teachers fully capable of teaching me, but they could not fit it into their busy schedules. GFS had a remarkable policy that it should offer any course if there was a genuine need for it. I'm sure someone would have been hired to teach Swahili if a student truly wished to learn it. In my case, they hired Alfred Mann to come out twice a week from the Curtis Institute of Music in Philadelphia to give me private lessons during my junior and senior years.

I began composing for the A Cappella Choir, and in my senior year Mary chose me to be student conductor. She even permitted me to select a work that I would train and then conduct in performance. In my youthful enthusiasm and true to the "fools rush in" syndrome, I selected a relatively new work: Randall Thompson's "Alleluia." Composed for the opening of the Boston Symphony Orchestra's new summer home at Tanglewood in 1940, "Alleluia" is one of the great American choral works of the twentieth century. It became one of my all-time favorite pieces to conduct—which I still do frequently. As a result of my writing to Dr. Thompson to tell him of the thrill of conducting his wonderful work, I began what turned out to be another lifelong friendship, voluminous correspondence with him, and the opportunity to claim him as a valued mentor. Far more will follow in later chapters.

Another of the special events for me during this period was being hired for a job that scarcely exists today: summer stock. During the summer of 1944, I was the juvenile lead in the company at Buck Hill Falls in the beautiful Pocono Mountains of Pennsylvania.

My grandfather, Neil Robert Montgomery, had a marvelous cottage in Buck Hill, where I had enjoyed many a visit over the summers. Now it became an ideal place to hang out and learn my lines for each play. My grandmother became adept at throwing cue lines—and the fringe benefit of spectacular pot luck lunches added to the appeal.

The exciting if exhausting season consisted of a new play each week: rehearse the next week's play all day and perform the current one each night. Two pleasant musical diversions that summer were composing a sweeping Viennese waltz, "Danubia," for S. N. Behrman's *Biography* and meeting three utterly fascinating refugees from the war in Spain. Marta and Mariuka Obregon and their brother Mauricio, from Barcelona, became dear friends and even prompted my first mature piano composition, Prelude No. 1 in C minor. It really is astonishing what one's brash and youthful enthusiasm can accomplish with two senoritas for inspiration.

Prelude No. 2 in E-flat minor came along in the winter of 1945. I remember premiering it in a morning assembly program at school—but that's all I remember. I don't recall its having been inspired by anything or inspiring anyone else in turn!

Shortly after my graduation from Germantown Friends in 1945, World War II ended, on August 15, and I was to enter Yale University. My godfather, Chandler Cudlipp, who lived with his wife in Wilton, Connecticut, invited me to come up one weekend to visit and see where I was to spend my next four years. When we walked through the New Haven campus on Friday, August 24, I found that workers were installing double-deck bunks all over the floor of a gymnasium. Yale had already accepted a full student body when, with the end of the war, veterans who had begun their college careers prior to the conflict were being let out as rapidly as possible to continue their education. I remarked to Uncle Chan that this was not the atmosphere in which to study painting and music composition, both of which require substantial individual criticism. He agreed and suggested that we go see his friend the dean.

I repeated my concern to the dean, who also agreed and suggested that I go elsewhere for two years and then transfer to Yale for my final two. He felt certain that by that time the university would weed out many of the students and be back to normal. My immediate reply was that it was now about two weeks before school was to start.

"Who would take me on such short notice whose credits you would accept two years from now?" I asked.

"Do you care where you go?"

"Not so long as you assure me it's a great place with great professors and you'll accept all my work from there in two years."

With that, he picked up the telephone and called his friend Emory Lindquist, president of Bethany College in Lindsborg, Kansas. *Kansas!* My only knowledge of Kansas—other than that's where you end up when you click red shoes together—was from riding through it on a train in 1941 and declaring it the flattest, most monotonous place I'd ever seen and the last place on earth in which I'd ever have any interest. On the other hand, I did know of Bethany College, as my father had twice been hired as tenor soloist for its internationally acclaimed Messiah Festival held each Holy Week.

The only train west that stopped in Lindsborg was on the Missouri Pacific Railway, and it stopped only at 2:00 A.M. So, very early on the morning of Friday, September 7, 1945, I stepped for the first time into my new life in Lindsborg, Kansas. So early in the morning, rather than head for the college I checked into the Carlton Hotel and spent a sleepless night wondering how this born-and-bred Easterner would fare on the plains. My walk through town after breakfast answered my question.

As I headed north on Main Street, I passed a man who wore white coveralls while he swept the street gutter. As his task progressed he was softly singing "The Trumpet Shall Sound" from Handel's *Messiah*. When I reached Old Main, the building where I would be living, I was astonished to hear a plasterer cheerfully plying his craft while keeping time with "Lord God of Abraham" from Mendelssohn's *Elijah*. These definitely were not your everyday laborers in Philadelphia!

I next went over to Presser Hall to pay my respects to the president, as I had promised Dad I would do. This, too, was an eye opener. In addition to the administrative offices of the college, I discovered an immense theater with twenty-seven hundred seats, a gigantic pipe organ, and a stage built to accommodate a symphony orchestra and a tiered chorus of five hundred! Upstairs on the third floor, I was confronted with a courtyard surrounded by thirty-two practice rooms—each complete with a piano—and additional studios equipped with practice reed organs and upright pianos. And this doesn't even touch on the classrooms and twenty-five faculty studios I saw throughout the building.

Across the street from Presser Hall was the Swedish Art Pavilion. This was the original structure built by Sweden as its pavilion for the 1904 Saint Louis World's Fair. Bethany had had the entire building moved and reconstructed on its campus to house its art department and studios. The gigantic central hall was a forest of easels and displays of truly fine paintings and figure studies. Between street cleaners, plasterers, Presser Hall, and the Art Pavilion, I knew what Bethany College was going to mean to me. It didn't pretend to be Ivy League, but it had many facets with which Yale never could compete. I was going to be extremely happy here.

My first dormitory was Old Main. At the time it was built it was reputed to be the tallest building west of the Mississippi River. I lived on the sixth floor. On the second was the college chapel, complete with a large, fine pipe organ. Advanced organ students were permitted to practice on this organ; it was equipped for this with a coin box on the side into which a quarter would be inserted to gain an hour of practice. At the end of the hour, the bellows would cease until the kitty was fed another coin. It also must be mentioned that the organ was of sufficient power and volume that any student sitting at its console possessed the grandiose feeling of piloting an aircraft carrier. As a consequence, very little impressionistic Debussy was played. The entire building vibrated much of the time with Wagner, Vidor, and Mussorgsky—fortissimo.

Late one night, I had gone to bed while a student still was testing the grander pipes. Sometime after midnight, he completed his labors and, just before his quarter gave out, proudly blasted his Great manual with "dum-diddley-dum-dum" hanging on a C7 chord. And then he left! However obsessive it may make me appear to confess it now, I lay there for nearly half an hour until I could stand it no longer. Padding barefoot down four flights of stairs in my underwear, I entered the dark chapel, inserted my quarter, and played the long-overdue E and F to complete the final "dum-dum." Content with this glorious finality, I retired to my sixth-floor bed and uninterrupted sleep.

Early in the first semester, the freshman class was called upon to present a program in that same chapel. For the occasion, I composed Prelude No. 3 in C minor. I can't explain why my piano output so far always seemed to fall in the minor keys, but my third prelude certainly wasn't sad. On the contrary, it was a broad, sweeping piece that foretold all that I hoped my Kansas experience would be. Today it sounds a bit Rachmaninoff-inspired, but even that, I think, is forgivable. I was unabashedly romantic about my forthcoming experiences, and my prelude simply set the stage for my destiny.

Bethany College lived up to all the hopes and expectations I had lavished upon it. I studied painting with a world-renowned master, Birger Sandzén, and with a series of more locally recognized painters including Lester Raymer, Charles Rogers, and Margaret Sandzén Greenough. I increased my study of my beloved music composition and conducting with Hagbard Brasé, Oscar Thorsen, and Arvid Wallin. I joined the Bethany Choir and the famous Oratorio Society. I was elected a member of Phi Mu Alpha Sinfonia, the national music fraternity, and of Delta Phi Delta, the national art fraternity. I founded a chorus in my social fraternity. I immersed myself in all things musical, artistic, and theatrical. I even paid attention to my scholastic work every now and then. But one endeavor, above all the others, occupied my time and interest and even proved to be the training ground for my lifelong career: I was a founding member of the Bethany Male Quartet, later known professionally as the PitchPipers.

Carol Anderson (bass), Russell Johnson (second tenor), and Meryl Volen (first tenor) joined me (baritone) to form the quartet, and we took it very seriously, rehearsing several hours every day. We covered all facets of music, from early contrapuntal to very contemporary to spirituals to show tunes to sacred to barbershop. Our eclecticism made us a desirable commodity appropriate for any locale or occasion, so we were off to a fine start and considerable touring right from the outset. At the end of our freshman year, however, Carol and I had the difficult task of informing Russell and Meryl that we felt we had gone as far as we could go with them. Actually, *I* had the difficult task because I would be leaving for Yale in only another year. We held auditions and finally settled on a wonderful lyric second tenor, Wayne Holmstrom, and an equally fine first tenor, LaRue Olson. With three "Svensk poikas" and me, we gave some brief consideration to calling ourselves "Three Swedes & a Scot." Fortunately, reason won out and we dismissed the notion. Our sophomore year took off like a rocket, our repertoire expanded daily, and I began learning the fine points of arranging and composing for male voices. Here was the embryo of my life's work.

During our sophomore year the college recognized our potential for spreading the word about Bethany throughout Kansas, Nebraska, Colorado, and

Oklahoma and presented us with a college car. Our dark blue Chevrolet had "Bethany Male Quartet" neatly lettered below the windows of the two front doors. Until now it had been through the generosity of LaRue that we made it out of town and, although the college Chevy was practical and even commanding with its tasteful lettering, it didn't really impress as readily as LaRue's maroon convertible lovewagon.

It was not the Bethany Male Quartet, however, that dramatically brought the college to my conscious admiration. It was the world famous festival that had twice hired my father as tenor soloist. In a record unbroken since 1881, the Oratorio Society annually presents Handel's *Messiah* on Palm Sunday and Easter and Bach's *Saint Matthew Passion* on Good Friday night. On the other days of Holy Week, concerts are given by the College Choir, the Bethany Symphony Orchestra, the Concert Band, the several soloists hired for the oratorios, and virtually all the various other student musical groups. In addition, important painting exhibitions are held in nearby galleries as well as student art in the Swedish Pavilion.

In a major article about this wonderful festival, *Reader's Digest* has likened it to the famous Passion Play in Oberammergau, Germany, and called Lindsborg's festival the "Oberammergau of the Plains." The orchestra and chorus are made up entirely of students, faculty, and volunteers who come twice a week from New Year's to Easter to rehearse, from as far as twenty miles—and from towns and farms and banks and schools and studios. What emerges from all this dedication is pure devotion and artistry that embraces all of central Kansas. Audiences come from all over the United States and many foreign countries. It has been broadcast worldwide and lauded by critics around the globe. It was an experience I had expected to enjoy because Dad had prepared me to. He did not prepare me to consider it one of the most moving and superb musical experiences of my life. It was so during my years in Lindsborg; it remains today on that same pedestal.

In short, the inevitable happened. I fell in love with Bethany College, with my classmates, my professors, Lindsborg, the plains, and even flat, monotonous Kansas. I stayed the full four years and never darkened the doors of New Haven again.

One of the early excursions of my freshman year was on Sunday, November 18, 1945, when a special Missouri Pacific train left Lindsborg for Kansas City, Missouri, with five hundred singers aboard. There we were the featured performers at the gigantic celebration of the eightieth anniversary of the Salvation Army. Evangeline Booth, daughter of the founder, was the special guest, and the address for the occasion was given by General George C. Marshall. The Oratorio Society sang six stirring choruses from *Messiah*, accompanied by the Kansas City Philharmonic. This was not your run-of-the-mill start to a college experience! My freshman year was further enhanced by my dad's being hired once again as tenor soloist for the Messiah Festival. Our great reunion on campus was especially joyful to this boy who had never before been more than fifty miles from his family. Not homesick, mind you, but awful glad to see his dad again.

My first composition of somewhat "programmatic" music depicted the feeling I had while standing before dawn atop Coronado Heights, the one tall projection in the pool-table plain north of Lindsborg, and watching the eastern sky become steadily brighter until, at last, the fiery ball burst over the distant horizon and bathed the fields with golden light and brilliant day. This was so akin to the exciting broad-brush-stroke landscapes of my beloved painting professor, Birger Sandzén—whose oils were once described by William Allen White as having been painted from "a palette of crushed jewels"—that, upon completion of my tone poem "Kansas Sunrise," I rushed immediately to Sandzén's home and played my "Kansas Sunrise" for him and his wife Frida. Impulsively, I thrust into his hands a copy of the manuscript already inscribed with my dedication to him. Many visits during the ensuing years included a request that either Frida or I sit at his grand piano and play it again for him. And incidentally, "Kansas Sunrise" later became the first of my compositions to be played by a symphony orchestra.

Meanwhile, the Bethany Male Quartet continued to grow in stature and repertoire. By this time it covered much of Kansas and a bit of Nebraska in its weekend travels. One particular 1946 job was of very special and lasting significance. Irene Thorstenberg, the college dietitian, asked us to entertain one day at a regular meeting of her ladies' club. In appreciation, she gave us "permission for life" to buck all lines at the cafeteria and break in right at the food. This daily maneuver probably was not met with as much enthusiasm by the remaining student body as that with which we greeted it, but it afforded us an extra hour of rehearsal every day. We sang for Mrs. Thorstenberg's ladies at her slightest behest that semester and all those that followed. And we built a huge repertoire.

By 1947, we had settled into the routine of being minor celebrities and took our bookings all over Kansas pretty much in stride. In quite constant demand, we began to get more and more confident with our showmanship as well as our music. We began parting ways with published arrangements, as Andy and I were arranging most of our music for our special sound and presentation. One of the most useful skills I learned in my undergraduate years was discovering and writing for the capabilities of male voices and how to play with the marvelous sonorities they presented when performed together. This will hold my fascination for the remainder of my life, and it became a major tool of my long career. By the end of the academic year, we were so confident of success that we booked a significant tour for immediately after final exams.

Our six-week tour began modestly. We stopped for "coffee" at Andy's parents' home in Russell. "Coffee" is an affectionate term the Swedes use for a six-course dinner. After three concerts in western Kansas, three in Denver, and another half dozen in northern Colorado, we crossed into Wyoming. Here we performed for several days before returning to Denver and Colorado Springs (Wayne's home) and then, at last, to Texas.

My most vivid Texas memories include, between our several San Antonio performances, our visit to the Alamo, which was very moving to each of us. Another was being given a very large hotel room in Austin with four single beds in a row. Hours after retiring for the night, Andy bounded out of his bed, threw off all our covers, and snapped on all the lights, loudly proclaiming to our groggy, not happy awakenings, "Dammit, men! I can't sleep! We're in the wrong order!" And the s.o.b. wouldn't allow peace in the room until we got out of our beds and trudged over to others so as to be in the order in which we customarily sang on stage!

In McAllen, our former second tenor, Russell Johnson, who was a student pastor there, joined us for a day's excursion into Mexico. We had no planned performances as we crossed the border at Reynosa but, after a delightful day in Monterrey, where we did a modicum of impromptu singing, we stopped for an extended time in Rio Bravo's town plaza and sang virtually a full program to the astonished people of the town, all out for market day. Every time we thought we were finished and headed for our car, we were brought back with shouts of "uno mas!" Further performances in Galveston, Houston, and Dallas completed our fabulous journey. In all, we had covered some fifty-seven hundred miles and had sung more than fifty performances, from full concerts to church services to private parties to a swim-trunk-clad beach party, before returning to Lindsborg and then going our separate ways until September.

Although this "biography" really isn't meant to be "auto," I'm spending more time on my Bethany experiences than I had originally intended. It was there that the foundations were laid for all that follows. So, in as quick succession as I'm able, I'll try to skim over the next events and get closer to the purpose of the volume. A few milestones will fill in the experiences of my learning cycle.

I continued to gain much from my participation in the Bethany Choir and the Oratorio Society. Among the many perks of membership in the Phi Mu Alpha Sinfonia fraternity was the several days the superb pianist Emil Gillels spent with us on campus, at which time we inducted him to honorary membership. I also continued my love for theater with the leads in several plays. And for Stunt Night each year, when each fraternity and sorority put on an original skit, I composed a one-act musical for my fraternity to perform. We even had a full pit band. Immodestly (why start now?) I report that we won prizes every year.

The Bethany Male Quartet continued to occupy much of my extracurricular time and yet I occasionally found time for academics. One of the more intriguing pairs of paintings of the year developed when Patti Taylor and I set up easels ten feet from each other in the Art Pavilion and painted each other's portrait painting each other's portrait. Hers, I'm quick to admit, was better than mine. But the most fun I had painting a portrait was the time Bob Seese asked me to paint him as concertmaster of the symphony orchestra. He wished to be in a seated position, wearing white tie and tails, and holding his violin vertically in his left hand while his right held the bow across his knees. His major concern was whether he could afford me. We struck a deal that pleased both of us greatly: I would paint him for free if he would then let me paint a second portrait of him as I wanted. Bob came to the studio after the initial formal painting wearing an open necked white shirt, a yellow sweater, and a tan corduroy jacket. He was to wear the same outfit each day but was never to pose—simply to practice. He ended his first session with Debussy's haunting "Le Plus que lente." It turned out to be the best portrait I ever painted, totally lacking in posed stiltedness, with an immediacy that never would have been caught had he frozen in a single pose. And it had the further advantage of permitting me to hear "Le Plus que lente" each day.

Around this time, Sandzén asked if I would teach an adult evening class one evening a week. I was highly flattered that he had such confidence in me but was nervous, to say the least. I had eleven adult students each Thursday after dinner and I planned what I was going to expect of them very carefully. I set up a still life of imperishable items (copper, glass, wood, pewter, and the like) that would not fall victim to the mice who relished our fruit-laden arrangements. I told my new charges that I wanted them to paint this same still life each evening for the first three weeks and that a painting must be completed each session. At the end of the third week, we lined up their paintings by the week they were painted. Only then did I confess my experiment. Without their being conscious of my intent, during the first week the hi-fi system was playing Debussy and Messiaen. The second week was Bach and Telemann; the third was Wagner and Mussorgsky. All this was played fairly softly and was definitely a subliminal influence of which the students were unaware. But their paintings certainly showed it! Each painting from the first session contained muted, almost pastel colors and diffused lines. The second week developed works that were considerably more rigid and precise; the colors were stronger than the previous week but grayer in tone. The third week produced wild sweeps of bold color and heavy blacks reminiscent of Roualt. All of us were astonished, and my delightful new students burst into applause when they learned how they had been duped. I have no idea what prompted me to try such an experiment and I'm still agog that it achieved its intended effect so convincingly.

The 1948 tour for the Bethany Male Quartet was to take us east to Saint Louis and then all the way to the east coast. With my house in Philadelphia as our home base, we sang our way up through New York State and well into New England. Donning heavy rubber suits and hip boots, we even sang for our own enjoyment *under* Niagara Falls. There is a guided tour with a rock wall on the right and the thundering cascade on the left. Even if no one heard us, we sang there! We did two television shows in Philadelphia and were the guests of James Francis Cooke at the Theodore Presser Foundation. It was Cooke who was instrumental in Bethany College's receiving its wonderful Presser Hall, and it was he who dedicated it in 1930.

While we were singing for Cooke, he picked up the phone and called his friend Fred Waring, then the most popular choral conductor in the world.

"How are you fixed for June 22nd?" he asked us while holding his hand over the phone's mouthpiece.

"We have a free day," we replied.

"Not any more," he said and turned to the phone again. "Yes, Fred, they'll be your guests on the 22nd. Yes, in time for lunch."

We had little idea what plans had been made for us, but from the side of the conversation we heard it sounded highly promising.

"Well, boys, you're going to Shawnee-on-Delaware, Fred Waring's home and summer camp for music teachers and conductors in the Poconos," Cooke informed us. "You'll have the run of the place and can attend any classes you wish, but be prepared to sing a program of about forty minutes for them that night."

We spent a fabulous and educational day with Waring and his chief assistant, Lara Hoggard. It was Hoggard, incidentally, who developed the phonetic system of choral singing for which Fred Waring gained so much fame and which taught choral conductors how to make their choruses' lyrics clearly understood. We sang for the assembled masses at 9:00 P.M. and were a decided hit. I believe it became a personal joke for Fred to put us and our repertoire to the test so that, whenever we thought we were finished and had sat down, he would declaim "Let's get them back for another encore." And, of course, the sheep followed the shepherd.

Before we left the east, we rather impetuously went to New York City one day and auditioned for the number one radio show, *Arthur Godfrey's Talent Scouts*. We recalled the event many times thereafter. We had seen dozens of acts before us ushered into the CBS studio by Judith Abbott, only to reappear two or three minutes later with "don't-call-us-we'll-call-you" hangdog looks on their faces. When our turn came, we expected much the same treatment. In the studio, we were instructed to sing a song into a standing mike. Then we were asked to sing another. And another. All the time, we could see more and more executives being invited into the control room. After about six songs, the producer, Irving Mansfield, entered the studio and informed us that we would be on the Monday, September 6 show at the start of the new season.

We returned to Lindsborg with the happy news and got the red carpet treatment. Bethany College didn't often get its students on coast-to-coast networks. Sporting the new name the PitchPipers (a name we came up with at the request of Mansfield, who felt we needed a more commercial, catchy title for national coverage), we went back to New York in September. We were told later that time stopped still in Lindsborg at 7:00 P.M. (Central Time) on September 6, and that Ray Hahn even stopped football practice in the middle of a scrimmage for the few minutes we were on. Perhaps the most nerve-racking feature of the broadcast for us was that Archie Bleyer and his studio orchestra gave us an impressive instrumental intro, and then we were on our own for our entire song a cappella, until Bleyer ended with a fortissimo orchestral stinger. If we weren't exactly on pitch at the end, the entire nation would know it. I guess we weren't called the PitchPipers for nothing. We aced it.

With our newfound fame and fortified confidence, we branched out into some recordings and auditioned for everything that came our way. One of the most popular dance and theater bands of the day was Horace Heidt and His Orchestra. We auditioned to do two live shows with him in Wichita and got the job. As I look back on it all now, today's collegiate a cappella groups are more savvy and have flashier showmanship than we had. I know—I've worked with a good number of them. But in the late 1940s, with very few people seeing slick acts every night on television, the PitchPipers still stood up pretty well and our musicianship was uncommonly high. Three of the four of us, in fact, went on to make music our life's work. Wayne and Andy taught music and conducted in the Kansas public school systems, and I made collegiate music my career. LaRue went into the family business of mortician and furniture store owner in Marquette, Kansas. He's the wealthy one.

The PitchPipers remains a high point in my life for its close-knit harmony in song and even closer genuine—and lasting—friendships. But all things come to an end, and LaRue left us early to attend mortician's school in Kansas City. When we broke up for good, the *Lindsborg News-Record* ran a feature story about us, which in turn was picked up by the *Kansas City Star* and then the Associated Press and United Press International. One item in our farewell story that caught the eye of the news services was our claim to have a repertoire of five hundred songs. They simply didn't believe it. To put their doubts to rest, we invited the AP to visit us on campus. This they did and were given a card file with well over five hundred titles in it. With their reporter choosing cards at random, we sang for over two hours—and he so reported over the wire services.

One of my classmates, Gloria Soice, was a marvelous soprano and a voice major. She was preparing her required senior recital in 1949 and asked me if I would compose a work for it. I took advantage of our mutual love of A. A. Milne's Christopher Robin poems and wrote "Christopher Robin: A Song Cycle," consisting of four of the charming poems. Gloria introduced it to perfection, but that was where the work ended. To my dismay, I discovered that Milne had assigned the exclusive music rights to a fellow Englishman and I could not obtain permission to publish my cycle. Happily, fifty years later, the work is seeing a new life, and it is my hope that Gloria's piece will be heard widely at last.

At Bethany, I continued to paint and sculpt nearly every hour I could spare from academics and singing. I even had my first one-man show, filling the Art Pavilion during the Messiah Festival week. I continued my pursuit of theater and directed and performed in several plays, including the title role in Molière's *The Imaginary Invalid* and Tom in Tennessee Williams's *The Glass Menagerie.* I also continued to write a new one-act musical for my fraternity to perform each year on Stunt Night in Presser Hall. And that led to my magnum opus.

Emory Lindquist, president of Bethany, called me to his office one day to discuss my senior thesis. Every graduating senior had to write a major research paper. Having seen each of my Stunt Night musicals, he sounded me out about participating in a wild, innovative idea. How would I like to write a full musical instead of a more formal thesis? I would research a plot, write the book and lyrics, compose the score, and design the costumes and sets and the college would produce it. This, he felt, would more than satisfy the college's requirements for a senior thesis. To this day, I am awed by the exceptional novelty and downright daring of Emory's plan. Emory Lindquist was every inch an academic. He was a Rhodes scholar, an esteemed author and teacher, and, after Bethany College, a distinguished university president. But, somehow, he had the remarkable originality of thought to deviate from the tried-and-true and dare to create a new set of rules for himself and his institution. He later became a close and dear friend, but on that day he was the object of my unbridled awe.

There's an old joke about Swedish immigrants arriving in America on their way to the very Swedish town of Lindsborg, Kansas, about which they had heard in glowing terms for years back home in Stockholm. In wide-eyed wonder at the bustling New York metropolis, one exclaims to another "Ya! And if this is New York, *what* must Lindsborg be?" My full-length musical, about the emigration of the Swedes to America in 1881, was a bright, colorful, and—though I say it myself—tuneful production. *If This Is New York* played to full houses in Presser Hall and received critical acclaim and considerable success. Jerry Harris did the tasteful orchestrations and conducted the large orchestra, Gladys Ekeberg directed the show, and (ever the ham) I played the role of J. P. Morgan Astor Vanderbilt Quist in the New York segment. I should add here that, as part of its celebration of the Kansas Centennial in 1961, Bethany produced a revival of *If This Is New York* and invited me back to conduct it.

In 1950, back in Pennsylvania, I hopped in my car one summer day and drove up to Fred Waring's Shawnee-on-Delaware without an appointment. I stopped at the home of Livingston Gearhart, his fine pianist and arranger, and laid out my mission. After an hour or so of hearing me playing my songs, Livingston left me to phone Waring. The side of the conversation I heard included, "Tell Bob Hope you'll finish the golf game later. I think you'd better come right away, Fred."

To cut to the punch line, I played and sang a dozen songs that Gearhart had put aside for Fred to hear. We chatted for a while. And on Sunday, February 4, 1951, the *General Electric Hour*, starring Fred Waring and His Pennsylvanians, on the CBS television network, included as a major production number "Candy Store" from *If This Is New York*.

In the meantime, I already had moved into my first office at 3810 Walnut Street on the campus of the University of Pennsylvania and had begun a career that was to last for fifty years.

✦ T W O ✦

One of the Best Investments

"**P**ARDON ME. Have you a light?"

It was intermission at the Schubert Theater on South Broad Street and the man came to me holding his pipe expectantly. I was able to supply a matchbook.

"What do you think of the show?" he asked between puffs.

I had no idea whether he was the author, producer, director, or simply audience, but I proceeded to tell him that I didn't think much of the production—and why.

"You're Bruce Montgomery, aren't you?" he said, after my critique. "I know your mother and father. My name is Frederick Gruber."

We chatted on for the remainder of the intermission and then returned to our seats in different parts of the theater. At the end of the show, Mr. Gruber was waiting for me in the lobby.

"I never asked you what you did," he said.

"I just graduated from college and I'm weighing my options," I replied.

"What are your options? What are you interested in?"

My undergraduate B.F.A. degree had been with a double major in painting and music composition, I told him. At his urging, I also told him of my interest in theater and a few of my experiences with the PitchPipers.

"Have you ever thought of working for the University of Pennsylvania?"

"No, sir, I haven't," I answered. Frankly it never had occurred to me. My father was a Princeton grad and my entire boyhood was spent rooting against Penn.

"Why not have lunch with me on Monday?" he suggested. "Meet me at the School of Education at noon and we'll see how it goes from there."

At noon I was ushered into the office of E. Duncan Grizzell, dean of the School of Education. At one, the three of us were having lunch at the Lenape

Club on McAlpin Street, and by two I had been hired for the munificent sum of twenty-eight hundred dollars a year! Mind you, this was 1950, and a daily newspaper cost three cents, a ticket to a Broadway show $4.80, dinner at Schrafft's $1.90, and a fully loaded brand new Plymouth $1,758.

I was hired to be the assistant director of the Cultural Olympics. A wonderful program with a bad name, the Cultural Olympics was the 1936 brainchild of Samuel Fleisher and George H. Johnson, president of Lit Brothers Department Store. They enlisted the University of Pennsylvania to be the developer and home site for the program, which was financed entirely by Johnson. The year 1936 was an Olympic year, and Fleisher and Johnson had the idea that, during a year when all the athletics were being presented, it would be interesting to bring the arts together as well. Music, dance, drama, and art all were featured in a year-long program of festivals. What began as a one-year project grew in scope and stature and became a continuing program. When Mr. Johnson retired from the presidency of Lit Brothers in 1948, the university assumed complete responsibility for the program.

By 1950, it had grown to a job beyond the capacity of Fred Gruber and his cohort Ben Rothberg to administer along with all they were doing already, as a professor of education at Penn and an administrator at Girard College respectively. Thus, the offer to me and my quick acceptance.

Ordinarily, I would have been hired to begin on the first of July, the start of the fiscal year. However, I was asked to begin immediately because of *Quiche Achi*. What on earth *Quiche Achi* was I had no idea. But I consented to start that weekend.

Quiche Achi was a Guatemalan dance drama, based on ancient Mayan legend, that had played for many years in its homeland. In a remarkable collaboration between the Cultural Olympics and the Pan-American Union, it had been translated into English, and the world premiere of the new production was to take place in Irvine Auditorium on Penn's campus. Ambassadors and dignitaries from the United States and Guatemala attended in abundance, and it became an event of major importance. My role, they tried to convince me, was of great importance, as well. I was unconvinced.

In one highly dramatic scene, great hordes of Mayan supers were to rush on from stage right and mount a massive ramp that led up to an impressive figure standing high and commanding. My invaluable contribution to all this was to stand, hip-booted, in a gigantic vat of liquid body makeup under the stage while what seemed like the entire student body of all-male Girard College, stark naked, climbed in with me, were painted from head to toe with my wide, wet brush, and then moved on to the drying fans, the loincloth station, and finally, their exciting mob rush onstage.

While Gruber and Rothberg were cozying up to the brass in the front of the house, I was sloshing in Sun-Tan-No.10 with fifty naked guys under the stage. Since this was far removed from the "artistry" for which I believed I was hired, I also was entertaining serious thoughts that my first day on the job might be my last.

But my job—and the Cultural Olympics in general—vastly improved in my mind after that initial stint and I settled into what became a fascinating workplace. The programs ran the gamut from high school marching band festivals which culminated in a thousand students putting on massive halftime shows in Franklin Field at Ivy League football games, to festivals of foreign-language theater, to painting exhibitions at the Cultural Olympics Gallery on Woodland Avenue or in conjunction with the Pennsylvania Academy of the Fine Arts or the Barnes Foundation, to dance recitals. In addition to helping to book and run the many and varied programs of the Cultural Olympics, I was given the golden opportunity of launching a tremendous sideline of commercial art opportunities. I designed posters and program covers for our presentations. I designed brochures and reports. This experience was to pay off handsomely later on.

One of the more ambitious Cultural Olympics undertakings for me personally was composing an extended dance drama for narrator, singing chorus, dancers, and orchestra. I chose for my work a subject of tremendous scope, a section of Homer's *Odyssey* called "The Stay in Phaeacia." The chorus of dancers and gymnasts was made up of performers from Temple, Penn, and the Cosmopolitan Opera Company. The singing chorus was from Lower Merion High School and was prepared by Gerald Woerner. The orchestra, also from Lower Merion, was prepared by Andrew Frech. Choreography was by Anthony Tudor and Malvina Taiz. *The Stranger* premiered at Philadelphia's marvelous Academy of Music on Friday, May 11, 1951, and I still wonder at the chutzpah that made me bite off so daunting a chunk. I also still marvel that it all came off so well.

At the same time that I was working for the university, some of my spare time was spent joyously in a new venture of my father's. He had worked for so many years in numerous companies devoted to Gilbert & Sullivan, gaining a world reputation as one of America's premier experts on the subject, that the natural next step was to found his own company. The Gilbert & Sullivan Players of Philadelphia generated considerable excitement. The pay wasn't high, but singers and actors flocked to Dad's side simply to have the opportunity to work with the acknowledged master in the field. And, although I was not a professional, I was given the marvelous good fortune to be with him in the venture. Our festive beginning was as beautifully staged a production of *The Mikado* as you're apt to find anywhere. What's more, I had the distinct thrill of playing Ko-Ko to my dad's Nanki-Poo. The new company was off and running and would gain accolades from press and patrons for many years to come.

Another of my "extracurricular" activities at this time was composing the music for the Air Force Hymn to words by Anne B. Hollingsworth. When it was formally introduced by the United States Air Force Chorus and Band, I was in attendance at a spectacular banquet whose principal speaker was President Harry S. Truman. After the dinner, Mr. Truman had a small reception to which I was invited. I was introduced to him as the composer of the work premiered that evening. He asked me if I had a copy of my music. I reached into my tuxedo pocket and produced the manuscript. Thoughtfully, he signed it and returned it to me. Not every composer owns a copy of his music signed by the president of the United States! He then asked me if I had another copy (I had dozens) and told me that he fancied himself something of a musician.

"It's noisy here," he said. "Let's go into my bedroom and go over your song." We sat on the edge of his bed and read through my hymn.

Mr. Truman was a charming man and one of those very rare conversationalists who can make you feel that you are the only person in the world to whom he wishes to be speaking at the moment. I was twenty-four years old, and that gift was an eye-opening revelation that impressed me then and continues to do so today.

As it turned out, my Homeric dance drama was the last thing I did for Cultural Olympics for awhile. After *The Stranger*, Uncle Sam apparently felt I needed a rest and drafted me to serve in the infantry in Korea. Since fighting a war certainly does not fit the parameters I've set for this book, I intend to make only two references to my army experience here.

Along with the other unwilling cattle, on my first day in the army I was herded in a railroad car down to Fort Meade, Maryland. There we were arbitrarily separated into platoons and given bunks in double-deck barracks. I was on the ground floor by the front door; the drinking fountain was at the opposite end, at the foot of the stairs to the second floor. Heaven knows what on earth prompted me to whistle on my way to the drinking fountain that gloomy first day. But whistle I did. Now, nearly everyone in my platoon was from West Virginia, and the barracks fairly reeked with country-western music—sung, whistled, played on portable radios, and blared on the intercom. Defiantly, I whistled the rondo melody from the last movement of Beethoven's Violin Concerto in D Major as I headed for a drink. I reached the fountain just as I finished the first ten bars. Then I nearly sprayed a mouthful over the walls when I heard the next eight bars continued upstairs! Both of us whistling loud and clear, we met at the halfway point on the staircase, astonished. This was my introduction to Joseph Willcox Jenkins, who became a dear and loyal friend for life. Cox is currently head of composition at Duquesne University in Pittsburgh, and we still exchange manuscripts and CDs of our latest outputs.

I went through my requisite sixteen weeks of basic training in the Fifth Infantry Division, with a red diamond patch on my shoulder, at the Indiantown Gap Military Reservation near Harrisburg, Pennsylvania. Prior to being sent to Korea, I was temporarily assigned to Special Services at "The Gap," where, among other duties, Corporal Danny Leone and I produced and performed the *Red Diamond Revue*, a weekly musical radio show over a Harrisburg station. Our modest fame produced a very touching string of events that deeply affected many lives—certainly mine.

One day a letter arrived at Special Services headquarters addressed to Danny and me. Mrs. Raymond Brandt from Harrisburg informed us that her twelve-year-old daughter Anna Mae was terminally ill with leukemia in Children's Hospital in Philadelphia. The only thing that seemed to lift her spirits was the occasional card from friends. Mrs. Brandt had asked everyone she knew to send cards to Anna Mae, but the list was severely overtaxed. Would Danny and I be willing to mention this on our radio program so that perhaps others would write to the little girl?

Major Francis McAuliffe, our commanding officer, gave Danny and me the go-ahead to do whatever we wished with the story and not check with him for permission for every idea that occurred to us. He trusted us and would back us all the way. We took the ball and ran with it. Given the army's propensity for code names, we labeled it "Operation Smile," and it became a regular feature of the *Red Diamond Revue*. We also got the entire military base involved. Fifth Division soldiers started mailing cards by the dozens. A buddy who had been shipped to Japan several weeks earlier began a campaign of cards from Asia. Major General Lawrence B. Keiser, commander of the Fifth Division, declared Anna Mae the official Division Sweetheart. The hospital had to put on a special employee solely to handle the mail for Anna Mae. One GI's father, who manufactured toys, had his company deluge the hospital with gifts for all the patients . When Mrs. Brandt informed us that she had purchased the last pint of blood she could for the daily transfusions and now was destitute, GIs were excused from field exercises to donate blood. The Red Cross informed us that we had amassed enough of a stockpile that the little girl would be supplied free for the remainder of her life. And finally, the Fifth Division sent an army bus with an entire soldier show to Children's Hospital.

The show was filled with music (we brought a full combo with us) and dancing and magicians and ventriloquists and clowns. I wrote a new song, "Anna Mae," for Danny to sing. And everything was fully covered by TV and the press and all the wire services. The story appeared worldwide, and Anna Mae's smiling photograph was on the front page of nearly every newspaper from New York to San Francisco. Saturday, February 2, 1952, became one of the biggest and happiest days in the life of Anna Mae Brandt.

Ed Sullivan told the story over and over, saying, "This thrilling exposition of tenderness indicates why American soldiers captured the affection of every nation they've ever invaded." In his nationally syndicated column, Jimmie Fidler urged Hollywood to take notice. "I think that there is, in 'Operation Smile,' an idea for a GREAT motion picture" he wrote. "As far as Anna Mae Brandt is concerned, it might have to have a tragic ending, but there is another side to the story, too—the effect of 'Operation Smile' on the men who are participating in it. We've had a dozen pictures showing what the horrors of battle can do to men. . . . Now how about one showing how those same men can forget their own troubles and find happiness in the process of trying to help a tragically stricken little girl?" Guy Lombardo and his orchestra played my song. In every respect, Anna Mae's last days were her happiest in years. She died shortly after I shipped out to Korea, and her pallbearers were her beloved soldiers.

When I returned from Korea in one piece in 1952, I picked up where I left off with the Cultural Olympics. In fact, one happy carryover from my army experience was the opportunity to commission a major ballet from my composer friend Joseph Willcox Jenkins. Fred Gruber and I talked at length about the success of *The Stranger*. Apparently this was the first time a musical work had been written specifically for the Cultural Olympics, and Fred believed it was a trend we should vigorously pursue. With my hearty enthusiasm about Jenkins and knowledge of the marvelous work he had done as arranger for the U.S. Army Band and a prolific student at the Eastman School of Music, the Cultural

Olympics offered a commission to Cox Jenkins. The result was a hauntingly beautiful and very exciting work entitled *Fortieth Parallel* (the latitude of Philadelphia), which premiered at the Academy of Music. It was a great success, and I believe that if the Cultural Olympics had continued for additional decades we would have introduced many fine works into the musical repertoire of America.

By now, while the University of Pennsylvania continued to pay Fred's and my salaries, Philadelphia realtor and philanthropist Albert M. Greenfield had assumed financial support of the Cultural Olympics. But as the years went on, more and more of the wonderful programs we had initiated were deemed indispensable by the Philadelphia public school system. Such items as the annual Band Festival, the Folk Festival, and the many dance programs gradually became regular public school activities. Thus, in the spring of 1955 the Cultural Olympics came to an end. It had functioned as a major force in Philadelphia education for nineteen years. Not a bad record for a program that was intended for only one Olympic year.

With the termination of this endeavor, Penn was faced with a dilemma: what to do with Montgomery. Apparently they liked my work and thought highly enough of me to keep me, so they came up with an appealing solution. For years, all the university's publicity and allied special projects had come out of the News Bureau, run by an old newspaperman, Henry Herbert, and his girl-Friday Florence Bell. Now Penn decided to have an Office of Public Relations and hired Donald T. Sheehan from the John Price Jones Company in New York to become its first director. Sheehan was never given an opportunity to interview me; I was handed to him, sight unseen, as his assistant director. The first day in my new job, my new boss asked me to sit down and write everything he should know about me: education, interests, talents, what I wanted to be when I grew up. I spent the day immodestly hunting-and-pecking at the typewriter filling him in on everything I thought he could possibly wish to know and, to this day, he has not let me forget that, at five o'clock, with trembling hands I delivered my autobiography carefully addressed to "Mr. Donald T. Sheehan, Director of *Pubic* Relations." We've been friends ever since.

My experiences with the Cultural Olympics came to real fruition in the public relations position. Don had me designing fund-raising brochures and university catalogs. I came up with handsome letterheads for numerous new programs. I was the first editor/writer of the *Almanac*, the university's faculty-staff newsletter. I designed LP album covers for several student performing arts groups. I rendered posters galore for everyone, it seemed. I designed the annual President's Report. I was fortunate to win several national and local awards from the printing and advertising industries. Don Sheehan apparently wasn't saddled with such a dud after all.

The Gilbert & Sullivan Players, meanwhile, continued to perform downtown with great success, and my dad and I had numerous opportunities to perform together again. Without question my favorite role was Jack Point in *The Yeomen of the Guard*. Perhaps the most demanding and difficult role in all of the operas, it was a challenge of immense proportions and satisfaction. It also was utterly delightful to play this wonderful court jester of the time of Henry VIII and be required to teach my father's character how to court a maiden! Among other joys, this gained us some remarkable press. With each new production, Dad gave me more instruction in his knowledgeable direction and permitted me to assist him with his fine company. I had the greatest of tutors in learning every facet of the immortal works of Gilbert and Sullivan. November 9, 1955, however, was to bring this happy collaboration to an abrupt close.

My father had been singing in Boston on Sunday and Monday. On Tuesday, he came home and that evening did a radio show with Gertrude Berg—known everywhere for her wonderful character Molly Goldberg. She gave him a huge jar of gefilte fish, which he laughingly presented to Mother as if it were a trophy of Stanley Cup caliber. On Wednesday, he was dead of a massive heart attack.

When his father (my grandfather Montgomery) died, Graddy was wearing a handsome signet ring with the Montgomery coat of arms etched in bloodstone and set in heraldic shield-shaped gold. It had been placed on his finger moments after his father had died. In his final breaths he said, "Bessie, the ring." My grandmother removed the ring and placed it on my father's hand. As my dad died, the ring's history was repeated as he said, "Connie, the ring." Mother removed the ring and placed it on my finger. It was as if the torch were being passed. The very last words Dad said to me were "Make sure the show goes on." We were about to open in Gilbert & Sullivan's *Patience* in which I was playing the comic role of Archibald Grosvenor. Being funny was unbelievably difficult, but the show went on.

And it continued to go on. Dad had been training me for this for years, so the transition was smooth and efficient. The Gilbert & Sullivan Players continued uninterrupted under my direction. The single major change was that the entire company met and decided that they would no longer accept their modest pay for performing but, instead, would donate all profits to the American Heart Association in Dad's memory. We gave the association tens of thousands of dollars over the years. And to this day we have not been able to bring ourselves to open that jar of gefilte fish.

We often run into irony in our crazy lives. But irony was never keener for me than at my father's funeral. He had been a member of Philadelphia's fine male chorus the Orpheus Club for many years. The OC had a long tradition of singing John L. Hatton's "Absence" at the funeral of any of its departed members. In the spring of 1955 it was decided that we really didn't have a very good arrangement of the song, and I was asked to make a new version for our special use. I made the arrangement that the club sings today, and the very first funeral at which it was sung was that of my father.

My alma mater, Germantown Friends School, possessed one of the finest choirs of any I have ever heard. Mary Brewer was a taskmaster, adored by her students because she always made them work hard and always let them know the feeling of accomplishment that resulted. It was she, I guess, who made me realize a truth that would follow me all the days of my work with college students: if you challenge students and help them work to meet that challenge, there is practically nothing they can't accomplish. I have spent my life daring young people to accept such challenges, and invariably they come through—frequently well beyond their perceived capabilities—and surprise even themselves. After my first few realizations of that observation, it no longer surprised me; it only delighted me and reinforced the trust and admiration I feel so strongly for the young people I know.

In 1956, the Germantown Friends School Choir undertook a concert tour of France, Germany, England, and Wales. It was conceived as an opportunity to visit some of the schools with which GFS had enjoyed an affiliation throughout World War II. During the war, Germantown Friends supplied school materials and moral support—as well as volumes of correspondence and even exchange students—with a school in Falaise, France. One of the French teachers at Friends, Lucille Hiatt, began the program at GFS, and a Monsieur Macary was chief correspondent on the French side. With that as impetus, the GFS Choir toured for some five weeks with great success and critical acclaim in the press of all four countries.

Recognizing the length and scope of the tour, Mary Brewer felt it advisable to have an assistant conductor along and invited me to fill that post. The job required me, of course, to learn the entire repertoire and be prepared to step in at any time. And in the back of her mind she further thought that I might gain the confidence of the boys in the choir and keep them in check. She never vocalized this, but she was smart, and I knew that I was along for more than musical emergencies.

Along with letting me serve Mary in the several capacities she had envisioned for me, the European tour furthered my absolute adoration of her. A decided fringe benefit of the tour was that my younger sister, Elizabeth, was one of Mary's featured sopranos. Liz not only possessed a gorgeous voice but was also fluent in French, so she became the choir's spokesperson all the time we were in France. She utterly charmed hosts and city mayors with her spontaneous repartee after they had delivered generally stuffy greetings and official proclamations. The one proclamation that I found singularly without stuffiness was that given by the mayor of Falaise. Upon realizing that William the Conqueror—who left his château in Falaise in 1066 to invade England in the Battle of Hastings—had as his chief officer one Roger de Montgomerie, and noticing that the coat of arms on my signet ring matched one that hung in his office, the mayor presented me with an impressive document declaring me "Citoyen d'Honneur de Falaise" (Honorary Citizen of Falaise) on June 23, 1956. This was my first honorary citizenship and one of which I am extremely proud.

Before I left for Europe, my happy work in public relations was continuing well when suddenly the spring brought some news of which I would never have dreamed. Gaylord Harnwell, president of Penn, told me that he had not been able to talk our Music Department out of dropping all applied music. This included the several performing groups, as well. Would I become Director of Musical Activities and take over the Glee Club, the bands, and all the other student musical performance groups? I'm certain that my boss put the bee in Harnwell's bonnet. Don Sheehan either hated me and wished to get me out of his hair, or loved me and wanted to see me burst onto a scene for which I was truly suited and in which I would be supremely happy. I tend to believe it was the latter.

The year 1956, therefore, was unequivocally the pivotal year of my life and the reason that I wrote this book. That first year I was hired on a part-time basis. My position with the Public Relations Office continued while I juggled daily rehearsals of the Penn Glee Club, the Penn Players production of *Kiss Me Kate*, and the Mask & Wig's *Ring Around Rosie*. I was cooking on all burners that year.

I entered my initial year with the Glee Club with a considerable case of the jitters. I had learned much about writing and arranging for male voices during my undergraduate years and even had conducted a male chorus or two. But that was more informal. It also was, for the most part, theoretical classroom learning. This time it was the real thing in the real world. This time, also, I was on my own, and I had to prove to everyone, not least myself, that I was exactly the right choice for the job. I was scarcely older than my students, and that always presents a difficult tightrope to walk. But, with a great gulp, I entered my first rehearsal, breezed through it, loved every second of it, and ended with a standing ovation and a round of applause from my charges.

Did you ever have one of those days when everything goes right and you can hardly wait for the next to begin? Well, that was the beginning of a relationship that seemed meant to happen—and the honeymoon didn't end for forty-four years! Now I had to set about making the Penn Glee Club uniquely mine, a showpiece for the university, and a chorus that would gain its rightful place among the country's best. My first step was twanging the heartstrings of alumni clubs throughout the Northeast.

"Aw, c'mon, Joe," I would shamelessly plead on the telephone. "That was the *old* Glee Club. This is a whole new ball game with a brand new pitcher. Give me a chance. Please book us."

All we required was a small donation toward a chartered bus, a meal upon arrival, a place to perform, overnight lodging in alumni homes, and breakfast with the host families the next morning. We'd take care of all the rest. I felt it essential that we finish my first year with a tour to put an exclamation point on the new era.

By coercion, bribery, blackmail, even tears—whatever it took—I called in some chips from my PR days and our business manager, Bob Suskind, and I booked a mini spring tour for the club. The day before we were to leave, I received a call from our man in Pittsburgh.

"I just wanted you to know that we've sold just nine tickets to your concert on Friday—and I bought four of them!" he informed me. "We'll stand by our commitment but you'll way outnumber your audience."

I told Bob the bad news, and he and I immediately began calling the other cities to which we were supposedly heading bright and early the next morning. The same tale of woe greeted us from Harrisburg, from Erie, from Cleveland, from Indianapolis. All would stand by us but it would be dismal. Since we already had contracted for the bus with Transport New Jersey, we had to go through with something. So Bob and I got very creative.

Early the next morning, the bus and the members arrived with their baggage. (Actually it was two buses; we didn't reduce the size of the club until

1969.) We told all the members to go get another cup of coffee and report back in an hour. Then we took the bus drivers to my office, informed them of our dilemma, and got busy on the telephones. Bob and I called the cities that were supposed to host us and canceled their obligations. We called everyone else we could think of, filled in the drivers so that they could change their trip-tickets with the bus company, and an hour later we let the members in on all that had transpired and were on our way to the most hastily planned concert tour ever executed.

Our itinerary included a village of appreciative orphans at Dobbs Ferry, drug addicts incarcerated at Brother's Island, prisoners on Riker's Island, and disabled veterans at what seemed like every service and veterans' hospital between Greenwich and Washington. These exciting venues invariably fed us in their cafeterias and mess halls and housed us in their barracks and wards. As it turned out, it was a marvelous tour of which its members still speak with great enthusiasm. The standing punch line throughout the tour was, "What day do we sing at a leper colony?" If I had known of one, I assure you we would have performed there.

The one distasteful experience of the tour occurred in Baltimore. Charlie Amos was the lone African American in the club at the time, and when the hotel at which we were to reside in Baltimore learned this they refused to permit him to stay. Needless to say, the hotel and the city lost our business. "Baltimore, after all, is still a very southern city," was the lame excuse they gave us. We skipped directly to Washington, where David Herrell's uncle—chairman of the Easter Seals Society for D.C.—put together an instant fund raiser for his charity and we gave a fine concert in a fine theater.

Our hastily planned tour was precisely what the club needed. Just the fact that we stayed together for the year, after a string of years that had witnessed alarming attrition, and even had a thoroughly unorthodox tour filled with amazing bonding, was the shot in the arm that was needed for the Glee Club at this particular time. We consciously built on this new esprit de corps and kept the club building repertoire and reputation. We even added production numbers and intricate dancing to our bag of tricks. The "big excursion" off campus prior to 1956 had been an occasional jaunt to Wilson College in Chambersburg, Pennsylvania. With a foot already in that door and a few lucky connections in other institutions as well, I persuaded Anders Emile at Hunter College, Willard Holman at Cedar Crest College, Lawrence Curry at Beaver College, and a few others who directed women's choruses to let us come to their campuses and perform for them and sing a few numbers with them—or even put on a major work together.

One incident from these early experiences that still haunts me was the joint concert Willard Holman and I planned by telephone. We decided to perform Marc Antoine Charpentier's Magnificat in G together at the end of a concert at Cedar Crest. His women would learn their parts and my men would learn theirs and then we'd put it all together in one brief rehearsal before the evening performance. What neither of us stopped to realize was that Charpentier had composed *two* Magnificats in G. His singers had learned one and we had learned the other! When we arrived at the rehearsal and discovered the fact, we, of course, were magnanimous and declared that we would skip dinner, borrow some of their scores, retire to a rehearsal room alone, and learn their version. Originally I was to conduct but, due to the revised circumstances, Willard conducted while I stood directly between the tenors and basses and assisted whichever part needed help. Remember, I was nearly the same age as the singers so I could get away with standing in their midst. Even with their director thus lousing up the preparation for a program, the idea of visiting women's colleges was greatly appealing to my guys. And I never again relied on a telephone conversation to determine a joint work.

It was about this time that the Penn Pipers—founded in 1950 by members of the Glee Club—were achieving considerable success and popularity with their performances in all the club shows and on their own. The Pipers were blessed at this time to have two of their members—Bill Tost and Bill Hoffman—arranging virtually all their songs for them. Therefore, their sound became uniquely their own. Brian Percival, Howard Spergel, Larry Turns, Bob Regaini, and Charlie Meredith rounded out the group with the two Bills. (In 2002, the Pipers celebrated their birthday with a gala concert/party on campus and two of the original founders from 1950, John Reardon and John Cox, attended and sang and danced with the rest. The "Two Jacks" were as spry as ever and were much loved for their active participation in the celebration.) Bill Tost, by the way, went on to play one of the fathers in the New York production of *The Fantasticks* for 7,500 performances during nineteen years and two months of its long run. I saw him at almost the very beginning of his stardom, and again toward the end before it finally closed in 2002. Astonishingly he—and it—were as fresh as the first viewing.

On occasion I've been known to refer to myself as the "worst marching band director ever to walk onto Franklin Field." That's not entirely true. Some years later, I hired a man who turned out to be even worse than I had been. So what does one do for a couple of football and basketball seasons when you're not very good at what you do? When you go through the paces but your heart's not in it? You change hearts, of course. And I was blessed with a most marvelous student whose heart was definitely in it and who was willing to save face for me. James DePreist, with the help of fellow student Joe Dalton, turned out to be the answer to my prayers. While we conferred regularly on what the marching band would do at each halftime show, it was Jimmy who made it happen. I stood on the sidelines each Saturday in awe of his command of the job. Jimmy is now one of the world's great symphonic conductors, and I own superb CDs of him conducting the greatest orchestras on earth. I just don't understand it: he's never asked me to fill in for *him*.

At that time, Elston Hillman was the official movie-maker for the University of Pennsylvania. Like most institutions, Penn needed films for promotion and for the entertainment of alumni at their club meetings throughout the world. There were frequent requests from television as well, for brief films for use, say, in the halftime breaks of an NCAA basketball game and the like. Many of Elston's films utilized the Glee Club's singing for their sound-tracks. At least one of his productions included the club in person, filmed in the dormitory quad. He even talked me into narrating that one.

In 1957, the club made one of its early appearances on television. Popular TV personality Marciarose invited us to explore and illustrate the history of college songs on her celebrated show *Concept*. In Heidelberg student uniforms and brandishing pewter tankards, we ranged from "Gaudeamus Igitur"—the granddaddy of all student songs—to one so new we actually composed it live on camera! "Pennsylvania, Here's to You" wasn't very good, but it made great theater.

Also at this time I began what became an annual event. I invited the entire Glee Club with parents, siblings, and girlfriends to my family home—a big hundred-year-old stone house in historic Germantown—following the last night of our campus run. Here our maid Marjorie (affectionately known as Mamoo!) yearly prepared two twenty-two pound turkeys, two hams, seventy pounds of potato salad, hundreds of rolls, pickles, mustards, olives, tossed salads, almost endless supplies of brownies, and a constantly refilled punch bowl. My mother was the most gracious of hostesses at this party, which was filled with singing and soon evolved into the occasion for the new men to put on a show making fun of our repertoire and the old men, as well as the director. To this day the New Man Show remains an annual travesty. One dares not have a thin skin when the neophytes attack!

In the mid-1970s, Kim Story added to the fun by writing a scathing "review" of the performance. This tradition was carried on by Greg Suss, who delivered his diabolical reviews at each year's party until my retirement in 2000. It always was to the delight of the maligned director, to the embarrassment of the singers and to the utter astonishment of the parents in attendance.

The Glee Club's weekend trips now became frequent to alumni clubs. The Richard Lyons Company and the William Honney Agency, both bookers of professional talent, began getting us into conventions in Philadelphia and Atlantic City hotels. We were building quite a following and improving the exchequer as well. And through it all we were adding considerably to the self-esteem and confidence of the club. By 1959, we were ready to really travel.

In 1959, the General Alumni Society of the University of Pennsylvania was to hold its week-long convention of all the regional U.S. alumni clubs in the Caribe Hilton Hotel in San Juan, Puerto Rico.

"Wouldn't it be great," I asked Leonard Dill, executive director of the G.A.S., "if the Glee Club could appear as a surprise entertainment at the final night's banquet?"

Len thought this was a spectacular idea and encouraged me to pursue it with all the necessary people. He would present it to his staff, and he felt certain he could come up with some underwriting. All along the way all queries were greeted with immediate enthusiasm. The student singers were ecstatic. The Penn Glee Club had never before left the continent. This would be a startling first! The convention grew nearer and nearer, and the enthusiasm of all in the know grew with it. The only thing that didn't seem to grow or even take root was the prospect of funds to fly us to San Juan and house and feed us there. Len finally told me that the idea was great but that funds would not be forthcoming.

All my life I've been accused of being impulsive, a dreamer, lacking a practical mind. But I've always felt that good things would happen if you made them happen. So, I decided, if no one else would make this dream happen, then *I* would. I probably wouldn't make this public today, but Jim Guthrie, who remains a loyal friend, let the cat out of the bag several years ago. To all intents and purposes, I worked the year 1959 for free and my savings account diminished considerably! Given the circumstances, however, I'd do it again without hesitation, and I still feel that it was one of the best investments I've ever made.

The Penn Glee Club timed its arrival in Puerto Rico so that its first day there was the last day of the alumni convention. The banquet went on as advertised at the Caribe Hilton and, at an appropriate moment, a boisterous rendition of Penn songs burst forth from behind the closed curtain at the end of the room. To cheers of delight, the curtains parted, revealing the University of Pennsylvania Glee Club in white dinner jackets, putting the final cap on the already successful convention.

We stayed at the Hotel Normandie (considerably cheaper than the Hilton) and continued for another five days of performing throughout the island. We even did two nightly shows at the Hilton. One of the acts was a hypnotist who, by the time the Penn Glee Club had been singing for a couple of performances, began using some of the students in his act. David Smith in a hypnotic trance was inveigled into singing a University of Pennsylvania song for the audience. Now, David was—and still is—a very deep bass, and the only part he knew for any Penn song was the lowest part as arranged for four-part male voices. I can't imagine what sense the audience gained from a lusty rendition of the completely *un*melodic bass part of "Fight On! Pennsylvania."

Robert Beecroft reminds me that we also performed the calypso "Marry a Woman Uglier Than You" with a local steel band, impromptu and unrehearsed, in the hotel courtyard, to the delight of many. Bob has been in the diplomatic corps ever since college and currently head of the OSCE mission in Bosnia and Herzegovina.

We performed two television shows in rather shabby commercial TV studios. But the real fun came when we were asked to present an hour-long show on the government-owned station. This was a first-class operation, and we presented a varied song-and-dance program to the commonwealth. As we were leaving the studio, there was an announcement on the PA system:

"Will Mr. Montgomery please return to the engineer's booth. You have a telephone call." Baffled, I went to the booth in the studio we had recently vacated and answered the phone.

"Mr. Montgomery?"

"Yes."

"I have just seen your performance. This is Pablo Casals."

Pablo Casals was, in 1959, arguably the greatest cellist in the world, and one of the world's great humanitarians as well. After the initial shock of realizing that I was talking with one of the great men of the time, I regained my composure.

"Maestro! What a pleasant surprise!" I replied.

"What are you doing tomorrow at noon?" he continued.

"Why, nothing I can't rearrange, sir."

"Fine. I would like you to come to my home if you would."

"I will have my student conductor take my rehearsal for me and I will be honored to visit with you," I offered.

"No," he corrected. "I would like to have your whole chorus visit my home."

"How wonderful!" I exclaimed. "What is your address, sir?"

Without a shred of braggadocio or false modesty, he answered, "Just tell the cab drivers you wish to be taken to my home. They'll know."

So out we went next morning in a fleet of taxis, all of whose drivers knew exactly where to go. Pablo Casals was then eighty-three years old. His beautiful wife and former pupil looked about the same age as my singers. The entire Glee Club was given a light and delightful lunch punctuated with lively conversation and hearty laughter. When lunch was finished, Casals abruptly indicated his plan.

"Now, music! Please sing for me some Bach."

I didn't know of any Bach written expressly for adult male voices and, I confess, I do not now recall what we did sing in his music room. I would venture a guess that we sang a male transcription of "Sheep May Safely Graze," which we seem to have had in our repertoire forever, but I'm not certain. We did, however, sing at some length. One of our selections was a charming folk song in Spanish, "Carmen Carmela." After we had sung for a while, I was bold enough to ask him if he would kindly play his cello for us.

"What can I play?" he asked, his shoulders shrugged and hands out to the side. Our accompanist at the time was one of the finest we had in my forty-four years with the Glee Club. Harvey Bellin already had played the Saint-Saëns Piano Concerto No. 2 in G minor with the Philadelphia Orchestra at a youth concert prior to coming to Penn. But, for starters, I thought Señor Casals would be more comfortable playing alone.

"Would you play one of the Bach unaccompanied suites?" I suggested.

His wife brought him his cello, and he set aside his pipe, closed his eyes, and played as if to beckon the angels. When he had finished playing, he made a confession.

"When I left my home in Spain many years ago in my very personal protest of the Franco government," he said, "I vowed that I never would play anywhere else without my little tie to my home. So whenever I play for others, I always add this."

And with that, he again closed his eyes and played "The Song of the Birds," a gentle Spanish folk song, and we could see the love and sadness in his face as he played.

From then on, for an hour, we sang, he played, we sang with an improvised cello obbligato—and generally had one of those remarkable days you remember and talk about for the rest of your life. When a fleet of taxis arrived, we knew that Señora Casals had determined that the excitement for her kind and elderly husband would now cease and our visit was over. There was time, he corrected, at least for a few group photographs by his wife. I seriously doubt that he kept any.

I do know we have proudly kept ours.

◆ T H R E E ◆

You Have Amateurs

WITH OUR GROWING SUCCESS in alumni centers throughout the Northeast and our much heralded performances in New York's Carnegie Hall and Town Hall and on the Ed Sullivan and Steve Allen shows, our joint concerts with women's colleges, our annual campus performances, as well as the word getting around about our leaving our shores for distant parts—all of which we made certain was widely talked about (I hadn't worked in public relations for nothing!)—the Penn Glee Club became a desirable goal for students. Nearly every September thereafter, freshmen men showed up in the hundreds for auditions.

One of the more moving moments of these early years, still talked about frequently and fondly by the men who participated, was singing Randall Thompson's "A Testament of Freedom" in the Jefferson Memorial in Washington, D.C., with the very words we were singing towering over us, carved into the walls of the magnificent rotunda. Never did the guys have a more impressive lyric crib sheet.

On another occasion we were doing a quick warm-up prior to singing at an important banquet in the University Museum. The museum has a very large—and resonant—men's room in the basement, an excellent place to rehearse before singing upstairs. While we were going through our vocal exercises, President Gaylord Harnwell, one of the speakers at the dinner, entered intending to take care of necessities. As we sang, Gaylord glanced over his shoulder and in his customary cultured way said, "Gentlemen, I've done this to Muzak before but this is ridiculous!"

It was at this time that I encouraged others in the club to emulate the success of the Penn Pipers and form new subgroups. One of the first to take me up on it was the Penndulums—whom I usually introduced from the stage as "our swingin' group." Walt Pepperman, Bob Graulich, Alan Emory, and Barry Kaufman auditioned for me and made it into all the club performances for the remainder of their years at Penn.

The Glee Club had a major concert scheduled in Fair Lawn, New Jersey, in 1960. The night before, I was rushed to the University Hospital with a rupturing appendix and called Bob Tabachnikoff, our student director, to tell him the news that he would be conducting in Fair Lawn. Throughout the concert the next evening, I would receive a phone call about every three numbers to let me know that Bob was doing a wonderful job.

A highlight of 1960 was being hired to sing at the 66th annual national Bankers' Convention in Philadelphia's Convention Hall. The thing that made it special was that another act on the bill was the beloved Metropolitan Opera star, Risë Stevens. After she and we had performed separately, it was planned that we would do the finale together. For this, among other things, I arranged a song closely identified with her: "My Hero" from *The Chocolate Soldier* by Oscar Straus. I arranged it for Miss Stevens, the Glee Club, and orchestra. She had sung this with great success in the motion picture version of the operetta, and music lovers of the world always thought of her whenever it was played. Backed by our men, it became a new sound, "effective and wonderful," she exclaimed.

At this time we also released our newest recording, *Whole World*, a stunning group of twelve folk songs from around the world. One of the songs, the Brazilian "Casinha Pequenina," was a gorgeous song with a glorious arrangement by conductor Leonard DePaur. And herein hangs a tale. I had first heard it sung by the DePaur Infantry Chorus, a great black male chorus formed during World War II. It never was published because of its tremendous range for male voices, including two almost stratospheric falsetto parts. I felt that I had the guys who could do it, however, and wrote to Leonard dePaur telling him so. He not only sent me the manuscript of his wonderful arrangement and gave me permission to perform it, but dedicated it to me and the Penn Glee Club. With Tom Ludlow's exquisite, bell-like voice on the rewarding tenor solo and Sven Borei and Paul Guida on the falsetti, we recorded it and, at the same time, began a valued friendship between Leonard and me that continues to this day.

During the summer of 1960, my friend Quentin Quereau and I were traveling all over Europe and had a great many very beautiful and impressive musical experiences. There were several occurrences in Yugoslavia that bear repeating. We went out in Belgrade one evening looking for a pleasant place for dinner. We roamed the streets by Kalemegdan, the ancient fortress where the city was founded by the Celts more than twenty centuries ago. It is at a wonderfully strategic spot at the confluence of the Danube and Sava Rivers. (Here the Sava is very brown and the Danube very blue, with an almost straight line of demarcation where they meet.) We entered a charming restaurant and were delighted to hear chamber music being played by a quartet off to the side. To the regular patrons, we were obviously American—perhaps the first ever to enter this decidedly nontourist area. Sometime during our meal, the quartet decided to acknowledge our presence and improvised the only American song they knew: "Deep in the Heart of Texas"! We nodded cheerfully and thanked them. Several days later we returned to that same restaurant and, right in the middle of a Mozart passage, they broke into a spontaneous "Deep in the Heart of Texas" with wide, proud smiles on all faces.

Another incident was later, back at the hotel. Quentin and I were hot and sweaty from our day of sightseeing. I wrote letters while Quentin took a bath. Then I went in to bathe. When I was drying off in the bathroom, at the very same instant in the bedroom Q and I began to whistle a tune we had heard that day—and in the same key! Astonished, I went into the bedroom wearing my towel and the two of us stood facing each other whistling away. But that's not the strange part of the tale. We were whistling the same music in the same key, and *neither of us was whistling the melody!* We each heard it in our heads, but Q was intoning a tenor obbligato while I was creating a bass line. We decided then and there that we had been traveling together too often and too long.

In 1960–1961, the University of Pennsylvania built an impressive new women's dormitory at the northeast corner of the campus. Hill House was designed by the great Finnish architect Eero Saarinen with a dramatic central court that extended from the ground to the roof. The student living quarters overlooked this court and had white wooden shutters that opened onto it. I believe the first public function to take place here was the annual dinner of the Benjamin Franklin Associates, the donors of large unrestricted funds to Penn. For this occasion I was asked to provide the musical entertainment. Throughout all my years at Penn, I always was grateful that the sponsors of such programs never dictated what they wanted from me. I assume they knew that it would be appropriate to the occasion and that I would come through with something that they themselves most likely had not envisioned. This BFA dinner was one of the more impressive and one of my all-time favorite campus dinner performances of the Glee Club.

During dinner, I had a string quartet playing on the lowest level, their music wafting up to the next level where the BFA were having their candlelight dinner. At the appointed time, the Glee Club was introduced, lights came on full, the shutters on the top of the north side of the hall flew open, and three heraldic trumpets pronounced an attention-getting fanfare I had composed for the occasion. Immediately after, the shutters on the opposite side burst open and the original fanfare was answered by another three trumpets. Then all six played the florid work together. As soon as these twenty-four bars were completed, half the Glee Club appeared on the east end and half on the west, one level above the diners, who by now were completely surrounded by music. It was one of those occasions when you really had to be there to fully appreciate the festive, stereophonic showmanship. It was also one of our flashier moments!

Fair Lawn, New Jersey, had been so pleased with the club the year before that it booked us again in 1961—this time hoping that I could make it too. I did—one has just so many appendixes. At the end of the performance, the mayor appeared on stage with us and, alluding to the year before, made me an honorary citizen of Fair Lawn and presented me with a handsome leather attaché case. Dangling from the handle was a very small gold key for the case. Holding up the tiny key, I remarked that I had been given the key to a city before, but wasn't this somewhat underdoing it? It may not have been my most diplomatic moment but the audience—and the mayor—loved it.

In 1962, the University of Pennsylvania Glee Club celebrated its hundredth anniversary with an active season befitting its milestone. For the actual anniversary concert we decided to hire our favorite opera singer, Risë Stevens, to join us on campus. Once again, I made special arrangements with which we ended the concert together. In addition to her marvelous singing and captivating personality, Miss Stevens further won us over with one of the most virtuoso displays I've ever witnessed. I'm certain that there is a technique one can learn to accomplish such a feat, but she wished to meet each man in the Club at the afternoon rehearsal and then dazzled us by calling each by name at the concert and reception that evening! The reception almost didn't happen. We had finished our last encore together and presented her with a big bouquet of roses. She went down in one of those deep, impressive operatic-curtain-call bows when, suddenly, there was a scream from the audience. I looked up to see the several-ton asbestos and steel fire curtain in a free-fall descending directly toward us. With spontaneous reaction and no grace, I shoved Miss Stevens backward on her rump. It missed us but sliced the grand piano in two! There was no question that the concert was over. She took it all in stride and thanked me with a kiss. I was thoroughly charmed by this gracious lady, and our paths would cross again in 1977.

The undisputed highlight of the early 1960s was the part we played in the commemoration of the centennial of the Battle of Gettysburg during the Civil War. Marciarose, a beautiful, brilliant, and well-known Philadelphia television personality, produced a remarkable program utilizing the talents of the Penn Glee Club to perform songs of the Civil War era. This war produced more songs—10,000—than any other American war period. We pretaped the soundtrack for the show and then, in period dress, lip-synced our songs all over the famous battlefield, taking care whenever possible to choose locales made familiar by Matthew Brady in his historic photographs.

I drove out to Gettysburg at about 5:00 A.M. with the producer and director and the cameramen. The Glee Club was to follow later by chartered bus. Perhaps the last thing I reminded the students the night before was, "Don't forget the costumes. They're in my office in Irvine Auditorium."

We had rented Civil War uniforms—both Union and Confederate—from Van Horn Costumes in Philadelphia, along with period muskets, flags, swords, and other regalia. When the bus arrived on location, the crates of costumes were not on it but were still sitting expectantly in the center of my office. Never underestimate the power of NBC television, however. Through collusions to which I was not privy, the hermetically sealed showcases in the battlefield museum were opened and the Glee Club men wore actual uniforms of the war and carried actual muskets of the day. All taken from the mannequins in the museum! What the viewers at home did not witness was that, just out of camera view, armed guards stood ready to pounce at any hanky-panky involving their uniforms and equipment.

For us and many viewers, the climax of the program was staggering in its concept then and remains daunting to me now. I had been commissioned by NBC to set Lincoln's immortal Gettysburg Address to music for my chorus.

Today I probably would refuse the commission; in 1962 I was a brash young neophyte who thought he could do anything. The remarkable thing is that it all turned out fine. To this day, I am proud of the work, which has remained in the Glee Club repertoire ever since. At least one deeply moving rendition will be recounted later, with the club in the Soviet Union in the 1970s.

For technical reasons beyond our control, the filming took considerably longer than anticipated and daylight began to fade. One final scene was made all the more effective by this happenstance. We built a huge bonfire and gathered around it to sing songs that soldiers might sing at day's end. To light the scene, cars were recruited to gather 'round, out of sight of the cameras, and play their headlights on the singers. Total strangers drove up to help. Since we had prerecorded the songs and did a convincing lip-sync on camera, the anachronistic whirring of engines to run the headlights was unheard by the viewing audience. What could have resulted in eliminating these songs from the program turned out to create a highly effective and theatrical mood, with fire and cross-lighting giving it an eeriness that the director could never have anticipated. Talk about spontaneous inspiration! The film in the can, we returned the borrowed uniforms and muskets to the museum and a great collective sigh could be heard from all concerned.

An exciting series of personal fulfillments began for me in 1962. I spent a good portion of that summer in a log cabin deep in the forest around Lady Dufferin Lake in Ontario, Canada. My friend Bill Boger had invited me to visit this idyllic spot, ninety-five miles from the nearest neighbor. It was a summer of blissfully getting to know oneself without the intrusions of civilization. Time was shared with moose, fish, bears, and Bill. By great good fortune, I found a book that I read and reread by the light of a kerosene lamp—the play *Riders to the Sea* by Irishman John Millington Synge. It gripped me in a manner that few things ever have. Then and there I began to formulate a musical in my mind. It took more concrete form, and I drew five-line musical staves on sheets of blank paper and began creating an Irish folk opera. I did not take Synge's one-act drama and stretch it to a full-length production. Instead, I wrote a new plot but included all the elements and characters of the original. Well, actually, I killed off Bartley, Synge's main character, and resurrected Patch, a character whose earlier death he merely alluded to. I thought "Patch" was a strong and provocative name for my male lead.

I came home at the end of the summer with a nearly completed folk opera I called *Spindrift*. The Penn Players produced it, I directed and conducted it,

Walter Keenan choreographed its dances, and it boasted exquisite orchestrations by Romeo Cascarino. The role of Patch was powerfully created by Robert Umholtz Taylor, and Margaret McGary was a marvelous and melodious Cathleen. The commanding, pivotal character of the Priest was created by Mark Busenkell. Four decades and several different productions later, I still consider it among the finest works I have ever created.

The direct result of the success of *Spindrift* and the accolades it evoked in the press and among producers led me to be hired to write the music and lyrics for a hit Off-Broadway show. *The Amorous Flea*, based on Molière's wonderful *L'École des femmes*, opened on February 17, 1963, in New York. *Flea*—and I, personally—racked up glowing reviews from all the papers and such magazines as the *New Yorker*. It starred the irrepressible old vaudevillian Lew Parker and Jack Fletcher, one of the funniest men I've ever seen. Imelda de Martin and Phil Proctor both won Daniel Blum Theatre World Awards as the most promising new personalities.

But since this isn't supposed to be my autobiography, I'll simply mention in passing that *Flea* was a decided hit on both coasts, won all sorts of prizes, enjoyed a TV special, and, happily, continues to this day to play all over the world. It also included a scene where I wanted a music-box tinkle to the music. I used my first composition, "The Sea." It was exactly right. And thanks to the railroad, I still made my daily Glee Club rehearsals. For nearly two months I commuted between Philadelphia and New York. At 1:50 P.M., I would finish a club rehearsal, have a taxicab waiting outside Houston Hall, dash to Thirtieth Street Station, rehearse and compose at a hall in Greenwich Village until midnight, confer with the producers and director of *Flea*, grab an early morning train to Philly, show up at my office, run another rehearsal, and tear out to the waiting cab.

For nearly two months my daily quota of sleep was achieved on the train. Each direction, I cultivated a regular conductor who knew when and how to awaken me. True to their instructions, they made sure I never woke up in Washington.

But I jump ahead. It's hard to control that in this sort of narrative.

The year 1962 also saw our first of many appearances in Macy's Thanksgiving Day Parade in New York. It almost didn't happen. Forty of us left for the big city before dawn in a blinding rain. The chartered bus didn't get very far before its windshield wipers failed. We tied shoelaces together, attached them to the wipers, and manually pulled them in and out from side windows so that the driver could see the road. Then the engine began overheating. Somehow, we limped along the New Jersey Turnpike, thus jury-rigged, and made it into the service area near Exit 7.

Station attendants told me they didn't have the parts to fix the engine. I called the bus company and asked them to send another bus post haste. I learned to my chagrin that the company had no additional buses, and even if they had, there were no spare drivers. "This is Thanksgiving, you know!"

I then called NBC and told them our disquieting news but instructed them to send our float through in its assigned place in the parade. We would get there somehow in time for our specialty act for national television, I assured them. With that, I marched the full club into the Howard Johnson restaurant and we burst into song. After one chorus of "Drink a Highball at Nightfall," the club went into a humming chorus while I addressed the astonished, coffee-drinking customers and told them our plight.

"If any of you are heading for New York City," I finished, "won't you please take one or two of these boys along?"

The Glee Club sang another chorus as cashiers and waitresses passed on the plea to those who had missed my announcement. Within five minutes everyone had a ride. I sent my student director in the first car and I waited for the last. Motorists stopped in the middle of breakfast or skipped it altogether to help the stranded singers. About twenty cars became involved in the auto brigade. The last of us arrived about fifteen minutes before we were to perform our song-and-dance for the TV cameras. While the spectators lining Broadway must have been surprised at the empty float being peopled one or two at a time along the route, the nation seeing our act on television was none the wiser. *Reader's Digest*, however, told the whole story in its September 1963 issue. We're darned sneaky how we get publicity.

The year 1963 began a new season opener for us. We were invited by the Inn at Buck Hill Falls to come for the Labor Day weekend as their guests. We would arrive Saturday night, spend Sunday rehearsing and at the pool, and give a reprise performance of the previous spring's concert (later *show*) in their wonderful theater. I found a charming song that had been written for the *Buck Hill Follies* decades earlier. Arranging it for male chorus, we took the audience completely by delighted surprise as we sang "Far above the weary world I'll take you . . . High above the world at Buck Hill Falls."

On our way home on Monday, we would stop at Penn's Freshman Boys' and Freshman Girls' Camps in Green Lane before returning to campus. The thing that always boggled my mind was how effectively the club remembered the entire repertoire from the previous spring after a three-month hiatus. Unhappily, the Inn was later closed—and remains so as of this writing—but it was a great free vacation for us and a leg up on the season, to say nothing of a bonding experience for all. This was how we began our year for nearly two decades.

Meanwhile, the Penn Pipers continued to enjoy great success in the Glee Club shows and at many a fraternity party on our and others' campuses. They further added to their fame and fortune by appearing on two extremely popular national television shows of the day: the *Perry Como Show* and the *GE College Bowl*.

One of the outstanding events of our 1963 season was being hired to perform with Bob Hope. We hit it off at once and exchanged a repartee on stage which seemed to delight him. Later in the year, in one of his television specials, part of his monologue was a skit about how lavish the entertainment had become that the airlines were providing for passengers.

"For example," he said, "I was flying to LA from New York the other day and we had to circle the airport an additional forty-five minutes so they could finish showing *Cleopatra!*" (Huge laugh.) "Now it's gotten out of hand. They're going to *live* entertainment!" He reached into his breast pocket and withdrew a schedule. "On the Pan Am flights on Monday, it's the New York Philharmonic. Tuesday, it's the Bolshoi Ballet. On Wednesday, it'll be the University of Pennsylvania Glee Club."

A thoughtful tip of the hat, yes?

With more and more of my choral music being published and the successful launching of my Off-Broadway show, 1963 also saw a nomination for me to join the premier music licensing organization, the American Society of Composers, Authors, and Publishers. When I received my ASCAP membership certificate in October, I was amused to find that the staff of music running around three sides of the imposing certificate was "Kiss Me Again," one of Victor Herbert's most sentimental ballads. It seemed to me an odd choice, even though Herbert was founder of the society. But I was proud to be elected and honored to be in the company of virtually every great American composer of the twentieth century.

In 1964, I presented a proposal to the Glee Club board to initiate an Award of Merit to be presented to an individual who, through his or her professional life, had helped to "create a climate in which our talents may find valid expression." The board of governors adopted the idea without debate. Consisting of a calligraphed citation and a specially sculpted bronze medallion—which I sculpted in clay and had cast by the Medallic Arts Company, then in New York City—the first of the many awards we have given to internationally acclaimed figures went, quite naturally, to my dear friend and mentor Randall Thompson.

All the wonder that his music and I had instilled in the singers was fully justified when Randall came to campus to receive the award at a banquet in his honor in the spectacular Upper Egypt Gallery of the University Museum. He was marvelous and inspirational to every singer and the many invited dates, parents, and guests, which then and always thereafter included the chaplain and the president of the university. The University of Pennsylvania Glee Club Award of Merit Dinner became a fixture. It also was refreshing to see tuxedos and evening gowns in an era when students really didn't have much patience or inclination for that sort of formality.

Almost as soon as I began directing the Penn Glee Club I began arranging and composing for it. One of the first arrangements I made was "A Pennsylvania Medley," a mélange of seven of the best-known songs of the university. It is now affectionately referred to as "the beast" (and is still sung frequently). The first work I composed for the club was a rather pretentious work entitled "Credo" (which isn't performed at all).

Two compositions from these early years, however, written specifically for the club when I was newly entranced by it, are now performed more regularly than any other music in its repertoire. The "Penn Glee Club Toast" was written to be sung to any group or individual by name.

> Oh, here's to [sing whatever name is being toasted],
> Fill up the tankard,
> Fill up the tankard and sorrows drown.
> Here's to friendship,
> Here's to pleasure,
> Fill up the tankard and drink it down,
> Drink it down,
> Drink it down.
> Oh, fill up the tankard
> And drink it down.
> Drink!

Somehow, it really lacks impact when written out and devoid of its four-part music! But it has served its purpose probably a hundred or more times a year since it was first composed.

The other work from my early blush of excitement with my job was "Afterglow." This frankly sentimental song was written to bring a tear of nostalgia to the cheek of the most callous alumnus. It was designed purposely to sound typically nineteenth century—although I believe that it is more interesting harmonically than most of that genre. It was first performed by the club at a Benjamin Franklin Associates Dinner for the big money-givers at the University Museum in January 1965. And it accomplished its purpose: they couldn't get their checkbooks out fast enough! What I could not have foreseen then was that it would become a standard and the virtual theme song of the Glee Club. It is sung at every collation of the club and is the last sentimental moment of every gathering. It is the occasion to put arms around each other's shoulders and sing one final song together. I am very touched and very proud that it has achieved this special place in the hearts and minds of the men, both past and current.

The Club continued to shine and prosper, singing more than fifty engagements a year from New England to Florida and as far west as Chicago. We made a new recording of fourteen songs, *Afterglow*, for RCA and appeared in a pilot TV show for the legendary Paul Whiteman. Among the more flamboyant performances of 1964, we sang in the Singer Bowl at the New York World's Fair.

Our record, *Afterglow*, began with a recording the club made in 1911. This faded and the remarkable voice of André Baruch came in over it. Wayne Baruch, the son of André—then the top announcer in radio—and my boyhood vocalist idol Bea Wayne, was president of the Glee Club, and I had the temerity to ask André to do a voiceover to begin the record. I also asked him to submit a bill. He did. Carefully itemizing the number of hours the recording took, the studio charge at NBC, the engineers' requirements, and his own fee, the bill came to $3106.23. He then itemized the pleasure his son had derived from singing with the club, the leadership skills Wayne had acquired as its chief officer, the number of hours of joy we had afforded him and Bea, and the value he placed on our personal friendship. Astonishingly, that "credit" portion of the bill exactly equaled the other half! No charge. Wayne, incidentally, is now head of Radio City Music Hall Productions.

In December 1964, a musical highlight was realized when the world-acclaimed contralto Betty Allen came to campus to sing Brahms's magnificent *Alto Rhapsody* with us. We had sung at Columbia in New York in October, so we decided to return the favor and invited the Columbia University Glee Club to join us for this very special concert. Miss Allen was marvelous, and she and her husband even came out to my home in Germantown for the annual December after-concert supper party. It was a jovial evening and a good time was had by all.

The Penn Pipers continued to be an awesome a cappella group, and now another group within the Glee Club made its debut. Jeff Hahn, Buzz Neusteter, and Skip Sullivan got together with their guitars, banjos, and voices to form a slickly professional group they called the Three Pennce. We were at the Channel 6 television studio, about to tape a TV show, when the three came to me and said that they wanted to add a fourth man to the group. The only problem was that Ron Hirasawa was not a member of the Glee Club. One of the requirements of the small groups was that all members must be in the club. Equal to the exigencies of the occasion, I broke with my own rules and auditioned Ron in the men's room of the TV station. Ron was wonderful and would have made the club under any conditions. But that night he went on with the other three, playing a string bass, and Three Pennce and a Yen was born. As I look back now, nearly forty years later, they still stand out as one of the most professional small groups we've ever had at Penn. They also remain four of the most continuing and loyal friends I've ever had. We meet for lobsters every now and then in Maine at their regular reunions.

The Award of Merit, meanwhile, continued to gain in stature and became one of the most eagerly anticipated events of the academic year. In 1965, the eminent conductor Robert Shaw, world-famous for his Robert Shaw Chorale, came to campus to receive our award. After singing a number of his fine choral arrangements at his banquet, we performed an exquisite folk song arranged by Marshall Bartholomew, "De Wind Blow over My Shoulder." Mike Thompson's silken-thread tenor solo captured the feeling of the piece. Afterward, Shaw came up to me with tears drenching his cheeks.

"I pay the highest prices for choral singers of anyone in the world," he said. "But you have something I can't buy. You have amateurs. You know, of course, the word comes from the Latin for 'lover,' and your men sing for the sheer love of it. I could never get that purity for mere money."

That just might be one of the most meaningful compliments I've ever received. I repeated the comment to Bartholomew when we sang the same song for him the next year as he received our Award of Merit. Barty had been a friend for many years, and as the acknowledged dean of American collegiate choral directors after his decades as director of the Yale Glee Club, he was one of the most deserving recipients we've ever selected. I don't imagine there are any male choruses in America that haven't half a dozen marvelous Bartholomew arrangements in their permanent repertoire.

It was at the Award of Merit dinner for Robert Shaw, incidentally, that the Club first sang the "Grace" that I had composed for them. The chaplain, Stanley Johnson, had provided me with a non-sectarian text from Psalm 145:

> The eyes of all wait upon thee, oh lord,
> And thou givest them their meat in due season.
> Thou openest thine hand and fillest all things living with plenteousness.
> Amen.

I set it to music to be sung by the Glee Club whenever it has meals together. Again, it is a source of considerable pride that it remains in the repertoire and accomplishes its original purpose these many years and many meals later.

On one of our frequent jaunts to New England, we sang at a number of places in and around Boston. We sang on the steps of Faneuil Hall and sang a concert for the alumni in the old Unitarian Church. Afterward, we were asked if we would like to go down to the crypt and see the tombs of John Adams and John Quincy Adams. We were ushered down to the vaulted crypt, and stood with rapt, reverent mien between the graves of the father and son presidents. We were then asked if we would care to sing. The first thought that came to my mind was Randall Thompson's appropriately beautiful "Alleluia." The first thought of the club members was different. They spontaneously burst into "Oh, here's to the Adamses, fill up the tankard . . . !" And you wonder why I stayed in my job so long.

In the summer of 1966 , I was in Europe and one memory looms large in my mind. You will remember that I had composed "Christopher Robin: A Song Cycle" for my classmate Gloria Soice. Here in London, a decade and a half later, I was with James Holroyd, an English friend, having lunch at a large round table in the smoke-filled, crackling-conversation atmosphere of the

Press Club. Part way through the lunch, James turned to me and said "Come. I want you to meet someone." With that we arose and I was introduced to the adult Christopher Robin. Somehow, he didn't look a bit like the original Shepard illustrations!

Back in Philadelphia, on a beautiful and balmy September evening, President and Mrs. Gaylord Harnwell hosted His Imperial Highness Takahito Mikasa, prince of Japan and youngest brother of the emperor, as well as other members of the Japanese court, at a formal dinner held at the Paley estate in Chestnut Hill. The entertainment was the customarily white-tie-and-tailed Glee Club. We sang a varied program and appropriately introduced a new work of mine, "Three Haiku," a setting of a trio of Japanese poems.

Following the program, the prince wished to meet each of the members of the Glee Club. Several days later there was a knock at my office door. There stood a liveried Japanese messenger who presented me with a blue velvet box containing an exquisite pair of cufflinks, each bearing the Imperial seal. They still are a happy reminder of a memorable evening spent with a gracious prince.

For many years, my choral music had been published in various series edited by various musicians. In 1966 I gained my own publication series: the University of Pennsylvania Glee Club Choral Series, Bruce Montgomery, editor, published by the Plymouth Music Company. For many years, Randall Thompson and I had carried on a voluminous correspondence and had exchanged our latest manuscripts and publications. I sent Randall a packet of the first half-dozen works that would be included in the new series. By return mail, he sent back a copy of my "Three Haiku" with a message: "I hope you don't mind, but I made one small addition to one of your manuscripts." I looked at the top of the page and discovered that a dedication had been added above the title in his familiar, beautiful handwriting. "To my good friend Randall Thompson," it read. From anyone else, this addition would be deemed unpardonably egotistical. From Randall Thompson it proclaimed to the world, "I endorse this composer and his fine new choral series."

The 1967 Award of Merit went to the great black conductor-composer-arranger William L. Dawson, identified for his entire professional life with Alabama's Tuskegee Institute and one of the all-time great champions of African American music, particularly the superb spirituals. I always have felt very privileged to number Bill among my dear friends and will divulge more of that friendship in a later chapter.

In many ways, the most remarkable Award was in 1968 when the flamboyant, world-renowned conductor Leopold Stokowski came to campus. At the time he was eighty-six years old, but in many respects he was the youngest person there! He was a rabble-rouser who exhorted the students to rise up together to get the things accomplished that needed to be done.

"Save the world from mediocrity," he advised, leaving the rostrum and wandering among the tables. "Don't go it alone. Gather your strength from each other and make it happen!" He later began a whole new recording contract with CBS at age ninety-five! He also told me later that, while Philadelphia figured prominently in many of his career milestones, this was the first time he had made the trip solely to receive an award.

"But I had to come," he said. "It's the first award I have been offered by young people. I would never refuse them."

The 1960s saw us frequently on the road. One of the most enjoyable jaunts for me was the spring vacation trip in 1967 that took us south to Kentucky and then west, where a "local boy made good" directing a performance in Presser Hall at Bethany College. It's nearly always fun when a ship docks at a welcoming and familiar pier.

On another occasion that year, in Washington, D.C., we paused to sing on the steps of the Capitol. Out of nowhere, police suddenly arrived to stop us. We were not aware that this was against the law without all sorts of permits arranged well in advance. We skillfully shifted gears and went immediately into "Lincoln's Gettysburg Address." Now I ask you, who would stop that in mid-measure? Our alumna hostess, Paula Green, waved an expired permit in the authorities' faces to keep them at bay. She succeeded—at least until we finished that song.

It had been many years since the Penn Glee Club had been asked to perform with the Philadelphia Orchestra. But in 1967 we made a triumphant return to the Academy of Music, then the Orchestra's home, and performed Randall Thompson's stirring *A Testament of Freedom* with them. We were back in the Orchestra's good graces (how we got out of them is a story from before my time) and were one of the rare choruses to sing a major work with them entirely from memory. They were duly impressed.

One memory that remains vivid, but for which I can find no validation (such as a program) to corroborate its precise date, occurred, I believe, in 1967 as we were starting a jaunt to New England. The generous alumni in Greenwich, Connecticut, treated us to an awesome dinner at Minero's restaurant. For many years it was a running gag among the Glee Club that wherever we were, whatever time of year it might be, it was invariably announced that it was my birthday, and all present were encouraged to join in serenading me! (Since my actual birthday is in late June, they never once got it right.) Minero's was famous for its unique rendition of the "Happy Birthday" song performed by its singing waiters. It wasn't until after their spirited singing to me that I realized that none of us in the Glee Club had brought along a pitch pipe, a necessity for our concert that evening. Our performance on stage that night was pitched courtesy of the generosity of Minero's waiters and their proffered pitch pipe. It also should be recorded that the consumption of garlic bread at dinner was immense and when the curtain parted and our initial massive chords blasted forth, the first four rows of our audience were effectively withered by our combined breaths billowing forth as an encompassing fog. Paint, I'm told, peeled from the walls.

Irving M. Felt, after whom the brand-new Felt Forum in the brand-new Madison Square Garden in New York was named, came up with an appealing idea to open his forum: a concert by each of the Ivy League glee clubs on successive nights. So on December 20, 1967, the University of Pennsylvania Glee Club gave its portion. From all reports, ours was the only club to leave the confines of a stand-up chorus and fully utilize the immense new space with our unconventional positionings, imaginative levels, and athletic dancing. A few arch-conservatives faulted us for our "modishness," but Felt praised our showmanship and invited us to return the next year.

It's incredible to me, considering my rather prominent early history of male quartet singing, that in all my years with the Penn Glee Club we had only one organized purely vocal quartet in the group. The Pennafour enjoyed tremendous success in 1968, when Jon Gailmor, Keith Neal, Tom Godbold, and Morgan Soutter brought the form to such a fine art that I thought I was back in Kansas as I turned out new arrangements for them from time to time. I wonder why no one continued in their proven footsteps. Jon, incidentally, is practically "Mr. Vermont" now with his songs, CDs, radio programs, and celebrity status at important events.

Morgan Soutter's parents had a wonderful house in Saint Thomas overlooking Magen's Bay. They generously invited me to spend each vacation between Christmas and New Year's there, a marvelous respite from the city life of the rest of the year. One particular time I recall with great joy was when Jon Gailmor and Wayne Baruch joined us and we were a decided hit as a quartet entertaining at the well-known local night club, Galleon House. We wowed them with "What's Your Name?"

The club continued to perform all over the Northeast and ventured south and west on long weekends and spring breaks. On a 1969 visit to St. Louis, we were fascinated by Saarinen's breathtaking Gateway to the West arch. The last time we had seen it, the two slender sides stretched high above the city but the final keystone was not yet in place. Now the arch was complete and we went to the very top and sang.

Nearly all special material for the Glee Club performances had been arranged by me over the years. In the mid-1960s we had a remarkable talent in our midst by the name of Mark Jordan. Mark created some of the finest choral arrangements we've ever done and, after graduation, went right on showing his expertise in Hollywood and Nashville.

By now, I had been in my job as director of musical activities and, of course, the Glee Club, for thirteen years. I am proud to say that I had demonstrated in that time that I was peculiarly suited to the job artistically. I'm not quite so proud to admit that I was less suited as a budget administrator or accountant. My artistic qualities far outweighed my practical ones.

Years before, I had displayed a singular lack of foresight and had turned down a talented auditioner for membership in the Glee Club. He was a fine clarinetist, but at the time I felt he didn't quite measure up vocally. I probably was correct in my appraisal, but I regretted it forever thereafter. Stephen Goff would have been a great addition to any organization and certainly was as a member and later producer for the Mask & Wig Club. Now, at last, I was going to work with him every day. To make up for my financial ineptitudes, Steve was lured away from his career as an architect to take over the money matters of all the student performing arts. And what a boon that was for all of us! He also became, in the bargain, one of the best friends I'll ever have. Now we were strong artistically and fiscally.

Early in January 1969, I saw a list of the people chosen as the University of Pennsylvania's honorary degree recipients that spring. I felt that the list was very one-sided and that someone in the arts should have been included. I promptly picked up the telephone and called Donald K. Angell, secretary of the university.

"Don, don't you think the arts should be represented in this year's honorary degrees?" I said.

"You know, several people have said that to us recently," he answered. "But it's too late now to do anything about it. It would be embarrassing to ask anyone so late."

"One of the great composers of the twentieth century is a dear friend of mine," I said. "If I were to call him and explain the situation, I'm certain that he would not be offended at the lateness of the date."

"Well, I'm equally certain that the trustees will approve if you are sure that it would not appear to be an embarrassing oversight."

"Let me find out," I said confidently. "I'll call you back."

Of course I called Randall immediately and received exactly the reaction I was sure I would. So at the university's 213th Commencement, Randall Thompson received an honorary doctorate and the Penn Glee Club sang his "The Last Words of David" at the ceremony in Convention Hall. After the program, the club and I ran to the University Museum, where the president's luncheon was to take place. When Dr. Thompson arrived with the rest of the honorary degree recipients and the president, the Glee Club was there and burst into "Oh, here's to Dr. Thompson, fill up the tankard . . . !" Delighted, he threw his arms around me and greeted the club. With all he had on his mind on that very special day, he still made time to bring a thoughtful gift to me. His *Frostiana* had been composed for chorus and piano. He had recently orchestrated it, and he brought me a recording of its premiere performance and the score of the new version.

This seems an appropriate time to mention my work with two other major student performing arts organizations on campus. Even though I will not be elaborating on them during the course of this volume, I would do each a disservice if I ignored them totally, as they were very significant facets of my endeavors at the University of Pennsylvania and contributed vastly to my enjoyment of my work there and the legions of students with whom I would not have come in direct contact if not for them.

I began working with the famed Mask & Wig Club in 1955, even before I started with the Glee Club. I was its musical director for five productions until 1960. Later, I was hired to be its stage director and staged nine shows, frequently composing major portions of its songs as well. I had several personal favorites. *H.M.S. Goldilocks*, in 1972, was a burlesque of the old fairy tale as it might have been written by Gilbert and Sullivan, containing twelve such songs as "A Simple Mailman, Lowly Born" and "We Are Dames with Special Unction." *Death Drops Its Drawers (or There's More to a Throne Than Meets the Seat)*, in 1975, was a spoof of nearly every international mystery ever written, including a dozen musical gems from "A Throne Is a Throne Is a Throne" to "It's Hot in Gstaad." My absolute favorite was *Cosi Fan Dudde*, in 1973, as if TV's Howdy Doody had been turned into a grand opera by Mozart, Verdi, Bizet, and a few others thrown in for good measure, boasting thirteen such important arias as "E' L'Ora Di Howdi Dudde" and "Quando Their Amati Are Away."

All three of these shows were the clever brainchildren of Stephen de Baun, and it was immense fun working with him on them. Steve had been a copywriter for the advertising firm of N. W. Ayer and helped conceive the *Howdy Doody* show for TV. My Mask & Wig tenure came to an end when M & W changed its schedule—particularly its touring times—and the new dates coincided exactly with those of the Glee Club, my major employer.

I also had the good fortune to be musical director, stage director, or both for a whole host of Broadway musicals with the Pennsylvania Players. With them I did everything from *Oklahoma* to *Kismet*; *The King and I* to *Once upon a Mattress*; *Kiss Me Kate* to *Pippin*. In addition, it was for the Penn Players that I wrote both *Spindrift* and *Why Me?* And it was the Penn Players, too, who presented the first amateur production anywhere of my *The Amorous Flea* after its original New York run.

While Penn Players and Mask & Wig were important to my happiness and career, the Glee Club became and remained my real first love. Besides, we were on an exciting roll. Now it was time to take the University of Pennsylvania Glee Club to a new and deserved level. Time to take it on a truly exciting, extended tour.

In May 1969, Marc Mostovoy and his marvelous Concerto Soloists played a half-hour concert before the Baccalaureate Chapel service in Irvine Auditorium. In the service, the Penn Glee Club was going to sing two anthems by Bach and

Copland from the top balcony. We had arranged for a small spinet to be delivered there to serve as our accompaniment. When we arrived, no spinet was to be found. Overhearing my frustration, Marc asked if I had any copies of our music. He looked at them briefly, then instructed his string players to go with me to the balcony and divide the spinet parts among them. With no opportunity for a rehearsal, the performance went off as if it had been planned that way all along. After the service I gratefully declared, "I owe you one, Marc."

Richard Nixon had been wooing a number of South American countries to display a bit more liking toward the U.S. than they had recently been doing. American oil interests were being threatened and "nationalized," and there were considerable questions about fishing and disputes over offshore riparian limits. Nixon felt that the time had come for a public display of goodwill.

We chose our venue to take advantage of this spirit of rapprochement In addition, we had been courted by several charitable organizations to assist them in raising funds so that some of the South American countries might send impoverished people with serious heart disorders to a hospital in Texas.

We began all sorts of strategic maneuvers to raise money for a trip unlike any in the previous hundred-and-seven years of the Glee Club. We solicited our alumni in a manner we had never tried before. Nearly everyone at the university knew our plans and helped create excitement. We literally begged on street corners. We set up shop on the corner of Broad and Chestnut Streets and sang and begged to passersby. We sewed sheets together, painted a map of South America on the huge cloth, and marched up Walnut Street singing and asking office workers high above us to throw coins from their windows onto the map. At the request of one knowing Penn administrator, I met the train of an arriving trustee to drive him home from Thirtieth Street Station. He asked me how our tour was progressing, and before we arrived at his front door he had pressed a check for five thousand dollars into my palm. Mine was an expensive cab ride for him.

In May 1969 we left on the first of our spectacular foreign tours: we flew to Ecuador and Peru.

✦ F O U R ✦

An Impressive Demonstration

THE GLEE CLUB ARRIVED in Quito, Ecuador, and immediately felt the rarefied air of 9,500 feet. I wondered how our athletic dancing would fare in our performances there. We also were keenly aware of the spray-painted slogans on walls everywhere: "Abajo Rockefeller" and "Yanqui Go Hom." Without even rudimentary high school Spanish, we understood these. It was 1969, and Vice President Nelson Rockefeller had been sent by President Nixon on a "goodwill tour" to South America. Many countries refused him admission. We felt the backlash.

After a tour of the city, we were taken to the homes of the families who would be hosting us for our two-night stay. Throughout all my years with the Glee Club, I attempted to make certain that, when we were housed in private homes on foreign tours, we were placed with at least two clubbers together per house. In a country where we don't speak the language at all—and they don't speak ours—it's exhausting to carry on conversations exclusively in sign language and smiles, and the presence of a fellow countryman eases the strain considerably. This "rule" of mine was established in Quito, where I was alone in a family. I loved my hosts, but I was in a household that spoke no English and was a happy but limp dishrag by the next morning.

That evening, we had our first performance. All went beautifully and I should have known that the guys would come through, whatever the problems of altitude. For this tour, I established a policy that would hold throughout my career. Always seek out, arrange, and teach the national anthems of the countries we would visit, and perform at least a few of their songs in their native tongue as well. We opened our concert with the Ecuadorian "Himno Nacional" and the "Star Spangled Banner." From then on, we could do no wrong. For two hours we captivated the huge audience with our singing and delighted it with our unexpected dancing.

At the end of our performance, all sorts of florid speeches were made from the stage and I was presented with a handsome gift. It always amuses me that well-meaning and generous people who wish to honor you never seem to realize that a concert tour lasts a bit longer than the single night in which they are involved. On the stage at Quito, I was presented a thirty-inch log! The bark still visible on one vertical side; the other side was carved with a three-dimensional Spanish conquistador in full armor emerging from it. We never stopped anywhere long enough for me to ship it home. So for three weeks I carried my suitcase, my garment bag, my music briefcase, and my log! It was worth the effort, however. It now stands proudly on the hearth of my summer home in Maine.

It was after our performance in Quito that I learned for the first time how lacking in adventurous spirit college men can be when it comes to food with which they are not familiar. Following our very successful performance at the theater, the whole club was given a spectacular midnight supper. The large dining room contained a U-shaped table where one delicacy after another was served. One dish in particular was making a decided hit with the members. They were relishing second helpings when I made a genuinely grateful remark to our generous hosts.

"I don't believe I have ever tasted more delicious brains," I said, innocently.

With that, the rattle of dropped forks all over the room was thunderous! The very men who had accepted seconds stopped instantly when they discovered what it was that they had been enjoying. This was one of life's minor lessons for me. Never again, in four decades of travel, did I articulate what we were eating—until after the fact.

One of our more bizarre lodgings for this or any other Glee Club tour was in the town of Riobamba. Mount Chimborazo, one of the world's highest volcanos at 20,577 feet above sea level, swoops down to the valley where Riobamba is located, and another mountain rises equally abruptly on the other side of town. On a terrace a few hundred feet up this new mountain a monastery had been built many years ago. Now deserted, it became our home for the night. There was no glass in the windows. Our "beds" were piles of straw in what once had been cells reserved for the ascetic austerity of the monks. Seldom have I heard the Glee Club gripe as they did that day.

From our strange aerie we could look down on the town. In the foreground was a high-walled prison where we could see the inmates playing volleyball in the courtyard on the sunny afternoon. With hours to spare, we descended to the prison. There I spoke with the warden, and soon we were marching into the courtyard to sing an impromptu concert. After our performance, we challenged them to a game of volleyball. They won decisively, but they and we had a great time. Many of the prisoners pressed little trinkets they had made into our hands to thank us for interrupting their monotony.

We returned to our cells and dressed for the night's concert. We had to walk through the town to get to the opera house on the other side. Since we were very early, we sang on street corners for the townspeople—particularly the children. Much like the storied Pied Piper, we amassed a loyal pack of little boys and girls who followed us wherever we went and led the cheers wherever we sang. When we reached the opera house, which, incidentally, was a jewel (sort of a smaller version of the Academy of Music in Philadelphia), we knew our ragamuffin pick-up disciples would be waiting for us after our concert. While we formed behind the closed curtain, as if by some prearranged cue, we all had the same idea, reached into our pockets for some pesos, and sent David Lauer, our business manager, running out the stage door to the box office with a hatful of money. Balcony tickets were purchased for all the children. Never has a chorus played to a more appreciative audience.

Writing later about the tour, David Bradley recalled, "Our job was not easy, and it was not all fun and games; we were hissed in Ambato and tear-gassed in Guayaquil. But we sang to them; music by our Copland and Thompson, by their Villa Lobos and Escobar, and by everybody's Bach and Handel. And as we sang the hisses and boos became tumultuous cheers." David is now a successful novelist and professor.

We also felt fear when the brakes of our bus burned out as we descended from twelve thousand feet to sea level on a roller-coaster ride. By jamming the front of the bus into the dirt bank on our left, our driver was able to stop the runaway vehicle, put out the fire, and somehow get us going again.

While he was working on the bus, we used the occasion to play Frisbee in the tall grasses that formed a small flat plateau before catapulting to the valley far below. We had been playing here for several minutes when one man yelled, "Spiders!" We looked down and discovered hundreds of spiders at our feet. All had the recognizable hour-glass configuration on their bodies. We were in a field of black widows! I don't believe a playground was ever emptied more rapidly nor clothes shed more quickly on the dirt road as we vigorously shook every item we had been wearing. But we also had time to serenade a single shepherd on the mountainside whose toothless grin was our applause.

In Ambato we were housed in a small private hotel. It boasted such charms as electric showers! The only way to achieve hot water in the shower was to turn on a switch at the showerhead so that electricity charged the water. The good people had the wisdom to supply wooden pallets to stand on to avoid electrocution. But even with these, you still could feel a tingle course through your body.

When we were in Ambato, I received a telephone call from the U.S. ambassador to Peru. He explained the strained relationship between that country and ours and that Rockefeller had been refused admission to the country. He had taken it upon himself, he said, to cancel our tour of Peru. We were supposed to leave for Lima in five days!

"Sir, are you *ordering* us not to come to Peru?" I asked.

"No, I can't do that," he replied. "But I don't advise it. Your presence will be the excuse for additional disturbances and demonstrations."

Knowing that I could not take the responsibility for the lives of other people's sons into my own hands, I asked an important question before I expressed any final reaction or commitment to him on where we stood on the issue he had raised.

"Sir, would our lives be in greater danger than, say, in West Philadelphia?" I thought that left him a bit of latitude.

"No, I don't believe your lives would be in danger," he answered. "But the situation here is untenable. I myself am leaving for Washington the day after tomorrow."

"Will the embassy be closed?" If it were, we definitely would not go.

"No. Our first secretary will be here."

"Then, sir, I believe we'll come. Perhaps we can do some good in what appears to be a lousy situation."

"Good luck," he said, and our conversation was over.

We continued on in Ecuador, hoping that we had made the right decision about Peru. We performed in Cuenca to standing-room-only crowds and received such accolades in the next day's newspapers that we were persuaded to put on our show that night as well.

Three days later, we flew from Guayaquil to Lima. We had, indeed, been tear-gassed in Guayaquil, and a bus next to ours had been set afire. It made me wonder if I had wrongly committed us to continuing our tour.

When our plane touched down, we were swarmed by excited press and television people. We were rushed from the Tarmac to a hastily arranged news conference in the terminal and from there to the most popular TV show in

Peru. It all seemed terribly, even frighteningly spontaneous to me. Then I learned the clever ploy initiated by our embassy. They had spread the word that we were *defying* our own government. We were heroes from the moment our plane touched down.

From the news conference in the terminal, we were sped to the major television studio, where a popular program was playing live to the nation and a large studio audience. After changing into our Penn blazer outfits, we went onstage singing. It was the same routine that had taken us to the Macy's parade: the men came on singing "Drink a Highball at Nightfall," then went into a humming chorus, and I turned and addressed the camera and the studio audience.

"Buenas noches, damas y caballeros," I said, hopefully rolling my r's correctly and speaking with all the right inflections. "Es con gran placer que el Club de Canto de la Universidad de Pennsylvania ha venido para compartir su musica y su sincera amistad con sus amigos en Lima. Y ahora, amigos, El Glee Club de la Universidad de Pennsylvania." I turned to the club and they burst into lyrics and finished out the song.

For the next eternity, live on camera, I tried to convince the program's host that I had memorized nineteen seconds worth of Spanish and did not know one more syllable. He seemed unable to grasp this concept from one who had just rolled out so fluent a speech. Finally Juan Arce, a member of the studio audience who understood both sides of the debate, jumped to the stage and explained all. He then took the next two weeks off from his job and became our interpreter who traveled with us everywhere. And our dilapidated clunker of a bus was exchanged for a fine, upholstered, air conditioned Peruvian Air Force bus. Sometimes it really pays to defy one's government—at least in the eyes of others.

We covered much of the country and were not ashamed of misty eyes when we sang in dusty schoolyards for children suffering from incredible poverty and malnutrition. We felt warm pride when a college student shook our hands and spoke in his best English, "If President Nixon had sent you before tonight, we would not know hate in governments—we would know the love of people." We were invited to special fund-raising dinners given by the rich to benefit hospitals of the poor and joyously sang and delightedly ate *anticuchos* and *animales*. It wasn't until we were back in the U.S. that I told the others they had enjoyed beef heart and guinea pig.

One very interesting visit was to the home of a gentleman who had turned the ground floor of his house into a private museum. Among the many fascinating objects on display was the box-like piano that had been in the possession of La Périchole—the "liberator" of Peru and about whom Jacques Offenbach would write his famous operetta. The generous curator even permitted me to play a brief Bach invention on it. I'm sure La Périchole played it better.

We scampered over the unbelievable ruins of ancient civilizations in Cuzco and Machu Picchu. I soaked up everything there was to see with a thrill quite impossible to describe. To this day, I remember the final turn at the top of the mountain which revealed the massive ruins of Machu Picchu spread out majestically before me, I was Hiram Bingham rediscovering them in 1911.

"Enjoy it all now, Monty," I said to myself. "You'll never be here again."

I couldn't know then that the Glee Club and I would, indeed, be there once again in 1987. And that I would be as thrilled the second time as the first.

Our final concert in Peru was to have been in a downtown theater in Lima. Our fame, however, had outgrown the venue and a stage was erected in the middle of a huge outdoor tennis club. Thousands showed up and, at the end of the show, we understood the experiences of the Beatles. Our shirts were ripped off our backs by screaming fans. One girl, holding my ripped shirt in one hand and a pen in the other, pleaded with me to autograph it, which, of course, I did with great pleasure.

We had also let it be known that we wished to send postcards to all the incoming freshmen males (we had brought labels with their names and addresses with us courtesy of the dean of admissions at Penn) but that we couldn't afford both the cards and the postage. Juan Arce's wife, Barbara, got on the radio to announce the change of location and added that anyone who was coming to our final concert should bring a new postcard to give to us. The performance ended with thousands of postcards being presented to me onstage. The forty of us wrote messages from South America inviting the freshmen to audition for our ranks in September.

We received almost unprecedented press coverage for nearly everything we did in Peru. But the *New York Times* sort of summed it all up for us: "The Penn Glee Club has created greater understanding between the United States and the people of South America than could be possible at this time on higher diplomatic planes."

Two very special Philadelphia friends, John and Mary Quereau, had recently built a wonderful summer home on Spruce Head Island in Maine, and I spent many delightful times there with them and their son Quentin. Prior to his marriage, Quentin and I traveled together to such fascinating spots as Yugoslavia, Scandinavia, Greece and Egypt, among many others, during numerous summer outings. I was best man at his wedding and we continue to count each other as closest of friends. While visiting the Quereaus' Maine home—which, by the way, they named Spindrift after my musical—I found the perfect land for me on the island, promptly bought it, and designed a house to go on my dramatic cliff cascading in four levels down to the sea.

Shortly after the Glee Club's return from South America, I went up to my new summer home. The most dramatic feature of the house is the dining room on a balcony overlooking the living room. The living room, consequently, is a story and a half high with an entire wall of glass facing the sea. It was just dumb luck that all my plans and blueprints for the house turned out right and that the man I hired to follow them, Forrest Adams, and his two sons built it exactly to my design. Named Connemara—from a reference to a section of northwest Ireland in *Spindrift*—the house has become the most wonderful and peaceful of "hideaways" for me. The quotation marks are because all of my family and most of my friends and students have found my hideaway.

I am making a conscious effort in writing these memoirs to avoid too many references to individual students. If I were to go into detail on each student who contributed vastly to the success of the groups or my personal growth and happiness, this little book would expand rapidly into multiple volumes. By limiting such personal references, I feel that I am being fairer to many who would not receive the special mention they deserve. But there are a few students over whom I simply can't just glide in a passing reference. James Kearney is one of these.

When Jimmy auditioned for me at the beginning of his freshman year in 1969, he looked about twelve years old. He possessed a fine tenor voice and superb musicianship, and I accepted him into the Glee Club without hesitation. That he lived up to his early promise is a considerable understatement.

"What do you want to be when you grow up, Jimmy?" I asked him that first day.

"Rudolph Bing," he shot back immediately.

Rudolph Bing was at that time general manager of the Metropolitan Opera Company in New York. After four years in the Glee Club—including being appointed my student conductor—Jim went on to create an arts management curriculum for himself which still is taught in Penn's Wharton School. From there he progressed to become general manager of the Santa Fe Opera and then the Spoleto Festival USA. My original appraisal and Jimmy's ambitions were more than justified before he died a tragic death at an unthinkably early age.

By the 1969–1970 academic year, the country was experiencing a strange new phenomenon. It was the time of "Do Your Own Thing," and it became unfashionable for students everywhere to join anything, particularly anything so frivolous as an all-male glee club. All over the country, glee clubs were rolling over and dying like mastodons. If the University of Pennsylvania Glee Club was to survive this trend, it would take more than an exciting tour to South America. And we determined to give it more. Thanks in large measure to an imaginative meeting I had with students Bob Hallock, George Vollano, Alan Rosenblatt, and Jim Kearney, a viable new direction was mapped out for the club and we would become a strong and vital voice in all that students were hoping to accomplish with their demonstrations on other campuses. With *Handel with Hair* we proved that we were a valid voice for more than just singing.

Handel with Hair was the first Penn Glee Club concert to be given a title, and it ably reflected the content of our performance: we covered the broad range from George Frederic Handel to the then current Broadway craze *Hair*. We put away the choral risers and built colorful wooden cubes and ladders for our elevations. Perhaps the most powerful scene in our show was one of stark contrasts and national moral immediacy.

Two large rear-projection screens were lowered and the club gathered around them. They sang my setting of "Lincoln's Gettysburg Address" while black-and-white slides of Matthew Brady's photographs of the Civil War were projected. As the song continued, an occasional color slide of Vietnam would interrupt the Brady for a fraction of a second on one or another of the screens. Then more would interrupt on both until ghastly color photos of the Vietnam war soon were all that the audience saw. The timing was such that as we reached the words "it is altogether fitting and proper that we should do this," the two screens showed the identical photograph of a blood-covered, horribly maimed GI being evacuated into a helicopter. The irony was not lost on anyone. When we reached the words "government of the people, by the people, for the people," the visual scenes were of a protest march on Washington, D.C. What once had been perceived as a concert chorus was now speaking the sentiments strongly felt by students on campuses throughout the nation. The Penn Glee Club had no intention of rolling over with the other dinosaurs.

Our final scene was one of great theatricality. We had built a large metal jungle-gym-like structure which the men used for numerous levels. Two songs from *Hair* were sung with clever effect. The first was done on a black stage with each man holding a tiny, moving flashlight emulating the movement of the planets as "Jupiter aligns with Mars." The concept for the second song was tipped prematurely by the downtown newspapers. They stated that we were going to "simulate a nude scene from the Broadway show."

The Reverend Jack Russell was provost of the university at the time. When he saw this in the papers, he called me to his office in College Hall.

"What do you mean by 'simulate a nude scene' in your production?" he asked.

I told him that only nine men would appear to be nude on the several levels of the jungle gym. They would be wearing body stockings while the rest of the chorus would be in black turtlenecks and jeans.

"What are you trying to say with the scene?"

"It starts with a writhing, primordial mass belly-down on stage and gradually rises to its feet in a danced sequence that culminates in God's greatest creation, man," I said. "It is a beautiful scene, mostly back-lighted, with nothing erotic about it. We also have no intention to use it as cheap publicity for the show."

"Do you believe in it?"

"Yes, Jack, I do," I answered.

"Then don't be a hypocrite," he said. "Take off the body stockings."

As it turned out, we found it more effective to have only one nude man climb the jungle gym and stand dramatically on the top with his arms raised high above his head. It was a scene of great beauty, and Will Fleissig never attempted to make his role anything more than the stunning tableau it was. His lithe, swimmer's build was exactly right for the Finale's centerpiece. *Handel with Hair*, also, was exactly right for its time, and we played it frequently and as far west as Saint Louis. It was interesting to us that alumni and even newspapers got wind of our "daring staging" and expressed concern beforehand but were unanimous in their praise afterward. Well, almost unanimous. There was one minor flap. Some official in Trenton, New Jersey, *who had not seen the show* when it played in a state-owned theater, heard the nude scene mentioned and wrote a letter of protest to Penn's president, Gaylord Harnwell. Gaylord, who *had* seen the show with his wife, Mollie, replied immediately and backed me and the Glee Club all the way. We never heard another word.

The following fall the Armstrong Cork Company hired us to revive *Handel with Hair* in its Lancaster theater the first week in October. The price was excellent, so we accepted even though a quarter of the original cast had graduated in May. All the new men had to learn the entire show—music, staging, and dances—in less than three weeks! It was a daunting task at best, but they came through splendidly. Our original nude, Will Fleissig, was one of those who had already left, so auditions were held for a body as much like his as possible. We found one in Dick Steiner. It wasn't until a while later that I learned that he was so fearful of disgracing himself on stage that he lessened the chance in a dressing room shortly before his dramatic scene.

Our Award of Merit dinners, meanwhile, progressed nicely. In 1969 we presented the award to Elaine Brown, founder and dynamic conductor of the wonderful Singing City Choir. Perhaps one of our most successful dinners was the 1970 evening with the "dean of American composers," Aaron Copland. He proved to be a most gracious and personable recipient, conducted us in "Stomp Your Foot" from his opera *The Tender Land*, and chatted with us for hours in a dormitory lounge after the formal dinner was over. We also presented a Special Award to Gaylord Harnwell at a convention of the Intercollegiate Musical Council that we hosted on our campus.

In the summer of 1967, my friend Morgan Soutter and I had spent a good deal of time in Greece. Climbing over the ruins of Sparta and standing in the pass at Thermopylae had an immense effect on me. Here we were at the scenes of major battles of nearly three thousand years ago, while three thousand miles away a bloody war was now being fought in Vietnam. Humanity never seems to learn from its past. It gnawed at my brain to the extent that, back in Athens, I bought a two-volume set of the *Histories of Herodotus of Halicarnassus*, with his definitive history of the Peloponnesian Wars. What a fabulous idea for a choral work, I thought. I began writing immediately, while I was on the island of Crete. I would create a work for male chorus and maybe a dozen brass.

For some two years that project continued to occupy my thoughts, and every now and then I would work on it a bit. I was a very good soldier in Korea, but I was dead against the Vietnam war, and virtually everything I was writing now reflected that position. One day, William Smith, associate conductor of the Philadelphia Orchestra, stopped me on Chestnut Street.

"What are you writing these days?" he asked.

I proceeded to tell him about Herodotus and my plans for the Glee Club and brass.

"Why don't you think a little grander?" he said. And then and there a definite commission was struck.

Now I worked every spare waking minute on the project. It became an obsession with me. It also became grander and grander. I figure today that, if I had continued with all the texts and sketches I made, the work would be slightly longer than anything Bruckner ever wrote. Fortunately, reason—and Bill—prevailed, and the final piece was a manageable half hour. David Madison, assistant concertmaster, Mason Jones, principal French horn, and Murray Pannitz, principal flute, asked me if I would write into the piece a small solo passage for each of them. The ironic twist was that Norman Carroll, the orchestra's wonderful concertmaster, played the performance, and therefore the specially written violin solo went to him. (Actually, Davey got his chance the next year when the Trenton Symphony performed the work.)

Herodotus Fragments was written for male chorus, female chorus, and symphony orchestra. It had its premiere at the Academy of Music by the University of Pennsylvania Glee Club, the Pennsyngers, and the Philadelphia Orchestra on April 28, 1970. Dear friend Randall Thompson, who had encouraged me all along the way, came down from Boston for the occasion. The work is in ten movements, and in the short break between two of them a woman sitting behind me in the audience leaned forward and tapped me on the shoulder.

"Pardon me. Aren't you Bruce Montgomery?" she whispered.

"Why, yes," I answered, flattered to be recognized.

"I thought so. You're obviously the most nervous person in the audience tonight!" she added—almost too frankly, I thought. My balloon thoroughly deflated, I slunk down in my seat to fidget through the remainder of the piece. Happily, my fears were unfounded, as the work ended with a standing ovation and considerable raves in the Philadelphia newspapers.

Penn's magnificent new Annenberg Center was finished, and the Royal Shakespeare Company from London was scheduled to open it. For some reason they backed out, so the very first production in the center was the University of Pennsylvania Glee Club. We packed the Zellerbach Theatre as we presented our 1971 show *See Hear!* The most memorable thing about *See Hear!* was that in it we introduced "Walk Him Up the Stairs" from *Purlie.* It's been in our repertoire ever since. On opening night we learned that the architect had created one major flaw in his design. In Act Two, there were times when I was bewildered to see a scene or song with five or six men missing from the stage. Then in the next scene they'd be back and others missing. This went on for half an hour or so before I got the message of what was going on.

There was an exit on each side of the stage's proscenium that led directly to the backstage hallway. In other words, the audience had access to the backstage, the dressing rooms, the stage, and all the other nonpublic areas of the building! This is not the accepted way to design a theater. During our Act Two, three men had simply walked backstage and proceeded to steal all our valuables from the dressing rooms. Rushing offstage for a costume change, several of the Glee Club men surprised the thieves and wrestled them to the ground. As those singers were needed on stage for the next number, their places on the hallway floor were taken by others. And so it went until the police arrived.

When I learned of our predicament, I decided that, since our audience must have been as aware as I that all was not going as planned, at the next opportunity in the flow of the performance I should take them into our confidence.

"I hope you're enjoying the show," I said from the orchestra pit. "Actually, you're missing the best show of the evening." And with that I explained the full scenario.

As it happened, Philadelphia's district attorney was in the audience, and feathers started flying immediately. Thanks to some heavyweight singers, the three thieves never got to their feet until the cops arrived. Then we spent most of the night at the police station until all details and bookings were completed. Since that first Zellerbach performance, to this day an usher has been stationed at those two proscenium exits.

In May and June 1971, the Penn Glee Club toured six countries in Europe. In Denmark, Finland, the Soviet Union, Bulgaria, Yugoslavia, and England we sang formal concerts, church services, our show *See Hear!*, radio programs, and impromptu sessions in airports and on street corners.

"You must enjoy a happy place at your university for it to send you on such a wonderful tour," a member of the Finnish Choral Union told us as we boarded our train for Leningrad at the Helsinki railroad station. "But I wonder if they know how much better we understand Americans now because you have been here? We will talk about this for a long, long time."

So, my friend, will we. That very comment is what our foreign tours have been predicated upon. That spirit has kept us going to other lands. That spirit kept us going on this exhausting nearly five-week 1971 tour—one of the longest we ever booked. We worked through a New York agency, Concerts Abroad, that specialized in foreign concerts, and they knew their business. Every facet of the tour was exciting, and we were blessed with some of the finest tour guides I have ever encountered.

Our visit to Denmark was entirely on Jutland, but we covered most of that. I had been to Denmark before and had seen much of the country, so perhaps the highlight of this visit was singing in Copenhagen's wonderful Tivoli Gardens. We wowed the Danes and, of great importance to me, we also wowed my aunt and uncle, Margaret and Eddie Chalif, who were coincidentally visiting Denmark at the time and were in the audience with my dear Danish friend Kirsten Leth.

From Denmark we flew to Helsinki. We had a concert that first night and discovered, to our dismay, that half our baggage had not arrived from Copenhagen. I made an instant executive decision. Half of us went on in white-tie-and-tails while the other half wore T-shirts and blue jeans! We created a bizarre impression at best, but I wanted the audience to know that we knew *how* to dress for them even though circumstances made it impossible. Just taking them into our confidence broke whatever ice there may have been, and they accepted everything we did from then on with wild enthusiasm. In this city of some of the world's greatest male choruses, we were highly flattered by our acceptance and our glowing reviews. In fact, we were asked on the spot to tape an hour-long radio show the following day.

The Mieskuoroliitto R. Y., one of Finland's great male choruses, invited us to spend an evening with them at their country cabin in the woods on the shore of the frigid Gulf of Finland. There's nothing formal or stilted about the manner in which they make you feel at home there. As soon as we arrived, both choruses marched stark naked into their huge sauna.

"There, we divide time equal between singing, sweating, and philosophy," one of their singers said to me later. The least philosophical part was running from the steam to the heart-arresting dive into the Gulf of Finland, just possibly a degree above the freezing point. And, as if survival initially seemed unlikely, we repeated the routine for hours.

Our train ride from Helsinki into the Soviet Union was uneventful except for the long delay at the border for passport check and emptying of baggage for customs personnel, replete with forbidding olive drab uniforms and submachine guns. Our next stop was a thirty-minute layover in Vyborg. It's difficult to describe the surprise and delight we saw on the faces of the townspeople—as well as fellow passengers on the train—as we formed on the outdoor steps of the station and burst into song. After a few songs betrayed to the growing crowd that we were from America, one high tenor voice in the crowd with a thick accent called out from the back.

"Sing 'Swanee River'!" he cried. It was probably the only American song he knew. Unfortunately, in a choral version it also was one we didn't.

When we arrived in Leningrad, we were met by our impressive Intourist guide, Zoya. I had been to the Soviet Union before and knew that all outsiders must have such a person attached to them. On this occasion, however, some uncommonly bright soul in the bureau must have looked carefully at our credentials, surmised that we were of more than average intelligence because we were a group from a university, and more sensitive than most because we were a singing chorus, and assigned us their very best.

Zoya had taken Harrison Salisbury around when he was writing *The 900 Days* about the siege of Leningrad during World War II. She had escorted John Erskine when he was writing on the same subject. It was Zoya who had accompanied the *National Geographic* team when they were doing a feature article on the city. We benefited greatly from her presence. Early in our first conversation, I told her how much we were looking forward to seeing and performing in her country and related the joy we had gained in South America singing spontaneously whenever we saw groups gathered in a park or kids in a schoolyard.

"Not in Soviet Union!" she stated deliberately in a slow, heavy accent. "Here, only where we say," she added emphatically.

It was the only time we locked horns: she proved to be a fascinating and knowledgeable guide and companion. Our first scheduled performance in the U.S.S.R. was at the Soviet American Friendship House. One of my favorite sights here was of Kim Story, Geoff Tozer, and Bob Hallock singing a uniquely American song beneath an immense head of Lenin. We sang half a concert, one of their fine choruses sang half, and we joined together for a song or two at the end. The first joint number suggested by their director was "Gaudeamus Igitur," the granddaddy of all collegiate songs and one that should have been known by every chorus in the civilized world. Although I knew it, I had never quite got around to keeping it in our repertoire, and the 1971 Penn Glee Club didn't know it. We—and I—appeared highly uncivilized that day. Now that the horse has flown, of course, the barn door has been shut. It's been in the club repertoire ever since.

On our third or fourth day in Leningrad, we had a free morning. Zoya proposed that we visit the Piskaryovskoye Cemetery. Here the bodies of those who did not survive the three-year siege during World War II are buried in mounds that seem to stretch on and on, ending in a colossal statue of Mother Russia. Under each mound, we were told, are thirty thousand bodies. It is a terribly sobering sight. It also is where Zoya's entire family, wiped out in the siege, are buried. She survived by eating sawdust and rats. Just inside the cemetery, before you descend the steps to the mounds, there is a sunken pit of granite with an eternal flame burning in remembrance.

"When we come here," Zoya told me, "we observe a minute of silence. Would you join me?"

"Of course," I answered, and we all ringed the pit.

I was standing right beside Zoya and, after a minute, I spoke to her quietly.

"I know you told me that we can't sing anywhere unless it is approved ahead of time," I told her almost tentatively. "But in 1963, I wrote a choral setting of Abraham Lincoln's 'Gettysburg Address' which we sang in a television show that was filmed on a battlefield of our Civil War. That, too, is now a wartime cemetery, just as this is. May we show our respects to you and your country by going to those stairs and singing that same anthem?" I assumed that Zoya was high enough in the Intourist bureaucracy that she was able to make such a decision on her own without having to check with some higher authority. I was right. She thought for a moment and then spoke.

"I think that would be appropriate," she said quietly.

We formed a choral stance on the steps and began, "Four score and seven years ago . . ." Within a few bars, we had some curious people stop to listen. Within a few more, dozens had stopped, then hundreds, then a very large crowd. I doubt if many understood the words we sang, but they couldn't have missed the intent of our singing. A few people went down on their knees. The singers began to have tears in their eyes. Some had tears streaming down their cheeks. A few were so moved by this moment that they simply couldn't sing any more and sat down on the steps. I find that I cannot possibly retell this incident and convey the emotion we felt. It was one of those situations when you had to be there to comprehend its immense effect on all—singers and audience alike.

Afterward, we returned to our bus. Zoya had been with us for several days and knew us to be a noisy and rambunctious bunch, but our entire trip back to Leningrad was one of awe and silence. I was the last to leave the bus, and Zoya was waiting for me by the front door as I exited.

"From now on," she said, "you sing wherever you wish."

Later that afternoon, we were driving along the Alexander Nevsky Prospekt when I spied a group of workers with their lunch pails gathered in a park. I looked hopefully over at Zoya; she had an unusual twinkle in her eye.

"I just remember," she said in her thick accent. "I wish to buy something in that store there. I will see you again in an hour."

With that, she left us to our own devices. We had won her over, but she could not be with us to condone our actions officially. We sang to the workers and amassed a large and receptive crowd. This sort of thing just did not happen very often in the U.S.S.R. I was reminded of the prisoners in Riobamba as people pressed small personal items, even books, into our hands. They didn't speak; they just wanted to say "thank you."

Throughout our stay in the Soviet Union we were painfully aware that our hotel rooms were bugged and our telephone conversations monitored. This gives uneasiness to nearly everything you do or say. In a group of inventive and imaginative pranksters, of course, it also gives rise to creative practical jokes. After David Bienenfeld ceased trembling from one bogus phone call he assumed was from the KGB, he decided to pull the same stunt on Tom Ulmer. Dave launched into his Soviet propaganda speech to fake Tom out. With a Russian-English phrase book in hand, he spieled off a series of transliterations he found without concern for their meaning. Occasionally he would interject a politically charged word like "Amerikanski pirate-ski" or "kapitalicheski." It wasn't until a genuine Russian began angrily squawking "Halloo, halloo!" that Dave realized he was actually talking (in his spurious Russian accent) not to Tom but to a Soviet monitor. Twice stung, I don't believe David tried it again.

Alan Brett's father had emigrated from Russia to the U.S. many years before, but his father's brother had not. Alan decided to telephone his uncle, but the conversation was difficult. His uncle spoke no English and Alan spoke no Russian. However, they both spoke Yiddish, and the talk proceeded in solicitous inquiries about all the relatives and in animated family anecdotes. At one point in the conversation, however, Alan was stammering and searching for a word that eluded him. With that, the omnipresent eavesdropper kindly provided the troublesome term! Unabashed, and without skipping a beat, Alan simply said "spasiba" and continued on with his uncle as if it were a common occurrence to include an intrusive monitor in his telephone conversations.

One extremely poignant moment in Russia occurred when some of us entered one of the rare synagogues as a shabbat service was about to commence. The expressions of fright that covered the faces of the elderly congregation were almost tactual. Here was their place of worship—always of deep concern in a country where religion in general had been nearly eradicated and the Jewish religion was a target of special persecution—being "invaded" by a group of young male strangers. When our Glee Club men proffered hands in greeting and said "Shalom," the anguish melted into warm handshakes and sincere welcomes.

One of the most valuable students on this tour was David Mechler. He didn't speak Danish or Finnish or Russian or Bulgarian, but he did speak German fluently. It seemed that whenever we were in trouble *someone* in the crowd spoke German, and our "instant interpreter" took over to our great relief. It was of particular value to me because as director I was forever being invited to private homes and small receptions. In self defense, I'd wangle an invitation for David as well. One occasion that I recall with more than a little humor was in Helsinki, when I was invited to visit the home of the much loved and venerable former conductor of a famous male chorus. As we arrived at his home, the entire family —wife, sons, daughters, their wives, husbands, and grandchildren—were in a receiving line at the front door. They all spoke German. David went charmingly into action for me. Introductions over, it was perfectly natural for us to strip and initiate animated conversation in the sauna! They're very civilized.

Shortly before we left Penn's campus on our trip, the senior class asked me to calligraph some certificates for them. When I delivered them I was asked for my bill. I told them that it was my contribution to their year-end ceremony. To my surprise, the president of the senior class showed up at the bus that would take us to the airport to begin our journey. He insisted that I take an envelope with me on the trip. On the plane I discovered that it contained a generous gift of cash "to be spent on something special on your tour." I decided that the generosity of the seniors would take us by hydrofoil to one of the most magnificent palaces in the world: Petrodvorets, several miles outside Leningrad. Arriving by boat in the manner planned by the czar, from the dock one approaches the palace along a gorgeous many-bridged canal and then is greeted by the immense cascade: steps of waterfalls and fountains, peopled on every level by heroic gold statues shimmering in the sunlight. These, in turn, lead you to the various, magnificently onion-domed and gilded pavilions of the palace. I have seen most of the world's great palaces, but this one is absolutely unique and unbelievably spectacular.

On one of our last days in the Soviet Union we were given a sumptuous dinner, part of which was a glorious mound of real beluga caviar—on each plate! Thirty-six of us were served marvelous dollops. Twenty-eight wouldn't touch them. Here we go again with the picky eaters. This time, however, I didn't admonish them in any manner. This time eight of us ate the caviar supplied to the entire Club. It's the only time in my life that I had all the caviar I wanted. I spent the next two days regretting it.

When, at last, we left Moscow to fly to Bulgaria, we played a raucous game of charades on the Aeroflot plane and the startled Russians didn't know what to make of these crazy Americans.

We arrived in Sofia, Bulgaria, and flew from there to Primorsko, a wonderful town on the Black Sea. People came from all over the Communist bloc to this most popular of summer resorts. Like little children, we romped on the shore of the Black Sea, had wonderfully refreshing swims and played with Frisbees on the beach. As always, we gathered crowds of onlookers who had never seen a Frisbee before. And as always, we lured them into the game and gave them the disks as we left the beach. After playing with us for a while, one Yugoslavian college student gathered his nerve and tried his English.

"Are you here for the tournament?" he asked.

"What tournament?"

"The International Basketball Tournament," he replied.

We learned that it was an open tournament and, with a borrowed ball, we put together a team on the spot. At this date, so many years later, I don't remember the exact statistics, but we beat something like three East German teams, two Russian teams, two Yugoslavian teams, and one or two Bulgarian teams. At any rate, we came in third, and Terry Tucker was photographed standing on the Olympic-style three-step winners' platform proudly holding a bouquet of roses and wearing the medal, which hung framed on my office wall for all the years thereafter.

I'm certain that it was as a direct result of our basketball victories and the many friends we made through them that our performance on our last night in Primorsko was more than just a success. One of the more remarkable feats of the evening was accomplished by our wonderful stage manager/photographer Bill Gilliss. Even though it harked back to another show of another year, we had decided to end our show in this huge outdoor theater with the dramatic nude scene from *Hair*. The effectiveness of the scene is greatly dependent on successful and artistic lighting. How he did it I'll never know, but Bill got every desire and every lighting cue across to the excellent professional stage crew—not one of whom understood a word of English! According to the Voice of America, "three thousand mostly young people crowded into the open-air theater at Primorsko and stamped and shouted their approval with rhythmic clapping after every song." There's no high in the world like that.

But even more meaningful than that kind of press were the remarks of a Bulgarian student after our show as he addressed us almost timidly through an interpreter.

"Some of us came to spoil your show tonight with shouts of Vietnam," he said to us as students were strewing our exit path with flowers. "But we saw that you brought only happiness and beauty and love to so many and your smiles became our smiles. For tonight we can say only thank you to President Nixon. We will talk of Vietnam tomorrow."

It is this kind of comment that makes any tour worth all the effort. We will receive many such encomiums throughout the years to come. We will never take them for granted.

After four wonderful days in Primorsko, we flew back to Sofia. From there we took a fine tour bus high up into the mountains on an extremely dramatic ride through the countryside. On the way, we entered the bustling town of Stanke Dimitrov and realized that it was market day. The town square, like those of most towns there, contained a statue in the center with steps leading to it. We can't see stairs, of course, without our minds instantly turning them into choral risers. So, at the height of market day, we stopped the bus and sang for the crowds of people there. It was so unexpected and so different from their customary market day routine that all sales ceased and a concert audience formed. One suspicious uniformed official insisted on being given a running translation to make certain that we weren't spreading any subversive message. But other than that self-important operetta factotum, the town adored us and thanked us profusely for stopping to give them such joy. Two women tried to give us live chickens. One woman insisted that we take along a live pig (we didn't). Meanwhile, Brian Maloney was sitting on a curb artfully turning the daily newspapers into fancy hats for all the children.

Nine thousand feet up in the mountains, we visited the Rila Monastery. Unlike the one in Ecuador, this monastery was active and fascinating. The cloistered triple tiers of arches surrounding the courtyard looked almost Moorish in their striped design. And the church was made up of five domes. We started to sing off to the side—not a planned concert, mind you, but just for our own benefit—when a monk came over and stopped us. Our location was not doing us justice, he felt, so he pushed us directly under the large center dome and gave me the high sign to go for it. Between the large center dome and the four smaller ones, the acoustics were breathtaking, and Randall Thompson's "Alleluia" was never more inspiring to us. I was no sooner back in the bus than I wrote a postcard to my friend to tell him so.

We returned to Sofia and were met by Mr. and Mrs. John Jones. Mr. Jones was the first secretary in our embassy. Mrs. Jones immediately endeared herself to us by inviting us to her apartment to launder our underwear in her washing machine. Now, that's how to endear yourself to a chorus on tour. It sure beats doing laundry by hand in a wash basin. So, before she could change her mind, six of us volunteered to collect the laundry for the group and take it to the Joneses'. As we entered the apartment building, we were keenly aware of suspicious stares from three men sitting there. We supposed it was our overactive imaginations and dismissed the notion. When we returned to our hotel, however, we discovered that the remainder of the club felt equally uneasy in their rooms, and the running joke—hopefully not understood by the people around us—was to roam the halls whistling the theme from *Mission Impossible*.

We knew that people entered our rooms during the day and found rather convincing evidence of newly installed bugging devices. Even more scary, men entered some of our rooms at night when we were actually or supposedly asleep. The outcome of all this is that eleven of us had our passports stolen. Eight were "found" the next afternoon.

I went almost at once to the American embassy and was ushered into the office of the ambassador. As he greeted me, he put a finger to his lips and pointed straight up. In other words, he knew that the embassy was bugged, so we exchanged simple pleasantries for a few minutes. Then, after pushing code buttons on a security device, we descended to the street, out the door, and into the park.

"We know about your stolen passports," he said when we finally were outdoors. "We've retrieved two of them, but Mr. Coppola's is still missing. I don't know if we can issue one quickly enough for your departure tomorrow. He may have to stay here and we will make every arrangement possible for him."

It was comforting to learn that *our* espionage was pretty good, too, but I did not want to hear that one member of our group might have to stay behind, no matter what hospitality was shown him. In order to make tracks as best we could to expedite the replacement of the missing passport, Larry Coppola and

I spent the early afternoon in the city looking for a photographer who would take passport photos and process them at once. In Bulgaria, this was harder than it sounds. Apparently there were no Polaroids there.

Larry's passport was found just about an hour before we were to leave for the plane. He was one very relieved young man. So was I. When we arrived at the terminal, all of us went through security check with no problem. The only person stopped and searched was Larry. Sofians may not have Polaroid, but they have excellent networks.

We stopped in Belgrade, Yugoslavia. Jay Skarzenski had long been teased for his prominent dimples. In addition to a little singing, the best thing to come our way from Belgrade was a bottle of Dimples Scotch, which was ceremoniously presented to Jay. Most of the remainder of our fabulous tour of 1971 was spent in England. We arrived in time to join all of London in celebrating the queen's birthday. I'm not certain if I fully convinced the club that the trooping of the Royal Guards, the bands, the Scottish Highlanders, and the entire royal family, including the queen herself, were assembled in their honor. But it was a most impressive and impeccably timed way to introduce the Penn Glee Club to England.

We sang pretty much all over England—in London, Cambridge, Oxford, York, and so on—but one of my very favorite performances was in the ancient Dry Drayton church outside Cambridge. We had been asked to sing a full evensong service and follow it with an hour's concert. Since the concert would be held in the church, I checked beforehand with the vicar as to what would be appropriate for it.

"How about dancing, for example?" I asked him.

"Once the service is over," he said, "you may be as secular as you wish."

When the performance was over and encores were eagerly sought and happily given, the old vicar stood in front of the altar and spoke in his loud, high voice with such a precise English accent that he sounded like a caricature of an ecclesiastical orator.

"I do believe," he intoned slowly, "that this is the first time applause has been heard in these walls in eight hundred years!"

After a concert in London, we drove all night to be on the Salisbury Plain in time for sunrise at the Great Stonehenge. We arrived as the first glimmer of the false dawn was beginning to appear in the east. To our dismay, there was a tall cyclone fence around the entire area, and it was closed until something like

10:00 A.M. This wasn't what we had driven all night for. Necessity is still the mother of invention, so we climbed the fence in time to see the ball of the sun rise over the heel stone. I can't imagine why it didn't occur to us that the fence was wired, but soon the constabulary from twenty miles around converged on us. After stating who we were and that we had traveled all night from a London concert, we paid admission for all of us and were permitted to remain. I went back there, incidentally, two weeks later and found that, in addition to the high fence, it now contained concertina barbed wire around the entire circumference. I can't tell you how responsible and guilty I felt.

We flew back to the United States a tired but supremely happy group. We all had various interviews with our hometown papers, all of great interest and highly complimentary to our university. But I guess the Voice of America said it for all of us on June 9, from Bulgaria:

"At a time when students throughout the world are demonstrating against nearly everything, thirty-six young men from the University of Pennsylvania in Philadelphia are staging an impressive demonstration for understanding."

✦ F I V E ✦

We Were Busy Boys

FRESH ON THE HEELS of our triumphs in Europe, the Glee Club got down to its more mundane business of functioning "normally." *Handel with Hair* and *See Hear!* had a worthy successor in *Paint the Яed Town*, which recalled some of our tour experiences, complete with rear-projected slides and movies. We also continued our string of very exciting recipients of our Award of Merit.

Impresario Sol Hurok came to campus in 1971. In the world of the arts in the mid-twentieth century, one impresario stood out above all others. In every corner of the United States and Europe—from the finest opera houses in the largest cities to high school auditoriums in the most out-of-the-way hamlets—the simple heading "S. Hurok Presents" at the top of a poster or program instantly informed the readers that tonight they would see a performance by the greatest artists in the world. A piano recital would be one of the world's paramount pianists. Ballet would be among the supreme companies on earth.

At the time, Hurok's roster of artists embraced every kind of artist and entertainment from Jan Peerce to the Black Watch bagpipers; from the Azuma Kabuki Dancers of Japan to Artur Rubinstein; and from Isaac Stern to the Bolshoi Ballet. It was a source of special satisfaction to us to be able to reverse the norm and have "The Penn Glee Club presents S. Hurok."

In 1957, two freshman women had come to me with an idea. Edie Herman and Meryl Moss felt that the all-male Glee Club was so successful that they wanted to found an all-female chorus. They called it the Pennsyngers, and I hired Ernest Wells to be their first director. Over the years, Ernest was succeeded by George Ganz, Denny Rittenhouse, and Susan Dash. Also over the years, the Pennsyngers sometimes found themselves outnumbering their audiences. They sang joint concerts with such all-male groups as the Kings Point Glee Club of the Merchant Marine Academy. They were a fine chorus that deserved better recognition than they were receiving. Apparently, there wasn't as much demand for a women's chorus on our campus as we all had hoped and envisioned. So in 1971 I took the bull by the horns and took it over myself. We also changed the name to the Penn Singers. The other seemed a bit too precious.

With the hearty support and encouragement of my boss, Alice Emerson, dean of students, the most drastic change was to make it a coed chorus. Our first performances together were sold out before we opened, because of the change in concept, not the change in directorship. Our first production was given a title, *Three Ages of Faith*, and consisted of the Buxtehude Missa Brevis, the Schubert Mass in G, and five numbers from *Jesus Christ, Superstar*—complete with a rock band. After the intermission, we presented a fully staged and costumed *Trial by Jury*, the only one-act operetta by Gilbert & Sullivan. There certainly was something for every taste. And it paid off with packed houses.

The following Tuesday was our regular rehearsal time, so in their euphoria of so successful a weekend, I sat them down in a circle and stated our case.

"OK," I said, "You've done some early music, Romantic music, and contemporary music. You've also done light opera. Which way do you want to continue, if any?"

Virtually to a member, they loudly selected light opera. They had had a ball doing G&S, and decided then and there to specialize in Gilbert & Sullivan with one of the famous operas every spring. Tish Emerson—who later would become the first female president of Wheaton College in Norton, Massachusetts—backed me all the way. The Penn Singers thus became one of the very few student performing arts groups that regularly used the Zellerbach Theatre in the Annenberg Center. As of this writing, they have presented thirteen of the fourteen operas, from *Thespis* to *Utopia, Limited*, some of them several times. One of these years they will do the last G&S opera, *The Grand Duke*, and become one of the few companies in the world to have done them all.

Award of Merit dinners continued to occupy our interest, and it was astonishing to us that such world-class musicians acknowledged its importance and came to our campus to receive the award. Eugene Ormandy, the highly acclaimed long-time conductor of the Philadelphia Orchestra, received our medallion for 1972. We were much amused when I introduced him to Mollie Harnwell, wife of the president. Each had had a recent hip operation and, they discovered, they had shared the same surgeon. They spent the cocktail period before dinner comparing walks and competing in jogging contests across the Rotunda of the University Museum.

In 1972, the Orpheus Club of Philadelphia did me the great honor of inviting me to conduct its two centennial concerts in the Academy of Music. The Orpheus Club had been founded by Joseph Clark Simms, Jr., just ten years after he had founded the University of Pennsylvania Glee Club. For the February concert, I was commissioned to compose a major work. "An Orpheus Triptych," a work for male chorus and piano, was a setting of three writings about Orpheus of Greek mythology. The first movement was to a text by Apollonius Rhodius (third century B.C.); the second was by John Fletcher (although it is frequently attributed to Shakespeare since it appears in his *King Henry VIII*); and I wrote the text for the third movement.

For the May concert, I arranged a medley of ten songs. For "Ten Decades" I selected one song for each of the OC's decades from what I considered a pivotal Broadway show of the time. It began with "Oh, You Naughty, Naughty Men" from *The Black Crook* and proceeded through Cohan, Herbert, Romberg, Gershwin, Rogers, Bernstein, and so on, to end in the latest hit of the 1972 decade: "Let the Sun Shine In" from *Hair*. I am happy to report that my offerings for the hundredth anniversary of the Orpheus Club were received with great enthusiasm by both singers and audiences.

In 1973, I was asked to come to the White House for lunch. That's not an everyday occurrence for me, so I was very excited by the invitation—a mild understatement. President Nixon held church services in the East Room regularly on Sundays, and the Penn Glee Club was being considered to do the musical portion of one of those services and a concert afterward. I was taken all through the stately home and felt very privileged to see the Lincoln Room, the location of Franklin Roosevelt's Fireside Chats, and all the other places I had heard about all my life.

When I returned home, it was but a few weeks before a bona fide invitation arrived. I gulped when I learned the desired date—we were already booked for that day. I asked if this were like England, so that a command performance meant that whatever else was booked, one canceled it and did the bidding of the president. No, I was told, we would receive another invitation at a later date. That indeed came but by that time the details of Watergate had surfaced and the club voted to turn down the invitation. I was sorry for this and attempted to convince the men that we would be singing at the White

House for the president of the United States—that we should not consider it a favor to Nixon. My argument was not terribly convincing and I went along with their feelings. I have had regrets ever since, but I respected and backed their decision.

Our 1973 show, *It's About Time*, looked cleverer on paper than on stage. The premise seemed intriguing: juxtaposing songs of wholly different time periods that told somewhat the same tale. A sedate Gregorian chant, for example, sung as it might have been by a group of medieval monks, was followed immediately by "God Said" from Leonard Bernstein's very twentieth-century *Mass*, wildly rhythmic and fully staged. The contrasts were startling and obvious. I hoped that our growing disenchantment in the show itself wasn't. The audience liked it, but we rapidly grew tired of performing it. And it had seemed such a good idea in the planning stages!

A genuine high point of the Glee Club's 1974 season, on the other hand, was our "staged concert" we called *Americ-O-Round*. Several of the highlights were a fiendishly difficult arrangement that Richard Broadhead made for us of "Turn, Turn, Turn," which was worth all the hard work; the premiere performance of "Prelude and Song for Jerusalem" which Jamie Lightstone had composed for us; a tremendously theatrical minstrel-show medley of songs by Stephen Foster complete with banjos, huge pink satin bow-ties, and tambourine drills; a piano solo by Jeff Dembo, one of our two phenomenal accompanists, of George Gershwin's "Rhapsody in Blue"; and another premiere of an extended, eight-movement, fully staged missa brevis, "Et in Terra Pax," which I had composed as the finale of the show. I didn't suspect at the time that it would have a life of its own and that we would perform it outside of *Americ-o-Round* in theaters, schools, churches and synagogues. Mark Rippel accompanied it on the organ in several of these venues. But the clincher, for me, was our performance of it in the John F. Kennedy Center in Washington, D.C.

The great contralto and lady-of-the-world Marian Anderson came to campus to receive our Award of Merit in 1973. Arturo Toscanini had declared that she possessed "a voice one hears once in a hundred years." Her Easter Sunday concert at the Lincoln Memorial in 1939 was one of the most heralded performances ever given in this country. She was special delegate to the United Nations and had been honored as highly as any American musician ever. With us, she was one of the most gracious ladies I ever have met and, I'm privileged to say, her friendship continued until she died.

The Pulitzer Prize-winning composer Samuel Barber received the 1974 honor. I'm aware that he was one of the finest American composers of the twentieth century and I love much of his work, but he seemed one of the most difficult men I'd ever met at entering into conversations. For a composer so very expressive in his music, he was distinctly taciturn with us. He had the habit of answering most questions with a single syllable. Whenever I tried to get something interesting started for the benefit and edification of the students, he had the incomparable ability to terminate every conversation with a word or two. His opera *Cleopatra* commissioned to open the new Metropolitan Opera House in Lincoln Center, for instance, was hardly a success, and I learned shortly before he came to our campus that he was about to rewrite it.

"I'm sure that the students here would be fascinated to learn how you embark on so daunting a project," I told him. "Will you share with us how you are going about rethinking and reworking such a massive undertaking?"

"I bought new manuscript paper." Period.

Shortly after I took over the reins of the Penn Glee Club, I had begun a marvelous tradition of inviting the club members, their dates, their parents, and other family members to my home in Germantown following the final performance of our major campus run. As I have recounted earlier, my mother and her wonderful maid, Marjorie, worked for days preparing for the occasion. For years I tried to convince them that it had become too big and I must hire a caterer. No such nonsense was tolerated and the two of them kept on with their labor of love until 1987, when the house was sold and we moved into apartments in Chestnut Hill. I relocated the party to the E. Craig Sweeten Alumni Center on campus and had several delicatessens prepare the comestibles. It was fun and delicious but clearly lacked the charm of home and family.

In anticipation of the country's bicentennial, we honored the world-famous folk singer Burl Ives with our 1975 award for his wonderful contribution to Americana. Not only was he absolutely at home with the students—and they with him—but he was irresistibly funny, charming, and generous with his guitar in hand to demonstrate the things about which he was speaking. When David Goldberg and I met his plane and took him and his wife to the hotel, the first thing he did was fling his toupee on the bed and ask whether Book-binder's restaurant was still in business "for lunch tomorrow." He then grabbed his guitar and we chatted and sang most of the night. We ate most of the next day.

Score! followed in 1975 and was about all sorts of sports. We often referred to it as "a knockout of a show," ending in a boxing ring. Little did we know that Lorenzo Walker and Mike Diamant had some offstage problems with each other and one performance actually did end with a knockout! *Score!* opened with "Magic to Do" from *Pippin*, and Michael Cianfrani bewitched us with his singing and dancing. We knew then that he would go places in show busi-ness—which indeed he did as Michael Corbett, becoming a popular soap opera star on *The Young and the Restless*.

Also in 1975 occurred a "Michel Huberism" that I believe should be recorded. The only time in all my years at Penn when I was angry with Mike was also the time I felt perhaps my greatest admiration for him. Mike was head of the General Alumni Society, and we were to leave for the weekend to perform for the alumni club in Pittsburgh. The bus had been chartered. Our social sched-ules had been cleared. Special music had been rehearsed. Housing had been arranged in private homes. Four days before we were to leave, I received a tele-phone call from a Pittsburgh friend expressing his disappointment at the can-cellation of our trip and concert. Canceled? That was the first I had heard of it! I was both angry and greatly embarrassed at hearing of it from a friend—particularly a non-Penn-alumnus friend.

I immediately contacted Mike and found out that it was indeed true. What on earth was he thinking, I asked, to let everyone know about it except the individuals most involved? When was he going to get around to telling us? I was furious and let him have it with both barrels.

Mike easily could have written an apology and an explanation that I could have read and clarified to the Glee Club. But that wasn't his style. He knew we rehearsed at 4:00 P.M. in Room 511 in the Annenberg Center and, unan-nounced, came to our next rehearsal and explained everything. (It seemed as if our first tour of 1957 was being reenacted: the Pittsburgh alumni club had-n't sold any tickets.) His remarks and the sincerity of his apology were deeply appreciated and I have no doubt that, as he left, the club spontaneously burst into "Oh, here's to Mike Huber, fill up the tankard . . ." I know for certain that he had won the total respect of everyone there.

Opus 76 took advantage of the nation's bicentennial and was devoted entirely to American music. We even subtitled it—brace yourself!—"A Bass 'n' Tenoral Celebration." Among the many songs in the show, this was the first time we performed my friend Bill Appling's arrangement of the spiritual "Rock-a Ma Soul." This was so popular—complete with our spilling out into the audience to encourage their participation—that it entered the club's standard repertoire. It also was for *Opus 76* that I wrote perhaps the corniest song I ever composed: "How Do You Spell the Fourth of July?" Even the metronome marking was too precious for words: "Tempo di every pseudo patriotic song you ever heard!" The song included four tableaux of famous scenes—Washington crossing the Delaware, Ben Franklin flying his kite, Paul Revere on his ride, and Betsy Ross making the first flag. But the pièce de résistance was the last gimmick: eighteen men held three-foot cards, each bearing a single letter. As they sang the words "that's how you spell" they rushed to form words across the stage from one proscenium to the other. Looking down at their labor, they realize that they are in the wrong order when it reads "FIVE SPORTS EXIST IN NY." They then scramble into "SPITE ON FIRST IVY SEX," then "IT PROVES SEX IS NIFTY," and finally get it right with "SPIRIT OF SEVENTY SIX."

One of the zaniest tours the Penn Glee Club ever undertook was the 1976 criss-crossing of much of the Commonwealth of Pennsylvania in its now-famous "graffiti bus." It all started with a terse memo to Cro Schaefer, director of publications in the Development Office, from Ed Lane, a special projects maven in the same office: "Please write me a bus!" Crosier Schaefer, Edward Franklin Lane, and Craig Sweeten, their boss, among my all-time best friends at the university, conjured up an idea that was to create a minor sensation. Ed wanted a tour bus to be repainted in red, white, and blue with almost every inch covered with some sort of fact about the University of Pennsylvania. They contracted with SEPTA (the Southeastern Pennsylvania Transportation Authority) to handle the job. Our preposterous multicolor almanac-on-wheels took off on May 13 with such information as "America's first medical school," "First full-scale archeological excavations in the Near East," "ENIAC, world's first digital computer, developed at Penn," and dozens of other salient but little-known facts about Penn painted all over it. There were even things painted on the roof for viewers on bridges and in tall buildings and helicopters. "Here

Comes the Penn Glee Club" was painted in reverse on the front so that drivers could read it in their rearview mirrors!

The Penn Glee Club went off for a week and played everywhere from the big cities to the smallest towns. (Well, *most* of the Club went off. Their director had to miss the bus: I was narrating a new work with the Philadelphia Orchestra and flew to Warren, Pennsylvania, immediately after my portion of the program at the Academy of Music.) *Paint the Яed Town* played to a packed house in Warren and to the first of our twenty-two standing ovations for the week. Also in Warren, we put on a free noontime show for the downtown shoppers. We sang and danced in straw hats and red-and-white-striped blazers on a huge flatbed truck parked for the occasion in the city center. With an average of three performances per day throughout the state, we were busy boys.

In addition, we wanted to tip our hats in sincere thanks to the commonwealth for the outstanding students, faculty members, and material help the state had given us over the years. We timed our arrival at the capitol so that our rousing performance on the grand staircase inside the rotunda would coincide with the luncheon break of the legislature. Startled legislators poured in and so rapidly gained the spirit of our fun that, almost to a man, they came out front and signed our bus!

Painting the bus especially for us—and then painting it back again—cost a bundle of money. At the end of the tour, however, I believe SEPTA canceled the bill. Their bus was on every newspaper and television in Pennsylvania and on the covers of the national trade magazines as well. You can't buy that kind of publicity.

At this time, too, a new small group appeared in the club. David Green, David Goldberg, Mitch Mudick, and Carlo Nalin formed a group of great showmanship. The PennChants Four used their fine voices and expert instrumental abilities to marvelous effect and were a popular addition to our performances.

In 1976, we presented our first Award of Merit away from campus. We were to sing at a Boston Pops concert in Boston, so we presented our medallion and citation there to Arthur Fiedler before the performance. I hardly need mention that Fiedler was one of the best-known and most popular conductors in the world; with the Boston Pops, he made whole new generations aware of great music.

Our firsts also included plot and characters in a Glee Club show. Each summer I went to my glorious Maine hideaway and planned an entire repertoire for the club's next season. When I was planning our 1977 show, it seemed to me that we had come far with staging a concert. Why not go the next logical step? So the 1977 show opened with an entire half-hour scene from the musical, *Why Me?*, which I had written ten years earlier for the Penn Players. It included an army locale that fitted well with the kind of singing and dancing for which the Glee Club had now become widely known. It also had an effective Arthurian Camelot final scene as well as picturesque period costumes that led us to the title *Extravagancelot*. And, what's more, it called for yet another innovation: the creation of a pit band to accompany the production. That year's club president, Mitch Mudick, wasn't convinced that plot and dialogue were the direction in which we should head, but to his immense credit he backed me all the way. *Extravagancelot* was a daring departure, and I had no idea whether the guys would welcome the idea or run me out of town. Fortunately, they welcomed the idea. They balked at the costumes at first, but gradually realized they looked pretty good in tights!

One mishap occurred in a performance we gave at Wheaton College, one of our favorite women's colleges (at least it was for me because I always stayed at president Alice Emerson's house). At the end of the finale, wielding his broadsword in the big production number, Peter McLaughlin hit his head on his sword's hilt while taking his final bow, hyperventilated, and passed out as the curtain was closing. Great timing. He spent the night in the local hospital.

That autumn also saw us in New York State. I confess that I can find no old program to remind me, but I believe that it was with the women of the College of New Rochelle that we sang a stunning performance of Carl Orff's *Carmina Burana*. We were accompanied by the Hudson Valley Symphony Orchestra, and a group of professional dancers interpreted the exciting work visually. To add to the three-ring-circus effect of the performance, we projected color slides of details from Hieronymus Bosch's fantastic *Garden of Earthly Delights* on walls, ceiling, stage, and any other surface that would accept them.

Our 1977 Award of Merit ceremony was one of the most pleasant of all. Having had two glorious experiences with the beautiful Metropolitan Opera star Risë Stevens, we invited her to receive our award. As always, she was charming and gracious, and she and her husband were two of the most interesting and animated conversationalists I've ever met. She was given a fine introduction by club president Mark Rubino, who was there with his girlfriend Denise. After Miss Stevens had received the medallion and citation and had given her delightful acceptance speech, she turned quietly to me and whispered, "That boy is never going to let that girl slip away, is he? I've never seen two people so in love!" (For the record, Mark and Denise have been married for years and have a devoted brood of kids.)

For the next twenty-three summers I wrote all but four of our shows. I still wonder at how I did it all that time and how I came up with ideas and plots (after all, even my idols Gilbert & Sullivan only wrote fourteen). The working regimen began with my retiring to Connemara on Spruce Head Island, spending three weeks creating a plot and characters and having at least a basic idea of some of the music that would fit into the general scheme. Then I would type up a full précis of the show to have ready when the current Glee Club president came to visit me for four days. We would immerse ourselves in discussing the forthcoming production, and before he left we would have a show. I would spend the next two months making choral arrangements, composing new music, writing dialogue, and generally completing the show to be printed and bound as full scores that were handed out at the first rehearsal in September. My bright idea about adding a pit band further required me to orchestrate each show. It all was a daunting task that makes me shudder now in retrospect.

An incident or two in the winter of 1977 garnered us several great bits of unplanned publicity. As we were approaching Milwaukee, Wisconsin, we were driving through a blinding blizzard. All day long we listened to news announcements on the bus radio about the endless succession of school, business, and theater closings. Sometime around 5:00 P.M. we finally heard the most wonderful announcement of all. "OK, Milwaukee, everything is shut down and canceled tonight except the performance by the University of Pennsylvania Glee Club! It's going on as scheduled at 8:00 P.M." With that, the announcer gave the location, and what seemed like the entire city turned out for our performance. A further perk of the blizzard was more contrived. As we were going along the Wisconsin highway the next morning, an idea for a quirky photograph occurred to me. Suiting action to the thought, I asked eight club men to change into their complete white-tie-and-tails outfits as we sped along the road. At an appropriate stopping place, the bus pulled off the highway, I got the photographer to follow us into the snow, and, with the huge

University of Pennsylvania Glee Club banner on the side of the bus as a backdrop, I instructed the men to have the most "formal snowball fight" ever recorded. Club president Peter Kurzina was pelted from all sides in a photo that made it into newspapers all over the country and onto the cover of at least one national travel magazine. I even saw it years later in Peru!

In the fall of 1977 we started our season by singing for President Jimmy Carter, who insisted on meeting each man individually. We were again booked to do the Macy's Thanksgiving Day Parade, and it was planned that our act on national television would immediately precede a song-and-dance act by Carol Lawrence, the original Maria in *West Side Story*. Some weeks prior to the stint, she and her choreographer came to Penn to see our tap-dance routine—performed, of course, in white tie and tails and top hats—and to plan how her act would proceed from ours. To her astonishment, we weren't at all the typical college glee club she had expected. After a quick phone call to New York, the question was answered. No transition was necessary; her act would simply be an extension of ours and we'd dance down Broadway together. It turned out to be a fabulous production, ending with our men lifting her over their heads with the camera shot from a "cherry-picker" high above Broadway. Announcing the whole parade, Ed McMahon waxed almost poetic on air as he assessed its effectiveness.

One of our more impressive jobs at about this time was in Atlantic City's huge Convention Hall. The Richard Lyons Company had booked us, and full stage band arrangements of our music had been orchestrated. After we did our stuff for the delighted crowd, Ed McMahon came on with his act. I'm certain that everyone has off nights, and this was Ed's. It was secretly satisfying but downright embarrassing when the low chant started in the immense audience: "Bring back the Glee Club! Bring back the Glee Club!" The finale of the show incorporated both the Club and McMahon, so it ended on a positive note. The Glee Club softly hummed "America the Beautiful" while Ed recited a patriotic monologue. When a few years later we were introduced again by McMahon on national TV, it took all the self-control I could muster to avoid reminding him.

It was at this time, too, that we began a concerted effort to organize our alumni. Spearheaded by David Goldberg, we distributed a handsome booklet, "It's Corny . . . But It'll Work!" to all our alumni, outlining our plans for the Glee Club Graduate Club. Upon their receiving the booklet, we could almost hear a cry from across the nation, "OK, when do you hit us for money?"

Actually, when you come right down to it, each time we'd taken a major tour out of the country we had contacted our alumni for assistance, and they had no illusions that we wouldn't again. But membership in the GCGC had no financial strings attached. The response was wonderful, and the first of the annual May bashes had alumni planning special acts for it as early as January!

The late 1960s and 1970s saw us covering much of the eastern half of the United States on numerous occasions. New England, of course, welcomed us many times. Women's colleges still were highlights of any season as we sang for—and with—Smith, Wellesley, Pembroke, Simmons, Wheaton, and many others. We even toured into Canada with them on occasion. One particular performance at the Oratoire Saint Joseph in Montreal stands out in my memory. What a glorious edifice. What acoustics!

We had crossed the border into Canada with the Skidmore College Glee Club, with whom we had sung the night before on their Saratoga Springs campus. After our performance in l'Oratoire Saint Joseph, we came back into New York State without a problem. Almost. All went smoothly at the border except for Brad Wilson, our fine accompanist. He was our only Canadian, and they gave him a hard time and removed him from our midst for half an hour.

In addition to the normal New York and New England concerts, the South and the Midwest hosted us with increasing frequency. Returning from performances in Kansas offered us special opportunities. And we were always ones to take advantage of special opportunities.

We had performed in Presser Hall at my alma mater, Bethany College, in Lindsborg, and were on our way toward Kansas City. Now, we knew that the national headquarters of the National Collegiate Athletic Association was in Kansas City. A new standard had been established by the NCAA requiring athletes to maintain a 1.6 academic average to qualify for NCAA competitions. The Ivy League presidents were not happy with this. "No athletic organization is going to dictate academic standards to us!" they said in effect. In our league, they felt, 1.6 would probably be quite different from 1.6 in some college in, say, Elephant's Breath, Montana, or Split Lip, Georgia. Consequently, they elected to withdraw from the association. And this in a year when Penn had a spectacular basketball team that might have gone all the way!

As we neared Kansas City, we stopped at a grammar school where we struck a bargain with an art teacher. In return for a few songs for the kids, we had use of her poster paints, and, taking a dozen cardboards that had come from the laundry with our shirts, we made mock protest signs with the NCAA as our target. We then headed toward Kansas City, having first made certain to notify our intent to the *Kansas City Star*, NBC, CBS, ABC, and the several news wire services. When we arrived at NCAA headquarters, everyone was there. We stopped our bus about two blocks from the building and then marched on the Association, singing at the top of our lungs. With signs proclaiming such inanities as "Really! It's Not Very Ivy of You," "1.6 Needs a Fix!" and the like, we made a considerable splash in what otherwise must have been a fairly routine day. The AP and UPI sent the story out on the wires. Television showed us in all their news programs. The newspapers covered it fully. We were on the *Today Show* the next morning. And the full story and the lyrics Morgan Soutter had written for the occasion were reprinted in *Sports Illustrated*. Of course the Ivy League still missed the NCAA season, but we caused some widespread mirth by lampooning the situation.

The 1970s continued with the Penn Glee Club as one of the most active and sought after activities on campus. The Penn Singers, too, were enjoying great popularity. By now I had directed *The Pirates of Penzance*, *The Mikado*, *The Gondoliers*, *Iolanthe*, *Patience*, and *Utopia Limited*, as well as a repeat of *The Mikado*. They were—and still are—the highly successful light opera company at Penn. In addition to their "big show" each spring, they branched out into a fall production. Sometimes it was a revue (with or without a theme), sometimes a full musical such as *Babes in Toyland*, *Once Upon a Mattress*, *Anything Goes*, or *Brigadoon*. One of my great joys was introducing students to a side of theater that, to most of them, was completely unknown. To develop devotees of Gilbert & Sullivan, for example, was a source of great delight and to know that they now are hooked for life gives additional purpose to all the initial hard-sell and the seemingly endless hours of work it entailed. What's more, they became a truly fine company.

One of my very good friends on the Penn faculty at this time also was one of the most popular professors at the university. Alexander Riasanovsky was professor of Slavic languages and a loyal follower of the Glee Club. In a moment of weakness, he shared with me the fact that he was a poet, as well— a sideline he had kept hidden from most—and presented me with several volumes of his works. With his permission, I set four of his poems to music and they became a powerful antiwar cycle for male chorus, piano, and six percussion instruments. Under the title *Anti-Bellum*, they were a featured part of our 1977 show and the season's repertoire. And I think Alex attended every performance that year.

Every now and then we all have stupid accidents that make us think how absurdly easily they could have been avoided. I had one of those when I dropped several ice cubes on my kitchen floor and, walking to clean them up, slipped on one and landed with a thud on my back. I lay there with the wind knocked out of me and severe pain in my back and chest. With hairline fractures in five ribs, I went to the theater that night and had to sneeze. That did it. I snapped all five of the injured ribs.

I was rushed to the Hospital of the University of Pennsylvania, and x-rays confirmed that I had indeed broken five ribs. I was to conduct a full two-hour concert by the Penn Glee Club the next day, and I asked to be strapped up tightly to get me through it. If I were to play a championship basketball game, I was told, they would strap me up—but not to conduct a concert! Strapping would force me to take shallow breaths and I might develop pneumonia. So sitting on a high stool the next evening, and only minimally medicated for pain, I conducted in agony. "Suffer for your art." I did!

Our 1978 Award of Merit went to conductor/arranger Leonard de Paur, who by then was director of all choral programs at New York's Lincoln Center. Leonard, you will remember, was the marvelous man who sent me his superb "Casinha Pequenina" back when we were making our record of folk songs of the world.

I had met a young man at a dinner party who was the embodiment of enthusiasm and energy. Bill Kelley taught in the Phoenixville public school system, and when he learned about the Penn Glee Club and our shows, he hardly waited a minute before laying a proposal on the table. Nobody, New York producers included, wants to open cold with a new show. The Glee Club should have a "try-out town." Why not Phoenixville? So, beginning with the 1978 production, we tried out every show there prior to bringing it to campus. Billy turned it into a major event. Townspeople were given an opportunity to subscribe to dinner with the Glee Club before the performance, and it became a full social evening. And, in the doing, Billy became one of the dearest and most supportive of friends and in 1987 was elected to one of the most exclusive of honors: Honorary Member of the University of Pennsylvania Glee Club. As of this writing, the club has been opening in Phoenixville for twenty-five years.

The 1978 Glee Club show continued the "innovation" begun the year before by including characters, dialogue, and plot, however contrived. *Next Stop: Manhattan* was a virtual travelogue of the Big Apple. Tim Crombleholme, as a New York cab driver, was taking Scott Arnovitz, a rube from Boise, Idaho, around to the many sights of the city. That was pretty much the plot of the show, but it permitted us to do serious music when "visiting" Lincoln Center, show tunes on Broadway, and a bit of everything at a Harlem block-party. Anything that didn't fit easily into a nice slot was relegated to the waiting room in Grand Central Station. A tidy package.

One really great feature of *Next Stop: Manhattan* was a wonderful assortment of rear projections shown while we sang a medley I put together of New York songs, "All Around the Town." In November, we had taken the entire club to New York for a photo session. We rode graffiti-covered subway cars in white tie and tails, to the stares of the other riders. We played basketball with some little neighborhood boys on 127th Street in Harlem. We danced a hornpipe in sailor uniforms down at the Battery. We wore robes as we stopped traffic with "Walk Him Up the Stairs" at Times Square, with photos being taken from the roof of a nearby building. One of the more surprising and humorous photo sequences was a view of the club singing at the fountain in Lincoln Center. The first shot was from behind the singers with the multi-arched Metropolitan Opera House majestic in the background. The Glee Club looked splendidly sartorial until the next slide showed them from the front. All were in tail coats and bow ties—and naught but white boxer shorts from the waist down!

But the pièce de résistance of the day was the forming of the word "Penn" by all the clubbers standing at the base of the Statue of Liberty, while I flew with the photographers, John Chimples and David Swetzoff, in a helicopter above the statue. Getting the permits to accomplish all this was a feat in itself, but its actual execution was definitely worth the effort. I used to brag about the fact that I bribed the helicopter pilot to bend the law on the way home and fly me between the towers of the World Trade Center. Now it is only a very sad and poignant memory.

One of the songs in the New York slide segment was to be "In Old New York" from Victor Herbert's *The Red Mill*. The last line of the song is

> You'll seldom see in Gay Paree
> In London or in Cork
> The queens you'll meet on any street
> In Old New York.

I thought that it would be a huge joke if, as that lyric was sung, we would interrupt the scenes of New York and show a meaning of the word that would never have occurred to Victor Herbert: drag queens.

A few days after I got this brilliant idea, I was downtown at a very formal dinner and thought that I would stop at one of the porn shops on Arch Street on my way home to purchase a magazine that featured a photo of men in drag with three-inch eyelashes, heavy mascara, and so on. I found exactly the right picture to illustrate the song's line and, looking around furtively to make certain that no one who knew me would see my transaction, I purchased the offensive magazine. As the clerk handed me the plain brown wrapper, he said "Thank you, Mr. Montgomery." My heart sank and only as I was exiting the store covered with embarrassment did I realize that I was wearing a very prominent name tag on my tuxedo. Since that night, I have never left a function that required me to wear a name tag without removing it before I left the premises!

We were later hired to perform the forty-minute "All Around the Town" slide segment at an important convention at the Waldorf Astoria in New York—this time with full twenty-piece orchestrations made especially for the occasion. It also was rechoreographed by Bob Wilson. One member of the audience who got a particular kick out of our songs and slides taken throughout his city was Mayor Edward Koch.

Mike Diamant, business manager in 1978, booked a spectacular tour that took us for the first time to New Orleans. We sang outdoors on a stage in Jackson Park, we sang in theaters, we sang for alumni and we sang at schools. We sang on board the old Mississippi side-paddle-wheeler the *Natchez*, which gave an excuse, of course, for us to sing my "See the Natchez," which goes in counterpoint with "Waitin' for the Robert E. Lee." And we were given a spectacular authentic red-beans-and-rice dinner prepared by one of New Orleans's premier Cajun chefs. To make it even more special, it was served to us at the legendary Preservation Hall, founded by Sousaphone-playing Penn grad Alan Jaffe.

Moon Landrieu, mayor of New Orleans, even made me an honorary citizen of the town and presented me the key to the city. When this sort of thing happened, I knew that the honor was given not for me but for the entire Glee Club. There just weren't enough imposing certificates and gold keys to go around.

After an evening performance, we went back to our hotel, changed into white cutaways and, led by our pit band, marched right down Bourbon Street in the French Quarter to set up shop outside the Royal Sonesta Hotel. We sang to the startled guests who came out onto the balconies and to the huge crowd that gathered on the street.

Mike, ever the practical one, stopped singing, held out his white top hat, began collecting from the people on the street, and then fielded the deluge of money thrown from the balconies. We had a great tour dinner that spring.

One of the most original shows we ever came up with was *The Magus*, for which we went farther overboard financially than for any show before or since. When the audience entered the theater, the stage was bare: no curtains, teasers, or legs, only the ropes, ladders, and customary mess of any backstage space. A lone boy was sweeping the empty stage by the light of a "ghost light"—the single self-standing light bulb one finds on every professional stage when everyone has left and the lamps are out for the night. "The Boy," as he was simply identified in the program, was played by a young man named Marc Platt. We had no idea that he would eventually become head of Universal Studios and a brilliant movie and Broadway producer. As the overture developed into Barry Scott singing "Magic to Do" from *Pippin*, wondrous things began to happen. Black velour drapes and legs and teasers flew in, hundreds of flowers appeared magically from everywhere, and we were off on an extravagant and exciting show.

Brian Kardon, our reed man par excellence in the pit, was also a professional magician and spent more time onstage than in the pit for this one. He performed some of the most marvelous illusions, not little parlor tricks but major stunts such as the "Metamorphosis" and the "ZigZag" and numerous others, for which we spent thousands of dollars!

The premise of the show was that while the Boy was sweeping he came upon a "ghost" inhabiting the theater: an old-time, has-been magician. As played by Tim Crombleholme complete with bald head and bushy gray fringe, the marvelously hammy magician was irresistibly befuddled by his "time medallion," which could grant any wish by the Boy. The only problem was that he didn't seem to remember how to command the medallion any more and, although the wish was granted, the Magus couldn't predict the age in which it would occur. For example, when the Boy took his baseball cap out of his back pocket and declared that he wanted to play with the Pirates, there was an incantation, a great flash, and a billow of smoke, and when it cleared he was with a cutthroat band of eighteenth-century Caribbean pirates singing "Come Friends Who Plow the Sea" from *The Pirates of Penzance*. When he remarked about the TV show *Charlie's Angels*, he wished to meet its star Farrah Fawcett. When the smoke cleared this time, the medallion had misunderstood "Farrah" for "Pharaoh" and he was now in ancient Egypt! And so it continued in other colorful venues and times with immense success.

When the University of Pennsylvania made it to the NCAA final four in basketball in 1979, the Glee Club was on tour in Indiana. Penn was about to play Notre Dame, so, displaying an uncommonly barefaced audacity (even for us), we taped signs of "Final Four Victors" and "We're Number 1" in our chartered bus windows and drove right into the main quad of the Fighting Irish, parked there, and sang. Expecting to be pelted with eggs at the very least and perhaps booed off the campus, we were greeted instead with wonderful jocundity and cheers and even were invited into the library to disrupt their studies. That's sportsmanship! Penn lost the game . . . but the club won the day.

Our 1979 Award of Merit was presented to the eminent music critic for the *Washington Post*, Paul Hume. Paul was a great choral conductor, but is best known as the critic to whom Harry Truman wrote his famous "s. o. b. letter" following Hume's panning of a concert by Margaret Truman. Paul later sold the letter for ten thousand dollars. If he had held onto it for a few more years, when Truman had grown considerably in history's eyes, he could have made many times that.

After the considerable triumph of *The Magus*, our 118th show took place aboard the U.S.S. *Flotsam* as a spoof on the popular TV show *The Love Boat*. It was titled *Hit High Sea*, and we already had opened in Phoenixville before some of the cast caught the pun! The characters were parodies of the TV version as well as a slippery, want-to-be Don Juan stowaway played by Barry Scott, who would come back year after year to work his magical choreographic skills for us. I wrote a song "All Aboard" that introduced the strange assortment of characters to Captain Stupid and the audience. They ranged from a barbershop quartet to an Olympic gymnastics team to a pair of stereotypical gangsters to three monks to an extrovert small town bowling team. The show was a hit at home and sailed successfully into Washington, Richmond, Louisville, Kansas City, Saint Louis, and Columbus. Club alum Larry Belger treated us all to a steak dinner in Kansas City.

That autumn, I was given the first surprise party that really was a surprise! I thought I was going to a dinner for the Arco Chemical Company at the Hilton Hotel, a black-tie affair. I was to be a guest for the dinner, and the Glee Club would arrive later to entertain. When Morad Madani escorted me into the ballroom, apparently all blood drained from my face and I, a nondrinker, was instructed to take a shot of whiskey to restore my composure. The first people I saw as I entered were Elliot Stellar, provost, my mother, my godmother Eleanor Brown from North Carolina, and Martin Meyerson, president, as the assembled singers, who came in from all over the world, burst into "Oh here's to Monty! Fill up the tankard! . . ." the toast I had composed so many years ago for the Glee Club. It was a surprise celebration of my twenty-five years with the club, carefully planned and meticulously executed by the current business manager, Scott Davenport, and 1975 graduate Greg Suss. They even had brought my dear former boss, Tish Emerson, from Wheaton to be my date for the evening, which was a bit awkward, since I already had brought Jane Thiry as my date. Since Jane knew of the surprise all along, she graciously sat with my family and all went smoothly. It was one of the most special evenings of my life.

Among the highlights were citations from the university, the Alumni Society, the mayor of Philadelphia, and the governor of Pennsylvania. The Montgomery Family Singers, made up of three generations of family, sang the "Battleship Song" I had written and sung spontaneously as a joke in Pisa, Italy, to amuse my mother and sister Liz when I used their bathtub since my hotel room didn't possess one.

> I love my little battleships I play with in my bathtub:
> My submarines and LSTs pitch battles all around my knees.
> And when I see the enemy I sink him like the Maine;
> And then I pull the stopper out and float him down the drain.

It never occurred to me that anyone else ever would hear it, and they sang it—from a folio-size illuminated manuscript courtesy of my niece Vicki—as if it were a just-discovered choral work by Palestrina. My brother Jim hired an enticing belly-dancer to surprise us and change the decorum!

Perhaps the most astonishing surprise of all was the appearance of the Glee Club to sing a song by William L. Dawson. I learned later that the club had written to Dawson months before asking his price to commission a new work for the occasion. He had written back, I'm told, refusing the commission. But, he added, he would write the work for love! Unknown to me, he had sent the music ahead and then come up to Philadelphia days before the event at his own expense. Greg Suss came in from New York to rehearse the new music each midnight. Then Bill secretly rehearsed the club in the piece and, on my big night, there he was in the ballroom to conduct the premiere performance of "Dorabella." I make no apologies for the fact that as I hugged dear Bill after the surprise performance, I wept freely from joy and love.

I don't believe that it is necessary to state it, but I'm going to, anyway. The tears of love extended far beyond just Bill Dawson that night. The unbridled love I felt for the wonderful men of the Glee Club who had planned such a celebration and even thought of commissioning a new work for it are the sorts of elements that have made me one the happiest men on earth. Can you really imagine someone who, for his entire career, would shave every morning and look at his reflection in the mirror and sometimes actually exclaim aloud: "You lucky son-of-a-bitch! You're going to work with students again today!" This is the way I felt for fifty years and continue to feel with every encounter today.

The Glee Club men also took it upon themselves to further honor me by having a Special Award of Merit medal struck for me. It was the only such award presented that did not include an imposing calligraphed citation. I always did those, and there was no way they were going to ask me to do one for myself! The official Award of Merit for the year was presented to the great Metropolitan Opera baritone Robert Merrill. As it happened, Mr. Merrill was rushed to the hospital the night before the event and his very first Met co-star, Licia Albanese, came to campus to accept it for him.

It seemed a good excuse, so we took advantage of my twenty-five years with the Penn Glee Club to exploit the show-stoppers of the past quarter-century in a rousing 1981 production entitled *Double Take*. In it we reprised such all-time hits as Handel's "Your Voices Raise," my setting of "Lincoln's Gettysburg Address," the celebrated "Aquarius/Let the Sun Shine In" scene that sort of started our new concept a dozen years earlier, one of our early danced folk songs "Tancuj Vykrucaj," a signature production number "Walk Him Up the Stairs," and even one of my rare cameo appearances in a kilt, tam, and sporran performing "My One Only Highland Fling."

This show also took us, for the very first time in our 119 years, to the Southwest and West Coast, where we performed in San Francisco, San Diego,

Phoenix, Las Vegas, and Los Angeles. And, of course, we did a stint in Disneyland. This also was the club's introduction to the spectacular, awesome beauty of the Grand Canyon. It was the first time I had been there in the winter and had the chance to see it in the snow. In San Diego we spent an afternoon at the fabulous Zoo and were particularly entranced by the penguins emulating us in their formal attire.

On our long bus ride from San Francisco to San Diego, we bribed our bus driver to avoid the main highway south and instead take us down the phenomenal shore route along the Big Sur, not the safest of roads for a bus. We nevertheless enjoyed every breathtaking vista and arrived in San Diego just in time to appear on a popular television show and a radio interview advertising our shows and Penn.

For our bus tour of the West, we had brought twenty-five-foot banners proclaiming who we were to go along the two sides of the vehicle under the windows. It wasn't until we were in San Diego that we discovered that one of the banners had come loose and disappeared somewhere along the coast. Weeks later, we received a box from California returning the long strip of muslin with a brief note: "You lost your scarf on the Big Sur!"

Some months before we embarked on this tour, the entire Glee Club was invited to the Los Angeles home of Mr. and Mrs. A. J. Carothers, parents of Chris Carothers, a freshman in the club. Mr. Carothers is a prominent Hollywood script writer of some of the best-known TV shows and motion pictures. The dinner party consisted of the Glee Club as guests of honor plus a roster that seemed like Who's Who in Hollywood. After dinner (with John Ritter as bartender), we gathered in the living room and sang a few numbers. Then Karen Morrow jumped up and did a hilarious nightclub act for us. We sang some more, and I sat down at the piano to accompany Maryann Mobley and Gary Collins. Then Dick Sherman took over at the piano to accompany us as we sang his Academy Award songs from *Mary Poppins*. And so it went until the wee hours of the morning. In a town of constant parties, this turned out to be something very special even to those who customarily make the rounds. It was one of the best tour-end parties imaginable.

The Penn Singers, too, decided to celebrate a "Monty Milestone"—the tenth anniversary of my becoming director of the group. Their board decided to skip a year of Gilbert & Sullivan and instead perform a revival of my *Spindrift*. While I had the final say in the choice of productions, there was no way that I would stifle this wise selection! I had so thoroughly believed in *Spindrift* in 1963 that its revival now seemed not only appropriate but almost overdue. I was also curious to see whether it held up with the passage of time. The show had received glowing reviews from the downtown papers, and we were able to spread on the new posters quotes from the original production such as the *Philadelphia Inquirer*'s "A merry Gaelic romp with only a trace of tears. . . . As Irish as Donnybrook Fair!"

The intense role of Patch was superbly recreated by Barry Scott. He became so immersed in the part that he even acceded to a barely mentioned wish of mine. He said he felt a bit foolish sitting among the women in a beauty parlor for a permanent, but his customary straight hair became a marvelous mass of curls for this Irish fisherman. The show held up. The revival, if anything, was even better than the original.

My nephew, Nicky Thomas, made a marvelous singing and acting debut as the little boy, Sean. He was so totally into his role that he flew off the sea wall right on cue. "Patch! You're back!" Barry suddenly remembered and wheeled just in time to catch Nicky in midair before he plunged headfirst into the orchestra pit.

The year 1982 was a fine one for the club, too, and *Casino!* took us to Miami, Orlando, Sarasota, and Tampa. Having already played in Disneyland, we thought it only fair to strut our stuff at Disney World. When we were in Sarasota we performed for three thousand people at the immense Van Wiesel Auditorium. This superb theater—painted a strange lavender inside and shaped sort of like a gigantic shell—was affectionately known by the natives as the Purple Conch. But what a theater it was! Our only slight reservation about the whole experience was that the manager of the theater failed to look carefully at our contract and raised the hydraulic orchestra pit to floor level and sold seats on it. We had a pit band and no place to pit them. My only choice was to scatter them around the stage amid set pieces. Somehow everything held together and we did the show. For *Casino!* I did something that I would do only one more time in my Glee Club career: I made a poster and program cover that included a caricature of each man in the club—all forty-four of them!—in this case, gathered around a roulette table. Each man came into my office and sat for me while I drew his caricature. It was something of a tour de force and, though I say it who shouldn't, highly effective.

But great though travel and performing to huge crowds all over the country may be, the true high point of the year—or almost *any* year, for that matter—

was the opportunity that Steve Goff, who by now was the managing director of the Annenberg Center, presented to us. We were the only student group asked to perform at "A Philadelphia Tribute to Grace Kelly, Actress." This was one of the most magical evenings ever dreamed up. The master of ceremonies was the legendary Bob Hope (the second time we had appeared with him), and the roster of people paying tribute to Grace Kelly was impressive in the extreme.

The Glee Club began the program in the Zellerbach Theatre with the two national anthems. Later, Princess Grace was to write me, "I was so touched to hear the Monegasque anthem sung so beautifully in French." A featured part of the program was the "Musical Tribute" by the Glee Club and our pit band. For this I made male choral arrangements of something from each of her eleven motion pictures. The movies that didn't have any songs were covered by my obtaining the sound tracks and arranging some of the underscoring for nonverbal voices. Philadelphia mayor William J. Green spoke, ambassador Walter H. Annenberg spoke, and touching personal tributes were given by some of her co-stars—Rita Gam, Brian Aherne, Celeste Holm, Stewart Granger, Jimmy Stewart, Ricardo Montalban, and Frank Sinatra. For the Grand Finale, I wrote special new lyrics for "What a Swell Party This Is" from *High Society*, and the Glee Club sang it, first from the stage and then pouring out to fill the two side aisles as well, completely enveloping the audience in this joyous paean to the career of this charming lady, mere months before her untimely death in Monaco.

The year 1983 had the Glee Club strapping on spurs and polishing guns in a rootin' tootin' Western spoof for its 121st annual production, *Saddle Up!* For the grand finale, I made a special arrangement of "America the Beautiful." Throughout the year, this was played with a split-rail fence across the upstage area against a fifty-foot painting of the massive arches and desert of the far Southwest. For one of our performances, Jeffrey Orwig, our business manager that year, booked us into the huge Masonic Hall in his home town of Williamsport, Pennsylvania. When we arrived at the stage, he looked up in the fly gallery and drew my attention to an immense American flag hanging on an upstage batten. It had been made years before by his grandfather. Instantly, the finale was revised and the flag was lowered to be the impressive background against which the moving anthem was performed. The capacity audience was on its feet in seconds and even joined the Glee Club in singing the last verse. There were very few dry eyes either on or off stage.

Andy Goldstein, president of the club, traveled with the group and *Saddle Up!* on our exciting trip to California, but he had already determined that it had been far too long since we had been to foreign shores. Therefore, he and Jeff had set about rectifying that serious oversight. We flew to Denmark.

Actually, we flew to Ostend, Belgium. We were supposed to catch our plane for Copenhagen in Brussels, but the airport was closed because of weather conditions and so we sat in Ostend. When Brussels finally opened, we flew there to find that they had held our connecting flight for us with passengers aboard awaiting our arrival. Apparently they had fed breakfast to the irate passengers on the ground.

When we arrived, we were hurriedly handed individual boxes of food. To the chagrin of the flight attendants, I told the guys to wait until every man had his box and then we'd come on singing. It was delightful to watch the sea of frowning faces melt into grins and then be greeted by hearty applause.

It sure pays to know how to make an entrance.

In 1963, Bob Graulich, Al Robinson, and Barry Kaufman were with us as
we taped a television show of songs of the Civil War for NBC on the
battlefield at Gettysburg, Pennsylvania. As you read in the text,
these uniforms were not costumes but actual uniforms worn
during the battle! Photo by Peter Dechert Associates.

Randall Thompson, world renowned composer and my dear friend, was the recipient of the first University of Pennsylvania Glee Club Award of Merit, in 1964. Jules Schick Photography.

The original Pennafour—certainly the best barbershop quartet during my years
with the glee club—was made up of the mellifluous voices of Jon Gailmor,
Keith Neal, Tom Godbold, and Morgan Soutter.

UNIVERSITY OF
PENNSYLVANIA

GLEE CLUB

CHORAL SERIES

BRUCE MONTGOMERY
EDITOR

UP 300   THREE HAIKU   T.T.B.B.
With Flute and Cloves

FOR MALE VOICES

THREE HAIKU

Music by

BRUCE MONTGOMERY

POEMS FROM THE JAPANESE

Plymouth Music Co., Inc.

17 WEST 60th ST., NEW YORK, N.Y. 10023

After my compositions had been published in numerous series for some years,
I finally was asked to edit my own series in 1965. The first piece to appear
in the University of Pennsylvania Glee Club Choral Series was my
"Three Haiku," which Randall Thompson had requested that I
dedicate to him. This was his endorsement to the world.

Over the years, the Penn Glee Club performed many times with the Philadelphia Orchestra. Here they are together in 1967 at the Academy of Music.

One of the sightseeing highlights of our first tour to South America, in 1969—or any other tour, for that matter—was our visit to the magnificent Inca ruins of Machu Picchu high in the Andes.

The lithe swimmer's build of Will Fleissig was the nude centerpiece for the spectacular finish to *Handel with Hair* in 1969. Photo by Brian Maloney.

One of the true highlights of our 1971 tour to the Soviet Union was visiting the magnificent Peterhof (Petrodvorets)—one of the lavish palaces of the Russian czars. The breathtaking combination of cascades, fountains, and gilded statues is unique in the world. It's a shame that bunch of American singers had to block so much of it! Photo by William H. Gillis.

In addition to sellout concerts, basketball tournaments, and frolics in the Black Sea, one of our more interesting stops in the mountains of Bulgaria was at the lofty Rila Monastery. Photo by William H. Gillis.

Perhaps our most flamboyant appearance in Macy's Thanksgiving Day Parade was the one in 1977, when we sang and danced with Carol Lawrence, the original star of *West Side Story*. We almost equaled her in our high-stepping.

In 1976 the famous "graffiti bus" took the club throughout Pennsylvania and attracted wide attention in cities, towns, and hamlets. It also made it into nearly every newspaper and television news story in the state as well as a national magazine or two. It's great fun—but a real drag—doing three to five performances a day.

One unforgettable experience was performing my dramatic missa brevis "Et in Terra Pax" at the Kennedy Center in Washington, D.C. in 1974. Photo by Rosie Mackiewicz.

Marc Platt was very trusting of his fellow chimney-sweeps as he was about to be flipped over in a flying leap in *The Magus* in 1979. Photo by Kenneth Kirshenbaum.

We were traveling in Wisconsin in 1979 when it began to snow heavily. As it continued, a funny idea occurred to me and I asked eight men to change into their white tie and tails as we sped along the highway. We stopped the bus and I instructed the men to gang up on Peter Kurzina, the club's president, in the world's most formal snowball fight.

Here I am in 1978, demonstrating a dance step at a rehearsal of one of the production numbers in *Next Stop: Manhattan*. I taught it backward, mirror fashion, so as to thoroughly confuse everyone. David Hopkins is at the piano. Jenson Hull Photography.

In 1978 I wrote a song called "See the Natchez" that went in counterpoint with "Waitin' for the Robert E. Lee." Here we are in New Orleans on the *Natchez* itself.

For *Next Stop: Manhattan!* in 1978 we photographed the Glee Club in locations throughout New York. These were shown on a huge rear-projection screen during our show. None was more impressive than the shot from a helicopter of the men spelling the word PENN at the base of the Statue of Liberty. Photo by John H. Chimples.

For the 1981 Penn Singers revival of *Spindrift*, John Cardoni and Andy Shoyer gathered their fish nets in a publicity photo taken at Cape May Point. Photo by Bruce David Rosenblum.

At a wonderful party in Hollywood in 1981, Dick Sherman played
many of his songs from *Mary Poppins* as we sang along.

In 1984 we sang informally in Hans Christian Andersen's home in
Odense, Denmark. The crowd in the background really wasn't the
audience fleeing from our singing. It's a mural on the wall.

Little John (Allan Polischak) fought his famous fight with Robin Hood
(Marcus Giancaterino) in *Ye Merrie Adventures of Robbin' Hoods* in 1984.

Several of us took time out for a visit to the Parthenon in Athens during our 1985 tour of Greece. Left to right: Peter Halverson, Monty, Richard Rosenberg, Brendan O'Brien, and Philip Schroeder.

The 1987 episode in the desert in Peru left us battered and bruised but highly pleased with ourselves. Here's one you'll just have to read about to understand.

Since our 1987 tour to Peru was at the request of Pilar Nores de García, wife of the president, it seemed appropriate to pose on the grand staircase in the presidential mansion in Lima.

After our 1969 visit to Machu Picchu, most of us believed we would never see it again.

I found it every bit as exciting the second time around in 1987.

♦ S I X ♦

The Sharing of Joy

WE ARRIVED IN COPENHAGEN and went through customs, how, I'll never know. We carried, among other props for our cowboy show, fifty pistols, several pickaxes, and half a dozen rifles. All this went on the airplane with us and passed through customs!

We took the boat train to Zealand, the mainland. I had never been on a train that broke into sections as it boarded a ferry and was fascinated by the full procedure. After the train was "put together" again on the opposite shore and we were underway, we were told that we had a three-minute connection in Fredericia for our next train south. I have heard people refer to a "Chinese fire drill" before but never had seen one in action. As our train headed west, we practiced our drill for our arrival. Some were assigned to exit the car immediately and take up stations outside each compartment. Others were to shove our 138 pieces of luggage out compartment windows to those on the platform. Still others would gather all the tickets, race up the stairs, across the bridge, down the stairs, and be ready to pass us through to the next train five platforms over. By the time we arrived at Fredericia, we were so well rehearsed that it ran like a well-planned production number. Reversing the drill into the new cars, we made the next train with about thirty-seven seconds to spare.

Our destination was Aabenraa. We learned that we were to perform two shows in Sønderjyllandshallen, the city's major concert hall, which pleased us very much. Our pleasure diminished when we discovered that all production companies were expected to bring everything with them. I mean *everything!* Our ingenuity and the cooperation of most of the town were called into play. Between 9:00 A.M. Sunday and our 4:00 P.M. matinee performance of *Saddle Up!* the chrysalis became a butterfly! A colossal ant colony (to thoroughly screw up my metaphors), we swarmed busily over the hall constructing a stage, jury-rigging battens and pulleys, building wings out of wooden screens, borrowing stanchions to hold batteries of rented spotlights, wheeling in a borrowed piano, setting up an orchestra pit with rented music stands and stand lights, and even enlisting the local fire department's hook-and-ladder to hang our 50 x 25 foot backdrop. By 3:00 the concert hall was a theater, and the show was ready for a spectacular scene of the Utah Territory in 1862—just about an hour before the crowd was due. I won't comment on how tired we were, but Bob Klausner as Wild Bill Hickok, during a scene where all the characters were supposed to relax around a campfire and sing a sentimental song, didn't get up when the rest of them did. He had fallen fast asleep on stage. Our finest first tenor, Howard Shalowitz, had lost his voice entirely and did a masterful lip-sync job for his entire stay in Denmark.

Although we sang in Tønder, Hojer, a side trip into Germany, a concert in Esberg, in Hans Christian Andersen's home in Odense, and the like, each evening we returned to our homes in Aabenraa. We lived in the homes of the students of the Købmandsskolen i Aabenraa (the Abenraa Business College).

After five wonderful days in Aabenraa with the most hospitable host families imaginable, we headed north to Aarhus. For me, a personal delight was my reunion with a very special Danish woman of whom I was extremely fond. Still am! Kirsten Leth entertained all of us when we were in Aarhus. After she gave us a delicious lunch at the hospital where she worked as an occupational therapist, we happily sang for the patients. That night we sang our show at the main music hall in town. I had not memorized a real speech of greeting as I had in South America some years before, but it is marvelously rewarding when a little bit of effort brings forth resounding responses from audiences. Since our performances in Denmark were shows, not just concerts, there was no real opportunity to sing national anthems or for me to say anything before we performed. Therefore, we sang the anthems as a sort of "third act" addendum, and I got a lot of milage out of a mere "God aften. Morer de dem godt?"—then, thunderous applause before I closed—"Tusind tak."

Of course we did all the tourist things such as seeing the Little Mermaid statue in Copenhagen harbor. It was a bittersweet visit for me. Thanks to some madman, she had needed a new head since I had last seen her. We bought countless souvenirs to add to our already overburdened luggage. At least one sweater store must have closed its doors for restocking after we left.

I have remarked before of my disappointment in some members of the Glee Club who on foreign tours will not even try foods that are new to them. This was brought home very graphically to me in Denmark. When we were in Aabenraa, I stayed at the home of the people responsible for housing the club members. Our first breakfast was interrupted by a phone call from one of the host mothers. She was in tears because the two students staying with her wouldn't eat a thing she had served them for breakfast. This, of course, was disconcerting for me but it was also the impetus for a short lecture that afternoon on common courtesy.

Perhaps an even more graphic incident occurred in Copenhagen toward the end of the tour, when we had a free night. We were staying at a hotel so there was no hostess to offend—only me. We had gone out pretty much together seeking a good place for dinner. Somewhere along the way, we divided into two groups. About three-quarters of us went to a delightful spot where we had delicious food, good Carlsberg beer, hearty fellowship with Danish and German students, and a lot of lusty singing and laughter. Returning to the hotel together many gleeful hours later, we found that the other quarter of the club had gone to McDonalds! It's beyond my ken that when a real opportunity is presented to some in a foreign land they elect, instead, to do what they can do any day at home.

Over the years I had visited Copenhagen a number of times and always stayed in very fine hotels—some even posh. But this time by lucky chance the Glee Club and I stayed in an inexpensive hotel that was infinitely more enjoyable than any of my earlier high-priced establishments. The Admiral was an old granary warehouse right on the river it had served. Each loft-type room had a pleasant living room and a steep staircase to a balcony bedroom. They also gave us a price break in return for singing for all their guests. The Admiral is now my hotel of choice.

The last night Tour Dinner is always a festive and frankly sentimental night, but the dinner in Copenhagen was a bit jarring to me. The president, Andy Goldstein, and business manager, Jeff Orwig made all the arrangements and reservations and chose a very fine restaurant near the Botanical Gardens. We had a private room and there was a good deal of toasting and singing. What they couldn't possibly have known was that in that restaurant a few years back, in that very room, at that small table over in that corner, I had proposed marriage to a Danish girl (not Kirsten, by the way) whom I had known for some years and whose parents' home I had visited several times over on Jutland. I had been refused primarily because she didn't wish to leave Denmark. Small world, isn't it?

We returned to JFK Airport in New York and passed the huge stone slab with Emma Lazarus's moving words carved in it.

> Give me your tired, your poor,
> Your huddled masses yearning to breathe free . . .

We weren't exactly huddled masses, but we definitely were tired and poor. Imagine our elation, then, when we found Barry Lites's entire family there to welcome us home with coffee and doughnuts for all.

A happy footnote to our Danish tour was the opportunity to return the favor to our wonderful student friends from Aabenraa. Fifty students from the Købmandsskolen came to America the following fall, and we hosted them on our campus. The guys stayed in the dorm rooms with our guys; the gals stayed with Penn Singers in their rooms. We were able to provide as many good memories for them as they had for us. Through generous friends in the Philadelphia Orchestra, for example, we had complimentary seats for all of them at the Academy of Music for an orchestra concert. We also arranged a tour of Philadelphia. The journal of their U.S. visit, of which they sent us a copy after they had returned home, indicated that their Penn stay was one of the highlights of their trip. It's great when kindnesses can be returned with kindnesses.

People often ask me about the "hands logo" on all Glee Club printed matter, from stationery to programs to brochures and ads and even this book. Years ago, I wanted a logo that would instantly identify the Penn Glee Club but would not become dated. At the time, Lillian Burns was an official photographer for the university. She set up a tripod on the stage of Irvine Auditorium about ten feet from my hands. When she said "go" I simply began to conduct. I have no recollection of what I conducted but I suppose it was at a fairly moderate tempo to avoid blurring. Lillian took about fifty shots of my hands in action, and I chose the pose with which Glee Clubbers are now familiar. With the photo in hand, I made a black on white dry-brush ink drawing, which I then had a printer reverse to white on black. That is the version we have used ever since. One flattering—but disturbing—instance of its use was on the program of another collegiate glee club in California. I promptly informed the director that this was a unique, copyrighted logo of Penn's chorus. Much embarrassed, he stopped using it immediately.

While the Glee Club was going along its merry way, the Gilbert & Sullivan Players in Center City and the Penn Singers on campus were building one success after another. The Gilbert & Sullivan Players had racked up an enviable reputation by this time and were considered one of the finest companies in the nation. We seemed incapable of doing any wrong, in the newspapers. As the *Philadelphia Inquirer* put it, "To laud this company for singing, acting, décor, and stage 'business' is merely to continue the string of encomiums." And the Penn Singers were constantly adding to their stature as well.

The Glee Club's 1984 show took full advantage of the fact that it was, indeed, 1984. I wrote an extravaganza called *Ye Merrie Adventures of Robbin' Hoods*, which depicted a pair of American backpackers, played by Larry Wolk and Jordan Foster, hopelessly lost in England's Sherwood Forest and looking for someone—*anyone*—to point them out of their confusion. The opening number I wrote for them, "Big Brother," included this deathless septet:

> Where's the Big Brother who is watching us?
> Where is the face we'd like to see?
> Where is the hellion
> So very George Orwellian
> We'd like to find
> Lurking behind
> Each and every tree?

As it turns out, they found themselves in a time warp and surrounded by Marcus Giancaterino as a swashbuckling Robin Hood (à la Errol Flynn) and his band of Merry Men in costumes of the twelfth century. We got to use the period costumes from *Extravagancelot* again and the guys still looked good in tights! Once again, we seemed to captivate our audiences on campus, and we took the show to Washington, Richmond, Tryon, North Carolina, Atlanta, Tampa, and then Puerto Rico. This time, someone else picked up the tab for our trip to San Juan.

The Glee Club gave its 1984 Award of Merit to composer Vincent Persechetti. Vincent was not only a great composer but the director of the Julliard School of Music in New York. He also was a personal friend from my Germantown Friends School days. At his dinner, we sang a haunting, beautiful work of his, "Song of Peace," which he claimed he only had heard performed once or twice before.

As I mentioned in Chapter 3, from the moment I took over the Penn Glee Club in 1956, a running gag had been perpetrated: to announce to the audience that—whatever the time of year, wherever we happened to be—it was "our director's birthday so let's stand and sing 'Happy Birthday' to him." It generally was announced, as well, that it was my *eightieth* birthday! Somehow, that's not quite as hilarious as it used to be. One particularly devious perpetration was at a joint concert at Skidmore College. One of the guys had a girlfriend in the Skidmore choir and "let it slip" to her weeks before we were to arrive that the very night we would be there was my birthday. "Don't let anyone know," he added, knowing full well that the word would be spread as quickly as a brush fire in Texas. At the pre-concert dinner in the large dining hall filled with students from throughout the college, the lights suddenly were dimmed and a cart with an immense birthday cake was wheeled in while the choir intoned "Happy Birthday dear Monty," joined by the entire student population. At times such as this—when considerable effort had been expended on my behalf—there was no way that I was going to let the cat out of the bag and proclaim that I was the last day of Gemini in June, not this early February weekend.

Each performance of *Robbin' Hoods* ended with a large sign saying "Ye Olde Penne Glee Club"—with travel-lights looking like the marquee of a downtown movie theater of the 1920s—descending from the fly gallery over the heads of the tap-danced finale. For the last performance of the year, the industrious Glee Club men, sometime between the late afternoon rehearsal and the evening show, had repainted the sign. It descended dramatically proclaiming "Happy Birthday, Monty!" As a rule, I vehemently disapprove of changing anything after a show has opened successfully. But this was such a crowd-pleasing punctuation mark to the entire season that I could do nothing but guffaw as loudly as the rest of the audience.

It has been my honor to serve on a number of boards of directors, due entirely to my work at Penn. Among them are Young Audiences, Franklin Concerts, the Intercollegiate Musical Council, the Musical Fund Society, the Garrigues Foundation, and the Presser Foundation. The Garrigues grants scholarships to music students and schools throughout the country each year, and it is a source of great personal satisfaction to be able to help so many deserving and talented young people continue their music education. But I guess my greatest efforts—and, with monthly luncheon meetings and additional committee duties, certainly the greatest allotment of time—are spent with the Presser Foundation. Little did I realize when I spent so much time and labor in Presser Hall in my Kansas alma mater that one day I would be serving on the very board that made that building possible. In addition to nationwide scholarships to music students, we grant considerable funds for buildings, instruments, special programs, retired music teachers, and almost anything else that furthers the cause of music and music education. This last is of great concern to us as we watch audiences for fine music get grayer hair every year and realize that something dramatic must be done to make it appeal to young people. We're trying to make a difference.

In 1985, our 123rd annual production was *Where'm I Goin'?*, concerning the Glee Club flying on Fly-by-Night Airways ostensibly headed for Boise, Idaho. With such a sleazy outfit of incompetent navigators, however, their circuitous route takes them by way of Denmark, Peru, Germany, England, Russia, Greece, and finally New York. They never do find Boise. It gave us a chance for numerous costume changes and five languages in addition to English, to say nothing of hilarious characters with amazing accents. After critical acclaim at home, it proved the perfect vehicle to take on a tour of Greece.

Before we left, on reviewing and assessing our equipment, our properties manager discovered that our traveling crates and footlockers for costumes, props, band instruments, and the like were in their waning days from our many travels and probably would give up their ghosts on another distant venture. The exchequer was strained to the limit and we saw no clear way of replacing our trunks with the necessary sturdy equipment. On the other hand, we have no shame in begging if the cause is just. I. Goldberg is a wonderful Army/Navy store, at that time at 9th and Chestnut Streets. Just who thought of it I don't remember, but somebody worked out a deal whereby Nana Goldberg had the whole Glee Club singing inside and outside her store one rush hour and our travel equipment requirements were taken care of for a flat hundred bucks! Off we went to Greece with newfound confidence in our baggage.

We were assigned to families in Athens who had signed up to house the members. Once again, there was an uneven number and I had to go alone to a family that spoke no English. I could say "good morning" (kahleemehrah, according to the Berlitz phrase book), "thank you" (ehfkhahreesto), and "where are the toilets?" (poo eeneh ee tooahlehtehss), which didn't help with more than the barest necessities. Brendan O'Brien and Richard Rosenberg, on the other hand, had the considerable help of an interpreter as they convinced my "family" that their director had arrived in Greece suffering from an acute intestinal disorder and that, no matter how much I protested to the contrary, for the sake of my health I should eat no native food but only the gigantic box of Fruit Loops they supplied! For nearly a full day I watched them eat succulent lamb dishes and moussaka and creamy homemade feta cheese while I choked down my Fruit Loops. Finally, I was able to convince them that it was a practical joke and that I would dearly love anything they served me. With some collusion of a servant in the house where Brendan and Rosie were staying, I was able to spread the remaining Fruit Loops in the beds they were to occupy that night. Pitifully small retribution for the hardship I had endured.

When we gave our major Athens performance that second night, it was a full house and an unqualified success. The next morning, a color photograph of the club in their red tunics and busbies—part of the costume for the London stop in *Where'm I Goin'?*—appeared in *Apogevmatini*, the principal morning newspaper, next to a glowing review. One thing about our performance that night that surprised all of us was the rapt attention the audience paid to our rendition of the Greek national anthem. It always was played at the close of each television day, it was heard on the radio, it led every parade, but it was always *played*, almost never sung! Therefore, it was a new experience for most to hear the words—and sung by an American chorus, at that!

We learned—well, some of us learned—that everybody in Greece makes the creamiest, sweetest feta cheese from local goat's milk that we had ever tasted. It's a very different experience from the feta we get in America. Pasteurization, while safer I guess, apparently makes the bitter difference in the U.S. We sang for children in a school and danced syrtaki in Delphi. We even learned the proper way to smash china dishes on tavern floors while dancing to the wild bazouki accompaniment.

One evening in Athens we were at Syntagma Square, the principal meeting place of the city, when what seemed like all of Greece was descending upon us screaming, honking car horns, and generally scaring the hell out of us.

Everyone, except the club apparently, had heard the news that the pro-American Papandreou government had just been overthrown and decided to show their spirit at the square. We were right in the center of what appeared to us to be a menacing mob. We immediately broke into the Greek national anthem, followed by a Greek folk song. The next day, a front page newspaper article quoted the president of Athens College who suggested that the United States "would be very wise to try a 10-year experiment of doing away with all professional diplomats and sending the Penn Glee Club on tour!"

My first encounter with a motorcycle took place on the island of Crete. The cycle won. When I picked myself up from the roadside, Rosie's major concern was not for my well-being but for the soft leather jacket he had lent me for my ride. It's always good to know someone's priorities. Also on Crete, in one corner of the ruins of the Palace of Knossos, is what is purported to be the world's first theater. Actually, it is a stone-paved area with several tiers of seats around three sides of it, but supposedly the first plays were performed there. Naturally, therefore, the Glee Club sang there.

On the plane on the way home, the PA system announced that a meal would be served shortly. "Will Mr. Cohen, Mr. Feldstein, Mr. Klein, Mr. Montgomery, and Mr. Katzmeyer please identify themselves to the flight attendant so that we may serve the kosher meals?" The first thing to cross people's minds, I suppose, was "What was his name before he changed it?" Of course it was another practical joke played on their long-suffering conductor by the Glee Club. But this time it was more practical than joke. The kosher meal was infinitely more appealing than what was served to the remainder of the passengers, including the perpetrators of the joke.

Our 124th annual production was planned with a specific tour in mind. I believe it was the only time I ever did that. *Holmes Sweet Holmes* was written because we knew that in 1986 we would be traveling to Scotland and England. With its frightful pun subtitle, *or Watson a Name?*, the show was an ideal vehicle to take to Britain. In Scotland and England we fitted right in. We challenged the experts in London and Edinburgh pubs to do-or-die darts matches and even learned to like the warm beer we ended up buying for everyone as the inevitable penalty of losing. Cue in hand, we mastered—well, almost mastered—the finer points of snooker. (Actually, there was that one shot . . .)

Our first performance of the tour was at Queen Ethelburga's School in Yorkshire. It was here that we were introduced to high tea. What a misnomer!

It was one of the few times on a foreign tour that I saw the club members completely empty their plates of the heaps of delicacies offered them. These were English foods, you know, and they're more like us. Therefore, naturally, the food would be edible! That evening, the show was made somewhat challenging by the fact that to reach the stage right dressing room required an outdoor dash in frigid night air. There were a few more left exits than as originally staged.

Following another day of sightseeing, including the beautiful York Minster, one of the world's great Gothic cathedrals, we boarded our bus once more and headed for Scotland. Here we sang in schools, in parks, even in a pub or two. Our major appearances were stand-up concerts at the University of Edinburgh and a fully staged performance of *Holmes Sweet Holmes* in the city's Saint George Theatre.

We performed several recording sessions for Scottish radio and television to be broadcast after we left the country, so we never had the opportunity to hear or see them. I'm told they were excellent and well received. A wonderful high point of our stay in Scotland was a marvelous reception and dinner given in our honor by the chancellor of the University of Edinburgh. In a way, it followed on the distant heels of a reception given a few years earlier for Benjamin Franklin.

The low point of the trip was an all-night bus ride to London. We arrived in London just as dawn was breaking, and the well-meaning Brits believed that our best introduction to the city would be a bus tour! We had a most charming tour guide who gave us the full narrated tour even though every man in the club was fast asleep, in the seats, on the floor of the bus, even in luggage racks. I kept apologizing to her and she graciously understood, but she was hired to do a job and, by George, she was going to follow through to the last halfpence-worth! Afterward, Brendan, Rosie and I split the cost of one of those blessed underground public showers and almost felt human again before we faced our hosts for our stay in England.

Holmes Sweet Holmes is still referred to on occasion by my Sherlockian friends. I am honored to be a member of the Baker Street Irregulars of New York (with the titular investiture of the Red Circle, in case you're interested), and some of my cronies there still rib me about my preposterous plot involving a missing glee club director, presumed kidnapped, and his cryptic note that stated only "12:58 Honey-bun." Throughout, I had George Pologeorgis as Holmes and Phil Schroeder as Watson chasing shadows due to Holmes's continuing misinterpretation of the note's meaning.

"12:58 Honey-bun," Holmes reads aloud to Watson. "12:58 is two minutes to one: 2-to-1. Honey comes from bees; buns from a baker. Don't you see,

Watson? 2-2-1 Bee Baker! Our old lodgings at 221-B Baker Street! Quick, Watson, the game's afoot! Together again on a case!" And off they run.

Or later, when several other deductions prove dead ends, "12:58 Honeybun" is reread to mean "It says '12:58 *Henry*-bun.' It is obviously referring to Henry the Third, King of England during the Rebellion of 1258."

"Oh, balderdash!" says Watson. "Then how do you explain 'bun'?"

"Elementary, my dear Watson. A bun is merely a flat-bottomed boat. Obviously their director was kidnapped and taken via bun to the Henry III exhibit at the British Museum, not far off the Thames."

And still later, and even more preposterous, "The early afternoon train from Scotland is due at Kings Cross Station at exactly 12:58. 'Honey-bun' is a code he left hoping that his students would be clever enough to decipher it and know that he would return for the performance tonight. 'Honey' is merely a misspelling of the French word 'honi'—meaning 'shame'—as in our own respected motto: 'honi soit qui mal y pense.' And 'bun' is but a thin disguise for our favorite English tea cake: a scone. Don't you see, Watson? He has avenged the shame of the English and returned the Stone of Scone to its rightful Scotland!"

Little wonder I'm teased about my contrivances.

While we were in London, I made my regular pilgrimage to the British Museum. I went to one of my two favorite spots (the other is the Elgin Marbles) to see the priceless manuscripts. Here are the original manuscripts of the greatest authors, poets, musicians, and playwrights from Chaucer and Shakespeare to Mozart and Beethoven. One glass case particularly interested me. Beside an open notebook in her tiny, meticulous hand, a small sign read "Emily Brontë's workbook open to her famous poem "Remembrance." I looked carefully and discovered that it was *not* open to "Remembrance"! I rather shyly went over to a nearby guard.

"I don't wish to appear the brash American," I told him, "but I believe you will find an error in that case. The Emily Brontë notebook is not open to the poem that the card indicates."

"Oh, thank you, sir," he replied a bit condescendingly. "But this is the British Museum, you know. But let's have a look, shall we?" We went to the case together and he leaned close.

"Oh, dear!" With that he took me to the curator of the collection and I repeated my observation.

"Oh, thank you, sir. But this is the British Museum, you know," he mirrored the guard's reaction. "But we'll have a look. Oh, dear!"

The curator then took out an unusual key and unlocked the case. Obviously, the page of the notebook had flipped over while they were placing it in the case. But instead of simply correcting the mistake himself, he did one of the most generous things imaginable: he handed the small book to me!

"Won't you find it for me?" he said as I took the notebook in trembling hands.

Of course it was but a page or so away, but I was thrilled beyond measure at his thoughtful gesture. He thanked me profusely. The thanks, of course, were mine.

Our major performances in London were in the large outdoor Bishops Park Summer Theatre and in the ballroom of the Portman Hotel—not the ideal venues for our show. The club is accustomed to setting up anywhere on a moment's notice, however, and we seemed to enchant the large English audiences with our flexibility as well as our performances. Our final tour performance was in wonderful Windsor, and we were elated by our visit to the castle before returning to London and the flight home.

In the meantime, the Penn Singers continued to add to their already fine successes and prestige with *The Yeomen of the Guard*, *H.M.S. Pinafore*, and repeats of *Iolanthe*, *The Pirates of Penzance*, *The Mikado*, and *The Gondoliers*.

In 1987, the Penn Glee Club celebrated its 125th anniversary. It was a festive year with many very special happenings. Our production that year was *Time In—Time Out*, a retrospective of the milestones of the century-and-a-quarter of the Glee Club. For the second time, I drew a caricature of each man for the poster and program cover. For the backdrop, I designed a fifty-foot-wide, twenty-five-foot-high page from a scrap book depicting many memorable photographs and newspaper clippings of the club's history. More about that later.

One of our winter weekend trips was to New England. I was going to be in Chicago on university business until the night before our early morning departure for Massachusetts. So, uncharacteristically thinking far ahead, I had packed my tails, blazer, underwear, and so on, and had it waiting in my office to pick up and take on the club bus that next morning. On my flight from O'Hare we circled Philadelphia for nearly an hour but didn't land, due to Philly being socked in by foul weather.

About 2:30 A.M. we were finally diverted to New York. I telephoned the Glee Club president and told him my plight. I instructed him to pick up my suitcase from the office and that I would meet the bus on the George Washington Bridge at 8:00 A.M. What I didn't know was that a pedestrian is not permitted to wait on the bridge—what's more, I had no idea whether the bus would take the upper or lower level of the bridge!

The police were unbelievably accommodating and arranged for me to wait in a police car. The toll-takers were alerted to tell them where our bus arrived and to hold it there. I then would be sped to wherever it sat. All went as planned, and I boarded the bus with an appreciative sung toast to New York's finest.

One of the most marvelous happenings of the year was the spectacular turnout by Glee Club alumni from many past years and from all over the world. After an afternoon rehearsal, all of us presented a "third act" following the Saturday night performance of *Time In—Time Out*. The stage of the Zellerbach Theatre was crammed with singers, and we presented another forty minutes of all-time hits with the magnificent sound of two hundred male voices. At one point, I even called Penn's president Sheldon Hackney up from the audience and had him conduct the massed chorus in a Penn song. A brilliant comic, Sheldon turned it into a ten-minute "shtick" to the delight of all.

In my position as director of the Glee Club, it was my great honor and pleasure to know as genuine friends five presidents of the University of Pennsylvania. Simply because we sang at every major function of the university, they could hardly avoid me. But they all went out of their way to befriend me and include me in many an affair that had nothing to do with the Glee Club. When Gaylord died, Mollie immediately requested that the club sing at his memorial service; he had directed that funds donated in his memory be assigned to the Glee Club.

Martin and Margy Meyerson followed right along with the friendship that had been shown by the Harnwells. They became supportive of almost everything I did and were—and still are—loyal annual patrons of the club. They also have been gracious hosts to me in their Spruce Street home and in many campus conversations and lunches.

The year 1981 began the Hackney era. Sheldon and Lucy Hackney included me in more activities than I can remember and a number of delightful meals in their lovely Eisenlohr Hall home. I had the distinction of writing a special (somewhat irreverent) musical piece "A Hackneyed Medley" for Sheldon's retirement dinner held at the Morris Arboretum. Sung by members of the Glee Club, the candid lyric scared the secretary of the university at the time, who thought it was offensive, but it was appreciated by everyone else—especially Sheldon and Lucy.

It was at the 125th anniversary performance, after Sheldon made a hit conducting the huge chorus in a Penn song, that the endowment of the University of Pennsylvania Glee Club was made public—the first student group at Penn so privileged. Begun by a generous gift of Bill Bolton, the fund serves to support club travels and any other projects of an extraordinary nature. It is administered by the Glee Club Graduate Club in New York and has already been of tremendous assistance to the undergraduate program. While I knew ahead of time that the endowment was going to be announced from the stage, Greg Suss took me totally by surprise when he proclaimed to all that it would be known in perpetuity as "the Montgomery Fund."

Without a doubt the most exciting happening of the year, however, was getting an invitation from Pilar Nores de García, wife of the president of Peru, to come once again to her country with the intent of helping to raise funds for her favorite charity, the Fundación por los Niños del Peru. So off we went to Peru again. This trip, no one discouraged us and we were made welcome everywhere. I also got many chances to recycle my nineteen-second speech from 1969, "Buenas noches, damas y caballeros . . ."

On our way, we stopped for a few days in Jamaica, where we swam and rested up prior to our rigorous whirlwind tour of Peru. The single most significant part of this island visit for all of us was the terrifying cliff-diving. All but two of the Glee Club did it, and I wasn't about to be among the minority. To me the scariest part was walking out on a tiny spit of rock. Looking down, you could see nothing but jagged needles of rock that would quickly impale you if you slipped. The dive itself was breathtaking as you plummeted sixty feet to the water below. It's the equivalent of jumping off the roof of a six-story building, and landing the wrong way in the water can be almost as injurious. The old man grew in the estimations of more than a few that day. Either that or they realized that I was as big a damn fool as they. Pain likes pals.

Perhaps the most foolish thing I did in Jamaica was to play a minor prank on some of the students, who still berate me for it. Several of us went parasailing over the deep azure of the tropical water. I was high up in the air and beginning my descent toward the four or five students expectantly awaiting my landing. To my students I was the old man fully capable of being their grandfather. So why not play it out? Before I neared them, my body went completely limp, my head sagged to my chest and, through my squinting eyes, I could see utter panic below me as they perceived a corpse descending. It was a thoughtless, nasty prank, and my jocularity was not shared by the clubbers, who set upon me without a shred of forgiveness.

Another couple of days in Jamaica, and we were off on the club's second jaunt to South America. We performed pretty much all over Peru. We would arrive bus-dusty at each of the orphan children's villages, change into our blazer outfits and greet Señora García as she arrived by helicopter. There are definite advantages to being the First Lady.

After performances in Lima and a reception at the presidential mansion, we headed north to Chiclayo. Here we sang for the opening of a brand-new children's village under the aegis of the Foundation. It was desperately hot most of the time we were in Peru, and our stay in Chiclayo was made pleasant by rousing games of pseudo-water polo in a large, cool swimming pool made available to us by thoughtful sponsors. From Chiclayo we drove south again, toward Trujillo. On the way, we made what proved to be a grave error by stopping in Huanchaco for lunch. Huanchaco is a charming seaside town of unusual, long, tied reed boats whose design must hark back thousands of years. We were charmed by everything except the lunch. It wasn't just the Inca Cola. or the grotesque charred chicken feet reaching up at us from the bowls of broth. Everything was unappetizing and foul-tasting.

We were scheduled to perform two shows—seven and nine-thirty—in Trujillo at a perfect jewel of an opera house. We were barely into the first act when it hit us. Every man in the Glee Club was experiencing food poisoning from our lunch in Huanchaco. No scene in the show was complete in its performers. Rushed emergency exits were the norm. Backstage was festooned with the foul evidence.

Somehow we limped through the first show. In the interval between shows, I was lying on my back in a little patch of garden behind the theater. I wasn't even modestly conscious enough to pull up my pants when Señora Poppi came to me with some coca tea she had made for us. It was the only thing we could keep down, and it helped immensely. It wasn't until much later that I learned that her magic brew contained the raw materials for cocaine. But it did the trick. When I went backstage to attempt to rally the troops for the second show, I found many of them lying prostrate offstage left, club president Brendan O'Brien among them. When he saw me, he first feebly raised his head to ascertain that it was time to begin our show. He then mustered every remaining ounce of presidential authority.

"Gentlemen," he murmured as best he could, "Monty will tell future Glee Club guys about this for years and years to come." Then, tapping an unknown source of strength and summoning his finest courage, he leapt to his feet and yelled "Let's *do* it!"

Challenged, the rest of the club, still horribly sick, rose to the occasion and the performance went on. Seldom over the years have I been so proud of the Penn Glee Club. The show went on, but at a real price. Four men were rushed to the local hospital immediately after the performance. I thought David Canaday was going to die. What on earth would I tell his mother and his doctor father? How could I handle the international ramifications of such an event? How could I counsel the remaining students in such a crisis? Strangely, it had never before occurred to me on a foreign tour that I might lose a student, and I wasn't prepared for the possibility. To our great good fortune—and in answer to my prayers—Dave recovered and continued with us.

For much of the rest of our South American tour we continued to feel the lingering repercussions of the travelers' time-worn complaint, "Montezuma's revenge." In my perverse sense of humor, I coined the more geographically and historically accurate sobriquet: the "Inca-Dinca-Doo." (How-to-feel-your-age 101: most of the guys never caught the humor and knew nothing of Jimmy Durante or his song!)

One of the most fascinating side trips of this tour was our visit to Chan-Chan. This gigantic adobe city was an ancient marvel in 1548 when Cieza de León observed that, "although they are so old, one can see that they must have been exceptional." To quote Ruiz's *Guide to Peru*, "Nowhere else in the world (not even in Mesopotamia, Russia, or Chinese Turkestan) do there exist adobe ruins as extensive as those of Chan-Chan. . . . No other adobe ruins in the world can be said to have so many embellishments or to be so perfectly laid-out."

In our Trujillo hotel, as we were having breakfast the morning after our ghastly illnesses and just before heading off to Chan-Chan, the restaurant and lobby television sets showed a promo of us singing and an announcement that we were going to do another show that night at the opera house. Adam Sherr, our wonderful, gullible, and now openly belligerent stage manager, simply refused to do another show in Trujillo. I, of course, checked with the necessary powers and learned that the announcement was an error. There was no performance in Trujillo that night. Sensing an opportunity to turn the tables on a student for a change, I let only Brendan and a few others know this, and thus began the only eight-hour practical joke to which I've ever been a party. It loses much in the retelling so I'll cut to the basics.

As we left Chan-Chan and were back on the bus again, with every passing hour Adam was getting more angry. By now, all the men except Adam knew the joke, and discussions became more and more heated, with the singers apparently dividing into strong pro and con Trujillo camps. Even our two police escorts and our bus driver, who spoke no English, got involved in the elaborate scheme. Our driver drove us into little towns and destroyed our sense of direction on side streets and town plazas. In one, he pretended a minor breakdown and proceeded to hammer things under the bus with a rock strictly for Adam's benefit. Shades were pulled down on one whole side of the bus so that Adam couldn't see which side the ocean was on and perhaps realize that we were going in the wrong direction for Trujillo.

Finally, as we were driving through the vast desert, the rowdy guys became so vocal and riled up that the bus simply stopped and the entire club erupted into the nearby sand dunes and engaged in a gigantic free-for-all fistfight. Adam sat in the bus astounded at what he saw. Naturally, I was busy trying to break it up, pulling flailing men apart and being knocked about in so doing. One of our police escorts even drew a pistol. Finally, some sense of order was restored and the disheveled men returned to the bus. Brendan and one or two other men continued a shouting match at the front as we got under way. Then he stopped abruptly and spoke to Adam.

"This was all for you, Adam, ever since breakfast! Raise the curtain. The ocean's on your right. We're on our way to Lima."

With that, the bus rocked with laughter—even the police and driver. I'm certain they thought that these were the craziest tourists they had ever escorted in their country. But after his initial disbelief and shock, by far the gutsiest belly-laughs came from Adam. The whole day had a salutary effect of letting off steam for the entire Club. No doctor could have ordered better medicine for a sick and spent group.

We returned to El Lima Tambo, the little hotel we had visited when we arrived in Peru, and were welcomed back warmly by the owner. We spent another few days there, were able to send out our laundry, and gave away another batch of Frisbees at yet another orphans' village.

We next flew to Iquitos on the Amazon River. We were met at the airport that night by dozens of screaming teenagers: a welcoming committee commensurate with a visiting rock group. Our major performance in Iquitos was held in the huge indoor bullring. A large stage had been built at one end of the ring, and wires and pipes were hung to accommodate a curtain and our huge backdrop. My first experience here was to stand to give a rehearsal downbeat, feet about twelve inches apart, and watch a 30-inch iguana slither between my shoes. I have no recollection of what we rehearsed—but I'll wager the tempo was faster than usual.

After this last performance of *Time In—Time Out*, we took down the scrapbook backdrop and each "photograph" painting was carefully cut out. Those who had spoken up for them took their muslin home and had it stretched on wooden frames to hang like a good-size mural. I sometimes wonder how many are still hanging.

Before we left the States, our drummer had canceled out on us and the tour. We had a young lad, Ken Williams, sit in with us at one of the high schools in which we performed, met with his parents, and obtained their permission for him to be part of our pit band in Peru. His entire town got behind him and paid for his air fare. Kenny was tall, slender, and blond, and the groupies adored him immediately. Señora García and her teenage daughter had come to Iquitos. The young teen, of course, fell in love with Kenny, and I believe it was reciprocal.

The finale of the first act was a medley of George M. Cohan songs ending with an exuberant tap-dance. The heat and humidity of Iquitos were almost unbearably debilitating, and our Cohan finale was performed in heavy wool World War I uniforms. As soon as the curtain closed, men tore off their sweat-drenched clothes and collapsed all over the stage. Of course, this was the very moment that Señora García and her daughter chose to visit us and Kenny. We somehow averted an international incident.

On a free day, we took a boat ride up the Amazon and were fascinated by the dense jungle that hugged the river throughout our journey. We stopped at one village and sang for the tawny-skinned natives among their straw and thatch huts. The men wore brief loin cloths and the women were topless. We never did determine whether that was how they lived or was a put-on (or take-off) for tourists who ply their river. I bought a poison-dart blow gun from one of them and it now graces the wall of my Connemara living room, which contains interesting masks and artifacts gathered from all over the world.

As we chugged along the Amazon, I cautioned the men not to let their hands get into the river's water.

"The voracious piranhas are small," I warned, "but they travel in schools and will take off your hand in an instant. Watch."

For the doubting Thomases, I threw a piece of ham from a sandwich into the river a few feet from the boat. As soon as it hit the water, the river was churning with hundreds of piranhas devouring it. It is a frightening sight and effectively discourages swimming in the Amazon.

Back in Iquitos, we played Frisbee with some of the little "river rats"—the children who live on the muddy banks of the river. Later, as we were having a sumptuous dinner given for us at our hotel, we could see the boys peering through the windows. One by one, each of us found some excuse to get up from the table, walk outside with our half-filled plates, and empty them into the upturned Frisbees of the grateful kids. Once again our proffered toys were put to excellent use.

The next day, we visited the long open market of awninged stalls where Iquitos does its shopping. Sloshing through inch-deep water, blood, entrails, and God knows what else, we were appalled by the stench and filth. Vultures perched on the ridge poles of the canvas stalls ready to help themselves to lunch whenever the crowd thinned out a bit. The scorched crocodiles and singed monkeys—both of which I'd eaten before—were heaped in unappetizing globs on piled wooden boxes. The makings for our sumptuous dinner the night before had, of course, come from this market, and it didn't now seem quite so sumptuous in retrospect.

Even though I was certain in 1969 that I never again would see fabulous Cuzco or unbelievable Machu Picchu, we all went high up in the Andes and spent some wonderful days there. In Cuzco we climbed over the immense stones of the fifteenth-century fortress of Sacsahuamán and again marveled at the ability to fit 200-ton stones together like a jigsaw puzzle with primitive tools. To my surprise, as we attained the top of the ridge where Machu Picchu sits unseen from below and, therefore, untouched by the Spanish, rounding the final curve of a wall and seeing the entire civilization spread out in front of me was every bit as thrilling this second time as it had been before.

The sole disappointment of the tour was that we weren't permitted to go to Lake Titicaca or the Nazda Plain. The Sendero Luminoso (Shining Path), a Maoist organization of revolutionists, was guilty of thousands of murders since 1981. The police simply wouldn't let us take the chance. This was very much on our minds when we took the railway to Machu Picchu with half-a-dozen of the most shifty-looking men I've ever seen in our car. I'm aware that that is a dangerous, unfair case of profiling, but we had been so forewarned that our imaginations made it almost inevitable. While no incident occurred with us, that very train was blown up several days later.

Back home after the last of the farewell hugs for the summer, I couldn't help but reflect on all the marvelous experiences and places that the Penn Glee Club had helped open for talented students—and the superb opportunities for them to utilize their talents. And I came, once again, to the conclusive belief that there is no academic course at any university that affords quite so hands-on a study of human nature, international relations, appreciation for art and history, and the sharing of such joy with so many diverse peoples.

They Always Gave Freely

WHEN WRITING AN ACCOUNT such as this—drawn from memory—it's sometimes difficult to stick to an accurate chronology. I already have referred to a couple of things in passing, but I haven't taken the side road to explain them because at the time I thought it would be an interruption to the narrative's logical progression. I'm going to start this chapter, therefore, by going back a bit to 1955, 1971, and 1967.

In 1955, my father asked me to take a stab at something he had dreamed about for a long time: writing the lost score for the first Gilbert & Sullivan opera. W. S. Gilbert and Arthur Sullivan had collaborated for the first time in 1871. At the request of John Hollingshead, they had written a work for a Boxing Day holiday entertainment at the Gaiety Theatre in London. What was supposed to be a very limited run far outlasted the holiday for which it was written. *Thespis, or The Gods Grown Old*, was not the hit that their later operas would become—but it never was intended or pretended to be.

For reasons that perhaps never will be fully known, the dialogue and lyrics were published (albeit in a rather hastily edited version), but not the score. Some time after 1878, when it was referred to in a letter from Sullivan as being stored somewhere in the Gaiety, the music was lost and has never been found. There were two survivors that we know of: "Little Maid of Arcadee" was published as a separate drawing-room ballad and "Climbing over Rocky Mountain" was lifted bodily and later placed in *The Pirates of Penzance* for reasons I won't go into here. In *Thespis* it was the entrance of the full mixed chorus; in *Pirates* it was the entrance of the women's chorus alone.

By 1955, my father's company had achieved such a reputation for excellence and authority that he felt he could present *Thespis* with a new score to show our loyal following what it might have been like. To that end, he asked me to compose the missing score in the style of the young Sullivan. Sullivan was twenty-nine when he wrote his; I was twenty-eight when I tackled it. I, of course, had the advantage of knowing what he was going to do for his next thirteen operas with Gilbert! Dad heard and approved my entire score and announced its production for April 1956. He died in November 1955. As I felt that it was necessary to show our patrons that the Gilbert & Sullivan Players would continue the immortal works with the same precision, devotion, excellence, and attention to detail that my father had brought to the repertoire, *Thespis* was put on a back burner until I had thoroughly proven myself. Then it was decided to put it off until 1971, the centenary of its first production. It was a real emotional wrench to have worked so hard on something—particularly at a young age when acceptance was important—only to have it lie fallow for sixteen years.

In 1971, however, the long wait was more than justified. We gained considerable publicity out of the fact that it was the centenary of its first production and that ours was the only company anywhere capable of so celebrating the anniversary. Devotees came from all over the U.S. and Canada for the production, and the press was ecstatic in its praise. One newspaper even went so far as to "hope that the original never will be found for we already have a definitive version." *Thespis* then became a part of our permanent repertoire, and we have twice presented it in international G&S festivals, as well.

When I returned from my Maine summer vacation in 1967, Steve Goff met me while I still had my briefcase in hand to inform me that Kathleen Quinn, who had founded the Penn Players in 1936, had resigned over the summer and that he was taking over the organization as executive producer.

"Everyone is predicting doomsday," he said. "Because the Players was hers for so long, many alumni are saying that it's all over now. Well, it's not over and we need a really dramatic way of letting everyone know it. That's where you come in."

"What do you want me to do?" I asked, puzzled.

"After the success of *Spindrift*, you've got a track record that will make people sit up and notice. How about writing a new musical for the Players?"

Stunned, I never even put my briefcase down, but said "OK," turned around, and went back to Maine.

Two weeks later, I returned to Penn with a musical. *Why Me?* went into auditions and rehearsals immediately. Following each night's rehearsal, I continued to tighten it and write new songs. If nothing else, the serious theater students gained first-hand knowledge of how a show is created—how new lines, new lyrics, new music are constantly being inserted to replace or improve what they've already learned. Somehow, it all came together and opened. Steve Goff produced it, I directed and conducted it, Walter Keenan choreographed it, and Roy Straigis orchestrated it. Once again, I was treated to delirious audiences and highly enthusiastic reviews. "For good taste, spirited dancing, an appealing cast, believability in story, and ear-tickling tunes," said the *Philadelphia Inquirer*, "accolades go to 'Why Me?' a musical that had its premiere Thursday night."

The plot of *Why Me?* was part fiction, part fact. Even the fictional part had its precedent in reality, however. It was a raucous musical comedy that took place during the Korean War, involving a young man who was just starting his career as a concert pianist when he was drafted into the army. This important role of Mark Maddox was played by third-year Penn Law School student Bancroft Littlefield, Jr. Already embittered, Maddox loses his right arm in the war. Before to going to Korea, his life was touched by a twelve-year-old girl dying of leukemia in Philadelphia's Children's Hospital. I knew that someday I would have an opportunity to tell the touching story of Anna Mae Brandt and her effect on me and many other soldiers during her last months. This proved to be the right time. And telling two very serious stories couched in a broad comedy was the way to treat them. With the character renamed Mary Ann Howard for the show, we were blessed with a marvelous twelve-year-old girl from a local school, Wendy Griffin, to be our guest star. In addition to all the Penn students involved, the stage was loaded with adorable pajama-clad children gathered from faculty, parents, brothers, and sisters. Two nieces of mine, Susan and Vicki Thomas, were among the kids making their stage debuts. Someone once said that a show could never fail if it had dogs or kids. I proved the point. Now let's get back to chronology and the Glee Club.

The club's 1987–1988 season began, as usual, with our singing the national anthem at a Phillies game. This time, however, Philadelphia was playing Montreal so we added "O, Canada!"—sung in English at the request of the management, even though we knew the French as well.

Our Award of Merit took a slightly different twist in 1987. We still sang a great many formal concerts with some of the finest works ever written by the great composers of the world, but much of our success was built on the fact that we balanced these with incredible showmanship and effective dancing. It seemed appropriate, therefore, to honor an individual who was prominent in the field that had made ours so popular a form of entertainment and to whom we owed a debt of gratitude for a good portion of the fame we enjoyed. Few met this description more deservedly than Sheldon Harnick, the brilliant cocreator of such milestone musicals as *Fiorello!*, *She Loves Me*, and *Fiddler on the Roof*. As we had expected, Sheldon was the perfect such choice and was a charming, articulate recipient who quickly endeared himself to all of us.

In 1988 the premise of our show was that the entire club was wiped out in a bus accident and we were trying to make it into heaven. *Heaven Help Us!* sported another of our fifty-foot backdrops. I painted a high wall with the pearly gates in the center designed as the double arches of McDonald's encrusted with gigantic pearls! On the wall such slogans as "Over a Trillion Souls" parodied the fast-food chain. In the blue sky above the wall floated typical Renaissance cherubs, each with a tiny, very circumspect appendage.

The plot required the Glee Club to pass certain tests in order to qualify for entrance to heaven. The tests took the form of the most popular of the TV game shows. When I cast Sean Barry as a hip Saint Peter and David Forbes as an unorthodox Saint Aloysius Jehosaphat to play the two moderators—and, therefore, the two principal characters—I was informed that there was no love lost between them offstage. I was a "damn fool to expect them to work together onstage." Sean and Davey not only were terrific in the show but became great friends in the bargain. The plot called for the club members to play "Celestial Jeopardy," "Ezekiel's Wheel of Fortune" (which, to my shame, even referred to an offstage sexy blonde Nirvana White), "Cherubic Charades," and "Halo Wood Squares." At the end, they failed, and the finale saw them tap-dancing in white tie and tails, each sporting small red horns on either side of his head and carrying a red pitchfork as if it were an evening cane.

We toured the Midwest performing *Heaven Help Us!* Starting with a twenty-hour bus ride to Saint Louis, we sang in a theater near Washington University in Forest Park. We also had time to go up the fabulous Gateway Arch, as we had done on earlier tours. We next performed in the Congress Hotel in Chicago, visited the Sears Tower, and attended a Blackhawks game. Then it was on to Detroit, Toronto (where I was involved in a remarkable episode with a zipper which will not be recounted here), Cleveland, and Pittsburgh. After eleven days on the road, we all agreed that one of the high points was in Saint Louis at a wonderful private Sunday tour that Augie Busch arranged for us to his Anheuser-Busch brewery.

The year 1988 also saw—at long last—the release of our recording *Brothers, Sing On!* which celebrated our 125th anniversary of a year earlier. This turned out to be the last lp recording we made. From then on it was Compact Discs. As a matter of fact, we were the first performing group on campus to make a CD.

For years we had performed on Parents' Weekend as part of the big entertainment put on by the university for the parents of the freshman class. On November 12, we started a fine new tradition of our own. We continually asked parents to understand why we must spend so much of our time rehearsing, performing, and traveling when they were seldom afforded an opportunity to be part of the fun. John Turbessi came up with a great idea: we invited all our families to a catered Parents' Brunch on Saturday morning before going to the football game together. It was a rousing success as the many parents got to meet and chat with each other, and brothers and sisters, grandmothers and grandfathers all compared notes. And, finally, we shared notes, too, and sang for about forty minutes. For some, it was the first time they had heard their sons in action.

For reasons far too numerous and involved to recount here, I disbanded the Gilbert & Sullivan Players in 1985. We went out, however, with a bang. Basingstoke (a G&S allusion that will mean something to the cognoscenti and not much to anyone else) was a 1989 festival that brought Gilbert & Sullivan nuts and companies from around the country and Canada to West Chester, Pennsylvania, to attend a week-long series of lectures, master classes, discussions, and performances.

I guess the most unusual feature of the festival was the brief resurrection of the G&S Players of Philadelphia as we presented, once again, my version of *Thespis.* It was a decided hit and walked off with stunning reviews both locally and in reports sent all over the country. Never before had the show been presented to so discriminating and knowledgeable an audience of G&S aficionados. Once again, my Sullivanesque score seemed to please everyone, public and press alike. I had contracted with a community orchestra to accompany this festive production. Less than a week before it opened, the conductor phoned me with the alarming news that they had rehearsed it faithfully but that it was too difficult for them and they would have to bow out. My immediate reaction was panic. My second was to call dear friend Marc Mostovoy to see if he could help me with the Concerto Soloists. At this late date, I told him, money is no object; I simply needed the best and could have only one rehearsal. As usual, Marc came through and hired the best in the business. I conducted, and their first reading was as if they had been playing the score for years. For the second time, Marc had saved my neck. Gosh, it's great to have such talented friends! I also made a vow to myself that one day I would repay his kindness.

Following the disbanding, I was hired to direct the newly formed Gilbert & Sullivan Society of Chester County in *The Yeomen of the Guard*. And I've been directing the company performances ever since.

I made one of my rare cameo appearances in a Glee Club show in 1989, playing Cecil B. DeMillions, a flamboyant movie director. Adam Sherr did an equally rare stint as my Gopher. Complete with the over-the-shoulders coat, an eighteen-inch-long cigarette holder, ascot, spats, and boutonnière, C. B. introduced two motion picture epics that he was directing. *Is This for Reel?* was about the making of two movie musicals. The first act was the old Jack-and-the-Beanstalk tale set to music as "Jack Bean Nimble" (the guys were still wary of tights). It included two of the more memorable characters to appear in a Glee Club show. Wizzen was an amoral con man extraordinaire played with extravagant hamminess by Michael Handler. Jack was played with tremendous charm by Jeffrey Coon, a freshman. And now I'm going to confess something that I've never truly acknowledged until this minute. Jeff was so spectacular and charismatic and possessed such a marvelous tenor voice that I make no apologies in admitting that I wrote the next three shows specifically for him. The lead was his for the rest of his Glee Club days! My assessment was right on target. Not only was he superb in the remainder of his work with us, but he has made a wonderful career for himself in the theater ever since.

The second act of *Is This for Reel?* was C. B. making a musical of Shakespeare's *Julius Caesar*. With Rich Gusick as Brutus and Marvin Lyon as Cassius, we had the current and next club president in starring roles. Nick Hunchak was our Mark Antony. The chorus was given so much hoofing that, at one point, C. B. called from the pit "Eat your heart out, Busby Berkeley!" But the wildest casting was Joey Arnel Sayson as the cool, hip Julius Caesar. The biggest groan of the show came when he took off his mod sunglasses after Brutus remarked that he is back so soon from lunch. I'm guilty of this unpardonable line:

"I have drunk my fill—and I have et, too, Brute."

Just in time for the '89 show, Mike Handler put together a new small group in the club. The PennChants received permission from the legendary PennChants Four of the 1970s to use the name, dropping the number because the new group was substantially larger, with Mike, Jack Ross, Marvin Lyon, Rob Biron, Thew Williams, Myong Leigh, Rick Aronstein, and John Shu.

As I look back now, writing from the vantage point of "retirement," many wonderfully successful Glee Club shows race through my mind with considerable joy. If I were pressed to name my all-time favorite, however, after much thought I believe it would be *Basses Loaded!* our baseball show for 1990. And because of that, I'll spend a little more time on it than on the others. (My sole regret of the production was that I didn't think of the better title *Perfect Pitch* at the time.)

Once again, my shameful admission: I wrote *Basses Loaded!* as a vehicle for Jeff Coon. And, oh boy, did he come through with a grand slam! As the curtain opened, the audience was treated to a bucolic scene of a Pennsylvania Dutch farm—complete with hex signs on the big red barn and fields of ripening corn—and five boys fishing, their pants rolled up and their bare feet dangling over the orchestra pit. It's county fair time, and the Yoder boys are scolded by their Pa for not aiding with the chores "already once." The county fair is the biggest event of the year here in Juniata Junction.

"That's one of those crossroads towns that's so small it oughtta have 'City Limits' written on both sides of the sign."

That, at least, is the opinion of Mike Handler as Chuck, anchor of the television crew from Channel 2 in New York that has been sent to the Amish country to cover the fair on assignment for the "A Day in the Life of" program. While singing a song, young Joe Yoder (Coon) absentmindedly picks up some apples and throws them at an offstage target. He is seen pitching by the TV men who are astonished at his speed and accuracy.

CHUCK: Did you see that throw?
HANK: Wow! What an arm that kid has!
CHUCK: (*handing Joe another apple*) Hey, kid. Do that again (*Joe is embarrassed*). No. I mean it. Do that again. Can you hit that same tree?

(*Joe winds up and throws the apple with more zing than the last.*)

MIKE:	Nobody has an arm like that! Not even Orel Hershhiser!
CHUCK:	Ever play ball, kid?
JOE:	Baseball?
CHUCK:	Yeah. Ever played it?
JOE:	Pa didn't like it much when we started but, yeah, we've got a team.
STAN:	A whole team?
JOE:	We're the Juniata Junction Jets.
HANK:	Any of them as good as you?
JOE:	Gosh, they're all better'n me. I'm only the pitcher.

And with this, a saga of immense proportions begins. The TV crew decides to forget the county fair—this is a *real* story. Chuck tells the boys all about the greats of baseball who started just as they have—on a sandlot. For this spot, I wrote a song that includes the names of thirty-eight all-time great baseball players, from Abner Doubleday to Ty Cobb to Babe Ruth and the rest, ending with the double-play legends Tinker to Evers to Chance. A lover of counterpoint, I then have the song repeated by all the baritones and basses while the tenors sing "Take Me Out to the Ballgame" in counterpoint. This turned out to be a show-stopper, and it has been performed out of context by a number of choruses ever since. I've even done it with an all-state high school mixed chorus.

Through all sorts of contrivances, it escalates into a national story and the Juniata Junction Jets are famous throughout the nation and even play an exhibition game with the New York Mets. After a fluke win over the Mets, Chuck has big plans for the boys.

CHUCK:	Well, you did it, boys! Never seen anything like it in my life! This'll go down in the books to inspire kids in sandlots for a hundred years to come!
JOE:	Thanks, Chuck, for givin' us the chance.
CHUCK:	Yea, but it's what ya *did* with the chance that counts. Well, Pop . . . I mean . . .
YODER:	No. Call me Pop. I kind of like it . . . Chuck (*they shake hands*).
CHUCK:	(*imitating Yoder*) Well, what're ya gonna do your boys with now, already once?
YODER:	Friends we are now—but don't push it! (*laughs*) Back to our farms we'll go, natural.
CHUCK:	After this taste of the big time? You're kiddin'!

YODER: No, sir. Our big day we've had already. And it's the biggest day ever we'll have. But still plain we live. And to plain we go back.

At this spot we performed a marvelous song called "Home" that a generous and dear friend of mine, Clark Gesner, wrote for an unproduced Broadway show. He gave his blessings to me to arrange "Home" for the Glee Club and put it in our 1990 show. I staged it so that the club spilled out into the audience and everyone in the theater sang the last chorus! Chuck narrated the ending, as he had the whole show.

CHUCK: Well, that's about all there is to tell.

He continues with some more details, then wraps up the show.

> When they got back from New York, they had one more day of it. The whole county turned out for the celebration. The Mets gave 'em fancy new suits an' the boys put on a real show for the folks. They even let me be a part of it—as an honorary citizen of Juniata Junction. "City Limits" written on both sides of the sign.

Chuck says this in front of the closed curtain. He exits and it rises to reveal the club dressed entirely in white. White tails, white tie, white vest, white shoes and socks, white evening canes and sporting white baseball caps. And the tap finale goes on.

The cast of *Basses Loaded!* was uniformly terrific. Those already mentioned came through with the goods, and Mike Weinmayr outdid himself as Yoder. I think even the Amish would have been impressed. Rob Biron once again was dance captain and it always makes me think back to his freshman year. He had never danced before and during the customary January rehearsals, when I brought the entire club back for a week of intensive work before classes resumed, we would break for lunch and come back to the rehearsal room to find that Rob hadn't gone out but had spent the entire time practicing the choreography he had been taught in the morning. No wonder he became so good, and the club continues to benefit from it. Though now a successful lawyer, he still choreographs and teaches dance numbers each year with great effect.

The plot of the show was more complete than any I had written before for the Club, and it gave more opportunity to develop real characters that did substantially more than simply tie musical numbers together. The music, too, was more integrated and thoughtfully considered an integral part of the story than had been our custom. So there! Now you know why *Basses Loaded!* occupies a very special place in my heart and memory. Thanks for humoring me.

One of the more unusual performances of 1990 came about when Nicholas Constan, long-time friend of the Glee Club and special advisor to President Hackney, called me to learn the availability of the Penn Band for a special reception for Lech Walesa, president of Poland, four days later. I assured Nick that the Band would be honored to play and we determined what sort of music would be appropriate.

"But," I added, "you know the Glee Club has gained something of a reputation for its singing of national anthems wherever we've traveled. How would you like us to sing the Polish anthem for President Walesa?"

This gratuitous offer, you understand, was made without any idea of how quickly I could find the Polish national anthem, who could teach me its pronunciation, how well I could arrange it for fast learning, or even if the club was willing!

The club, of course, was willing, and I found the anthem readily enough. To my good fortune, there was a gentleman who worked in the bowels of the main library who spoke flawless Polish. He patiently taught me just how to teach the correct pronunciation, and the club learned it forthwith. As it turned out, we were asked to sing it—and Walesa rushed over to us to join in its performance—but, in addition, we were requested to sing my setting of "Lincoln's Gettysburg Address." Among the special guests at the reception was author James Michener, who generously gave each man in the Glee Club an autographed copy of his book *Poland*.

We had applied to various organizations and bureaus and even the Chinese government over a period of several years in the hope of arranging a tour to China. The most promising was in 1989 for a tour in the summer of 1990. Everything seemed to be going along well and plans were developing quite positively. But then the student uprising and massacre happened, and Tiananmen Square erupted into a horrible nightmare. We withdrew immediately from any idea of going there in 1990. Business manager Chris Geczy, with the aid of his Hungarian father, shifted gears and expertly pursued a trip to Hungary instead. So *Basses Loaded!* flew off to Budapest. Well, actually, we flew to Vienna,.

Many years ago I was taken to task by a student who felt that I should perform a work every time precisely as I had rehearsed it. I'm not certain that he was convinced by my defense, but I replied that many factors played into my conducting and interpretation of a work from performance to performance. Acoustics, for example, can change my tempo slightly depending on reverberation. The sickness or wellness, alertness or fatigue of the singers can make a difference; so can reactions of an audience. But even if none of these enters my consideration, neither that student—nor any other—will ever convince me that my inspiration or emotion is not affected when I stand to conduct where Mozart stood in Saint Stephen's Cathedral in Vienna.

We stayed in a hostel on the outskirts of Vienna and commuted to the city. After some performing there, we took a boat down the Danube heading for Budapest. The Danube curved into Czechoslovakia, and we stood in a choral bow on the boat and gave an impromptu forty-minute concert. This was a legitimate—if sneaky—way to add a country to our growing list. Of course, we later clinched its legitimacy by performing all over the newly divided Czech Republic and Slovakia. I suppose it's principally due to Johann Strauss's influence, but there's something instantly romantic about going down the Danube River. Once again our supersensitive sides came to the fore and we treasured every ripple of the "beautiful blue Danube," even though it was quite brown at the time.

We couldn't have asked for a more propitious time to have arrived in Hungary. We docked in Budapest on the very day the first democratically elected president in forty-two years took office. The entire country was in a state of euphoria.

After concerts in Budapest, we went on the road to the hinterlands. At one point, we arrived at a summer camp on the south shore of Lake Balaton. The wooden barracks-like cabins became our homes for the next several days while we went off each evening to a different town to perform. One of the largest lakes in Europe, Lake Balaton is exceeded in size only by a few in Russia and Scandinavia. But the sight that boggles the mind is that—at least where we were—it's so shallow that we actually saw a man begin to walk across it! We had time in the afternoons for refreshing swims and vigorous games. The camp on the shore was filled with delightful children. We became friends almost at once and while we beat them at basketball, they skunked us at soccer. Of course we had our customary stash of Frisbees to hand out and the air was filled with flying plastic. The children, in exchange, wore and gave us T-shirts that said "God Bless Penn" on them.

On our last night at the camp, we returned from a performance of *Basses Loaded!* (which they had translated to mean "drunk fish") in Csopak, arriving at the camp shortly before midnight. The kids and their counselors had dug a pit, lined it with stones, and built a colossal bonfire to welcome us home and to say a final farewell. We all gathered around the fire and sang to the delighted campers. After an hour or so, I quietly spoke to the soccer coach, with whom I had become friends several days earlier.

"It's getting pretty late for the little ones." I said. "Do you think we should end this wonderful party and let everyone go to bed?"

"I think that would be wise," he admitted.

"Let us sing our two national anthems and have that end the program."

When we finished and were beginning to give our goodbye hugs, one little boy started to sing very tentatively. Then a little girl joined him; then others; then all. I asked the coach what it was that they were singing to us.

"That," he said proudly, "is the Transylvanian anthem. None of them has been officially allowed to know of its existence. For forty-two years mothers and fathers have been secretly passing it down. Now we are free. Now we can sing it aloud."

We built up lifelong memories singing Schubert in a Budapest concert hall and a folk song in Vorosmarty Ter, dancing a Broadway show tune in Kaposvár, singing Aaron Copland in the Cultural Center in Siófok. American spirituals in Szekszárd, and Randall Thompson in the tenth-century church in Veszprém.

Our last performance in the south was at Pécs. This was the biggest performance of the tour, and one of the true delights for me was when we sang Clark Gesner's "Home" and the guys spilled out into the audience. The Hungarians didn't pick up the words very readily, but they certainly caught the melody and sang heartily. Clark was very pleased when I related it to him later. For the second time on a foreign tour, we had a drummer back out on us just before leaving, but this time there wasn't a Kenny Williams to call upon. Adam Sherr, our stalwart stage manager for many years and a fine musician in his own right, performed the herculean dual job of playing the drums in the pit while wearing a headset and calling the show.

Back in Budapest, we had more performances but none so touching as one at the Peto Institute for crippled children. The ability to respond was limited;

the display of love was limitless. It was on occasions such as this that I was particularly proud of the manner in which the men of the club handled themselves. They always gave freely.

Our last night was, as usual, our tour dinner. It was in a charming restaurant on the shore of the Danube. I don't quite know why it occurred to me there, but I decided to start a tradition. Without the club members knowing it, I bought a large bottle of champagne at the restaurant and took it with me as we left the dinner. We went to an impressive old Turkish fortress overlooking the river. In a huge round corner turret, we stood in a circle as I explained that I was about to steal a marvelous leaf from the Orpheus Club, the fine male chorus to which I belong in Philadelphia. Marvin Lyon, our president, was standing to my right and, popping the cork of the champagne bottle, I turned to him and sang:

> Here's to you, Marvin Lyon.
> Here's to you my jovial friend.
> And we'll drink before we part for sake of company
> We'll drink before we part.
> Here's to you, Matt Larsen . . .

And so it went, around the circle, the whole club quickly catching on to the melody and singing in unison to each man toasted by name, and each man taking a swig from the bottle of champagne until it came back around to me to end the song. This stolen tradition has continued to this day as the final event at the club's last dinner together. I don't believe the Orpheus Club will fault me for this one. It's a beautiful tradition, and it's fun to spread the good ones.

We partook of one of the most relaxing spas imaginable, complete with truly expert masseurs, compared notes in the Worst Souvenir Contest, and then dressed for an embassy reception. Among the dignitaries present was the mayor of Budapest. Long before we left on this tour, I had asked Wilson Goode, mayor of Philadelphia, if he would give me an appropriate gift to present to the mayor of Budapest. He generously gave me a handsome miniature replica of the Liberty Bell with the plaque below engraved as a greeting from Philadelphia to Budapest.

One important 1990 performance we were proud to have been invited to do was the celebration of Penn's 250th anniversary. We shared the stage in Philadelphia's Convention Hall with Bill Cosby, Dolly Parton, and Kenny Rogers. Our song-and-dance routines, I add immodestly, were a great hit with the capacity audience.

In anticipation of the Commencement exercises in 1990, the university had commissioned me to compose a work for the 250th anniversary. It would be performed outdoors in Franklin Field and required a large chorus. I planned it, therefore, to be for mixed chorus and concert band. Greatly honored, I set about selecting the perfect text. None I could have found was more appropriate than Benjamin Franklin's "Proposals relating to the education of youth in Pennsylvania." I advertised on bulletin boards and publications at Penn for singers who would be interested, and we amassed a fine Commencement Chorus from Glee Club, Penn Singers, faculty, staff, and even a few parents. The United States Second Army Band from Fort Meade, Maryland, was hired to play the accompaniment, and my "Academic Festive Anthem" became a featured part of the ceremony. I conducted the performance. I'm proud to report that it has become an official anthem and has been performed since at numerous commencements as well as the inauguration of Judith Rodin as president—that time, since the ceremony was indoors in Irvine Auditorium, with the massive Curtis organ for its accompaniment. Once again, I conducted, and Christopher McCutcheon played the organ.

The Glee Club's 129th production, *Step Right Up!* (I don't know what we'd do if there weren't an exclamation point in our language), was about "the great carny caper," complete with sideshow characters and slide projections—the latter on a giant rear-projection screen forming the side of an ornate circus wagon. Taking place in a traveling carnival, the show gave me an opening for one of my better puns. David Zlotchew, Mansoor Movagar, Scott Romeika, and Barend Pennings were members of the high-wire-trapeze act I called "The Flyin' Mysoop Brothers." It also gave Zee another opportunity to appear in a Glee Club show stripped to the waist. Actually, if I possessed his physique I think I'd go around all the time without a shirt. I'd wear a bow tie, of course. This 1991 show also was another that I wrote for Jeff Coon—to be the Ringmaster. The show took us pretty much all over the east from Toronto to

Atlanta with many stops in between. This was not a tour but numerous extended weekends.

I think my favorite performance of *Step Right Up!* was our last, on Alumni Weekend. On May 18 we did the show as usual. Then the curtain rose for a "third act." The club was grouped around—and hiding—a grand piano. We began singing "Que Sera, Sera," and then a piano accompaniment snuck in. We gradually stopped singing and I asked a puzzled question.

"How do you know our song?" I asked as the Club parted to reveal two men sitting at the keyboard.

"Because we wrote it!" was their tandem reply.

"Ladies and gentlemen," I announced to the audience with a sweep of my hand to the two at the piano, "Jay Livingston and Ray Evans." We then began "Que Sera, Sera" again and finished it out.

For the next forty minutes we sang "Mona Lisa," "Tammy," "Silver Bells," "Buttons and Bows," "Dear Heart," and a host of other wonderful popular and Academy Award winning songs by our guests. They had sent me practically everything they had written, and I arranged the songs for male chorus and FAXed my arrangements back to them in Hollywood. We were able to do our joint act, therefore, with minimal rehearsal time that afternoon. Jay and Ray were great fun to work with and fast became loyal friends with whom we kept in touch regularly. Tragically, Jay died in 2002, but Ray and I continue our coast-to-coast friendship. Our most recent exchanges have been CDs. I sent him one of a number of my compositions; he sent me one of Michael Feinstein performing his. Not an altogether even trade!

In addition to all the performances of our show each year, of course we did many other gigs of other repertoires. In 1991 these included a return engagement to the Macy's Thanksgiving Day Parade, a new CD of Penn songs called *Hail Pennsylvania*, another concert with the Wellesley College Choir, and numerous others.

The Penn Singers continued their successful way as I directed them in *The Yeomen of the Guard* in 1982, *H.M.S. Pinafore* in '83, *Iolanthe* in '84, *The Pirates of Penzance* in '85, *The Mikado* in '86, *The Gondoliers* in '87, *Patience* in '88, *H.M.S. Pinafore* in '89, *Ruddigore* in '90, and *The Pirates of Penzance* in '91. The year 1992 was another year when the board of the Penn Singers surprised me by asking permission to revive my re-creation of the lost Gilbert & Sullivan opera, *Thespis.* I, naturally, found this an appealing suggestion. It was wonderfully cast and performed in the Zellerbach Theatre; the Singers outdid themselves with this lavish production.

Another time that year, I answered the insistent ring of the telephone.

"Is this Monty?" the pleasant male voice asked.

"Yes, sir."

"How old are you, Monty?"

"I'm sixty-five. How old are you?"

"I'm fifty-five. You'll do."

"Who is this?"

"This is Bill Cosby. I understand you know every song ever written."

Well, that certainly wasn't true, but it's a flattering reputation to have. Bill went on to tell me that he was making a movie for Disney in which he was playing the part of a tutor to a shut-in boy. He remembered that when he was a kid at summer camp they sang a song with a lyric that indicated that, from reading about distant places, "I've been 'most everywhere . . ."

"I want to sing that song in the movie and I don't remember it. Do you?"

"I've never heard of it but I'll do a little sleuthing for you," I replied.

The sleuthing turned out to be more difficult than I had anticipated. The Library of Congress determined that it had never been filed for copyright. No one I called who generally was a well of such information had any knowledge of it. I asked around everywhere and very nearly gave up on it.

Mike Huber heard of my plight at the Faculty Club one day and suggested the name of a person who had been a counselor at Green Lane Camp about forty years ago. Within hours I was taking down the words and music on the telephone and FAXing them to Cosby. Hardly a week passed before I received grateful phone calls from the Disney people and a box of appreciatively inscribed books and CDs from Bill.

Over the years, the Glee Club covered many thousand miles fulfilling its performance schedules, with nearly all our travels in the U.S. by chartered bus. We bused so frequently and so far that I'd go to almost any extreme today to avoid getting on a tour bus again. There were bus rides in the southeast, the midwest, and the far west that had us sitting for as long as seventeen hours. On these excursions, we were required to have another man meet us part way to relieve our original driver. Even some of our shorter jaunts *seemed* like seventeen hours! I could fill an entire chapter with the exploits and shenanigans of our bus travel but will spare you, save for a very few that serve as examples of the variety of our road-runnings.

One vivid memory is of a time when we were traveling in two hired buses along the Kansas Turnpike at about eighty miles per hour. At one point, the bus in which I was riding was in the process of passing our other bus. Always up to the challenge of such an inspiring occasion, several men in my bus took advantage of the situation by "mooning" the men in the other bus. With their bare bottoms hard-pressed against the windows, I'm certain that it created a thoroughly disgusting display for the enjoyment of the other half of the club. A short time later, reciprocity seemed in order and the other bus sped past ours. This time virtually the entire bus was "mooning" us. All went as planned until one man pressed so hard against the glass that the panic window suddenly flew out, hinged only at the top, and a great bare rump hung out speeding precariously over the highway. I believe that was a permanent moonset for the club and ended the questionable practice for good.

One weekend we were returning from performances in New England and were approaching New York City late in the afternoon. As I lazily peered out my window, I saw two planes low in the sky coming toward each other. "They're going to collide!" I yelled to the men on that side of the bus. The words were hardly out of my mouth and all eyes trained in that direction before they did, indeed, intersect in a shattering collision. Pieces of aircraft hurtled to the ground less than a mile from our astonished eyes. We learned in the next day's news that the occupants had been killed along with people in an apartment into which one of the wrecked planes fell.

Once, on the Pennsylvania Turnpike, the entire bus burst into laughter as we passed two roadside signs we believed had nothing to do with each other but whose juxtaposition gave them an entirely new meaning. About twenty feet apart, they read in succession: "Jesus Saves" "S&H Green Stamps."

Many years ago, I had learned a valuable procedure consisting of part yoga/part self-hypnosis. With this technique I was able to put myself to sleep in a total trance in about thirty seconds. It proved indispensable in high school, college, and the Army. It also was great for bus trips. The only downside is that the trance is so total that it is extremely difficult to awaken me. (I even experimented with it once for a dentist, who did root canal work on me without the benefit of Novocain!) On more than one occasion, the highly creative club took full advantage of the fact that I would not wake up and carefully lifted me up and placed me in the overhead luggage rack. It's very strange to wake up with a roof a scant few inches above your face, giving much the same sensation you would experience opening your eyes inside a sealed casket. Once we were at the Wright-Patterson Air Force Base outside Dayton, Ohio. We had given our performance and, while waiting for the service bus to take us to the barracks in which we were to be lodged for the night, I fell asleep in the lounge. Only the next morning did I discover that the Club men had twisted me in and out of the bus, undressed me, made my bunk, and put me to bed for the night. I awoke in a barracks without any memory of getting there.

We were late getting to Providence, Rhode Island on one occasion, and feared that our audience was already in place as we were making our way through the town toward the theater. There would be no time for a vocal warm-up and even less for us to change into the white tie and tails required for the concert. The bystanders on the sidewalks of downtown Providence must have wondered at the apparition that passed them as bare chests, arms and legs protruded from open windows as all of us tried to change clothes hurriedly in severely cramped, mobile quarters.

In the later years, our handsome buses even had the luxury of television sets and VCRs to amuse us on our long journeys. The members, whose tastes varied widely, brought video tapes with them for the long rides. I remember with considerable amusement one trip that presented the remarkable immediate succession from *Rugrats* to *Debbie Does Dallas*.

I never was one to let mere anachronisms deter me from telling a good story in a Penn Glee Club show. In fact, I frequently inserted them for their comic value. I had Julius Caesar wear mod sunglasses and own a microwave. Saint Peter was the MC of *Jeopardy*. I put the *Looney-Tunes* theme into *Robbin' Hoods* as a fanfare. And so on. I also was not about to let an obvious anniversary slip by without taking full advantage of it. The date of our 130th show was 1992. There was no way that I would allow the five-hundredth anniversary of Columbus's historic voyage go unnoticed by us.

Cross Chris, Cross took place on the deck of Columbus's nao *Santa Maria* from August 3 to October 12, 1492. Jeff Coon, of course, was Columbus. The passengers included such out-of-time personages as Sir Francis Drake, J. Cruz, El El Bean, Lance Endez, and El Gapo. With a few lyric changes, I was able to recycle "Bon Voyage" from *Hit High Sea* to introduce Columbus's passengers. Perhaps the biggest departure from former Glee Club shows was the opening of the second act. By 1992, we had become so confident about the club's ability to dance that we opened the act without a single sung syllable. We performed the "Sailors' Dance" from Reinhold Gliere's *The Red Poppy*. The entire show was a tremendous success and ready to be taken across the ocean in the opposite direction from Chris's crossing.

One of the most frequent questions I am asked—particularly now in retrospect—is what was your favorite foreign tour with the Glee Club? That's nearly impossible for me to answer. My favorite tour was usually the one in which I was engaged at the time. Certainly, some tours had higher moments than others: Machu Picchu comes to mind, twice. So does Piskaryovskoye. And Syntagma Square and Saint Stephen's and Pablo Casals and about a dozen more. But among the favorites I would have to include the fabulous trip that business manager Jef Pollock planned for us to the Holy Land in 1992.

After the tour Seth Bloom would write, "As we boarded the El-Al 747 bound for Israel's Ben Gurion Airport in May of 1992, all 36 members of the club had different expectations. This was the land of Abraham, Moses and King David. This was the land of Jesus and his Disciples. This was the land of Muhammed. So much history . . . so little time. Yet, without a doubt, in the two weeks of song, dance and sightseeing that followed, all of our expectations were met and surpassed!"

We arrived in Tel Aviv, Israel on the shores of the Mediterranean. Arik, our tour guide who was with us at all times, was a major in the Israeli army. His idea of the tour was to point out all heroic spots identified in any manner with the Six-Day War of 1967. Ancient Hebrew sites or important Christian locations were there to be tolerated, but tanks and entrenchments of 1967 were of far greater concern and were pointed out in detail with enthusiasm and military pride.

While we were staying in a small hotel in Tiberias on the west bank of the Sea of Galilee, one morning we made an excursion of about twelve miles north to Capernaum. A town of considerable importance to Christians, it had a sign at the entrance to the ancient ruins: "Visitors must wear long sleeves and long trousers." Some of the Glee Club were wearing T-shirts, some were wearing shorts. Only five of us were dressed in appropriate garb. Arik, therefore, dismissed Capernaum. I strongly objected.

"Arik," I protested, "this is a site of great importance to Christians. It was here that Jesus lived for three years, and the ruin of the house of Peter and

Andrew where he stayed is still standing. His ruined synagogue is here. It was here that he performed most of his miracles and called to his disciples, 'I will make you fishers of men.' We are not going to skip this place. You should have known the dress requirements in advance. Please take the bus back to Tiberias and let the rest of the club change clothes."

"But I have jeeps waiting to take you through some interesting battle sites of the '67 war. If we go back to Tiberias we will be late."

"We will be late, then."

Grudgingly, Arik took the club back to Tiberias. The five of us entered the ruined town and were deeply moved by all we saw—as were the others when they returned forty minutes later. On our way to the jeeps we passed hurriedly by the hill believed to be the site of the Sermon on the Mount. While I objected to the perfunctory mention of its importance as we whizzed by, I did not make an issue of it. At least we saw it, and I already had won one battle of wits.

When we reached the ridge where we were met by the jeeps, we were fully attentive to Arik. This was important, too. It simply wasn't the *only* important area of interest in our visit to Israel. There is one student whose name I will not record here. As we walked along a ridge and followed a carefully delineated path edged in barbed wire, one reckless man in the club, as if to test the vivid yellow and red signs warning of the dangerous mine field through which we were gingerly walking, picked up a sizable rock and tossed it twenty feet into the field. Arik was furious. This time I agreed with him.

At one kibbutz on the Lebanese border, we sang to its inhabitants. Because we were performing our show, we put off singing "Hatikvah" and the "Star Spangled Banner" until right after the finale. No script writer could have asked for better timing. As we reached "And the rockets' red glare, the bombs bursting in air," there was a tremendous thud of incoming rocket fire from Lebanon. Our performance was over.

Whatever the political conditions, however, we sang all over the country. One memorable performance was outdoors on the bank of the Sea of Galilee. Another time, in Caesarea, we did not have a scheduled performance, but the ancient Roman theater, built at the time of Herod, beckoned to us too strongly to ignore. So we went to the stage, formed a choral bow, and sang a brief concert to the tourists and townspeople who drifted into the time-worn seats. I think it was here that Arik realized fully that we were not his typical American tour and he softened considerably in his appreciation of us and our wishes.

As a result, he assessed the dangers and braved a trip to Arab-held Bethlehem where we were awed by the Church of the Nativity.

One day we will remember always—at least, I will—was spent in the River Jordan. Yes, I mean *in* the River Jordan. I suspect collusion with Arik, who demanded that he take our valuables, including our passports, for safekeeping as we kayaked down the river. I believe that the club informed him that their deepest mission of the journey was to make absolutely certain that I would be drenched to the skin. We got into our tipsy kayaks and paddled down the river. Then, in an ordered and malevolently conceived phalanx, the entire club descended on their trusting old director. With paddles smashing the surface into tidal-wave-like walls of water directed solely at me, with speeding bows aimed at ramming my little boat, I was as sodden as if I had simply scuttled my craft in mid-river. My second baptism. It must be recorded in the annals of the trip, however, that I fought back like a puissant water serpent, and no man escaped with a dry square inch of clothing. Now I understood the wisdom of leaving passports with the major.

One of the planned drenchings of the tour was the remarkable "swim" in the Dead Sea. I have been in America's Great Salt Lake but that is like Poland Spring water compared to the Dead Sea. It's impossible to swim or sink. It is so dense with salt that the shores are lined with pillars and cliffs of dried salt. You dare not open your mouth or eyes in the water. The novelty of it was fascinating.

A more pleasing swim took place at the beach in Eilat, Israel's southernmost town, right on the Red Sea. (That completed the rhymed seas for this trip: we now had swum in the Med, the Dead, and the Red.) The only disconcerting thing about our Eilat stay was the two rubber-suited, aqua-lunged terrorists from Jordan who came ashore armed with submachine guns and hand grenades, prepared to mow down anyone on the beach. They emerged about a hundred yards west of us and were quickly subdued by some courageous men on the beach, who stifled their advance. The ever efficient Israeli police leapt into action and arrested them immediately.

As with other foreign tours, some members of the club were not willing to try the native cuisine. They missed out on falafel and shwarma. But even more tragic, they didn't try the spectacular Saint Peter fish, which is only found in the Sea of Galilee. While we were relishing exotic delicacies served with hummus and tehina, they were sticking to the unadventurous Pizza Hut and Ben & Jerry's fare that can be found on Walnut Street. At least there wasn't a McDonald's in Israel!

Arik and I had another run-in as we sped by the Mount of Olives and the Garden of Gethsemane. There was a dramatic field of wrecked tanks and burned pillboxes over on the Gaza Strip that had to be seen.

"Fascinating and important to modern Israel," I told him. "But on our next free day, we're going to visit the Garden of Gethsemane. This was where Jesus spent the last night of his life and where he was arrested to be taken to his trial and crucifixion. There is no way we're going to miss that visit, even if we see one fewer tank."

He'd met his match. And it wasn't many days before we were walking through the peaceful garden of twisted, gnarled, ancient olive trees, some of which are old enough to have witnessed the events of Jesus' last night with his disciples, the kiss of Judas, and the arrest at the hand of the Romans. Incredible!

Some of the other sites we savored were the field where David met and slew the giant Goliath; the stables of King Solomon and the phenomenal well and water system at Megiddo; the home of David Ben-Gurion, virtually the father of modern Israel; Abraham's well in Beersheba; the ruins of Jericho; the Church of the Holy Sepulcher; the Via Dolorosa; the Dome of the Rock; donning yarmulkes and praying at the West ("Wailing") Wall; the cave where the Dead Sea Scrolls were found; the haunting sadness of Yad Vashem. All this, and so much more, we visited utterly fascinated. Places about which we had read and studied for our entire lives—no matter what our religion or background—came dramatically to life for us.

One frightfully hot day we assisted in a dig at an ancient tel. We dug deep into the colossal mound and came up with buckets of dirt, which we carefully passed through a large sieve to separate the pottery shards and bones of two thousand years ago. One clubber even came up with an almost perfectly preserved clay oil lamp.

Of extraordinary interest because of its historical significance was our visit to Masada. Few places on earth are more dramatic and possess a more heroic tale than this clifftop fortress. Although it was built by Herod the Great in the first century B.C., its greatest significance lies in its providing refuge to Jewish fighters who retreated here to continue their struggle with the Romans after the destruction of much of Jerusalem in A.D. 70. When the Romans, under Silva, after three years of unsuccessful attempts to scale the manned cliffs, built an immense ramp up which to attack the nearly impregnable fortress, theirs was a hollow victory. Seeing the inevitable end, all the Jews—men, women, and children—committed suicide or killed each other, and Silva's long siege was for naught.

One of the people we met on the top of Masada was the American entertainer Pat Boone. He was in Israel taping a TV program of religious songs. He told me that he was very disappointed not to have known of our presence in Israel or we would have been in his program. Of course his soundtrack was pretaped and he was doing lip-sync on Masada, so he couldn't just "work us in."

There were formal performances in Israel and informal ones as well. We sang in theaters, outdoors, at holy places, at colleges and universities. But the singing most of us will remember beyond the planned locales happened each night on Ben-Yehuda Street in Jerusalem. Like the Stroget in Copenhagen, this is a walking-shopping street closed to vehicles. Everyone in Jerusalem, it seems, shows up sometime each night on Ben-Yehuda Street! So, therefore, did we.

We would arrive at about 11:00 P.M. and take over a street corner. After setting out two hats for contributions to our tour dinner, we would sing for an hour or so. I should add that it's somewhat disconcerting to sing informally and see uniformed Israeli soldiers at the edge of the crowd, each sporting an Uzi submachine gun. ("Look, men. You've *got* to stay on pitch here!") When I arranged Carly Simon's "Let the River Run," I arranged it for chorus and piano. I also made an a cappella version, which became the most popular song on Ben-Yehuda Street. It also became our sign-off song each night.

With all the wonders of Israel—its history, the Bible, the hymns and beliefs of my lifetime—coming into a marvelous new focus, the "Eternal City," Jerusalem, will always be for me a true highlight of a visit to any land. I am certain that I would have arrived there at some point in my life, but I am forever grateful to the Penn Glee Club that I made it to Jerusalem with them in 1992. To the chorus, doors were opened and experiences were possible that seldom are available to the lone, private traveler.

Todah rabah!

It Sure Works on the Popular Level

WHEN SHELDON HACKNEY FINISHED his tenure as president of the University of Pennsylvania in 1993, Claire Fagin was named interim president for 1993–94. I had known Claire for years when she was the head of our School of Nursing. In her new position she and I got along very well except on one extremely contentious subject. She wanted to accomplish some things for which she would be remembered and not just be a lame-duck administrator. Well, I certainly remember one of her actions. She virtually ordered me to turn the Glee Club into a coed chorus.

There already were five coed choruses on our campus—I was the conductor of one of them—as well as half a dozen smaller coed a cappella groups. I saw no logic in terminating a group with a hundred-and-thirty-one year tradition of fine male choral singing simply because it was all male.

The male choral sound is unique and rich and marvelous. So is its glorious repertoire, contributed to by nearly every great composer in history. If we hadn't already had numerous outlets for the choral aspirations of women on our campus, I probably would have acceded to Claire's wishes with regrets but without another thought. But there were a good many such opportunities, and I felt to destroy a unique artistic expression in order to make it sound like every other group was downright ludicrous. Not surprisingly, a sizable and powerful group of alumni supported my stand. A tuba player could wish to play with the Curtis String Quartet, but it would drastically change the sound and repertoire. I fought the edict tooth and nail. The exchange went on for Claire's entire term of office.

She heard, I know, from many quarters. The debate ended when she sent me a postcard—showing a long-skirted tennis player of about 1900 holding a U of P pennant—and the terse message: "You win!—Claire."

Judith Rodin, to her everlasting credit in my mind, informed me at our first meeting that she was fully aware of the situation between Claire and me and that it would not continue in her administration. She not only has been good as her word but has been a wonderful supporter of the club and a delightful friend. I'll always cherish a most remarkable poem that she wrote and delivered at my retirement party years later. She was also the instigator of a wonderful minute adopted by Penn's board of trustees and presented to me in 2000. In addition, she develops the most charming and becoming blush whenever the Glee Club sings its very special anthem to her: "We love our president . . . So-o-o-o-o-o much!" all to the tune of "My Country 'Tis of Thee."

We all thought that Chaucer's *Canterbury Tales* would make a great vehicle for the Penn Glee Club's 1993 production and would open all sorts of character and plot opportunities for the men. David "Guapo" Goldsmith, the new president, came to Maine the last week of June, and together we worked on what I still believe was a good book. It was a series of tales that Chaucer *didn't* get around to telling. At the same time, Stuart Draper and Dan Coelho decided to work independently on a book. The problem was that Stu was spending the entire summer in Jerusalem at the university and was, therefore, pretty much out of contact with the rest of us. Guapo and I came up with a tight and usable book, but we bowed to Stu. This sounds like sour grapes, but I'm sorry that we backed ourselves into this corner quite so readily. The book was long overdue when we began working on the show in September and, while we made progress on the music, it always was without any real knowledge of how it would fit into plot and dialogue. When, at last, we received the completed book, it was considerably more dark and sinister than any we had expected or desired, but timing was against us and we had to proceed. At any rate, *The Canterbury Scales* became our 131st annual production and played successfully on and around campus and in Hershey, Pennsylvania, and Owego, New York. It was a fine experiment to have the show student-written and Stu and Dan learned that it is a fairly gutsy task.

At the campus run in February we added a new feature to the Saturday night performance. Still strapped for cash from our Israel trip, we added an innovative "third act" to our weekend. We had let it be known to our alumni that we were instituting a silent auction and that the man who bid the highest amount would have an opportunity to sing a solo backed by a special choral arrangement by yours truly. It surprised us how many alums jumped at the chance. Miles Cary Leahy, College 1978, sent us a wonderfully generous check and won the right, hands down. He sang "Time Was When Love and I Were Well Acquainted" from Gilbert & Sullivan's *The Sorcerer*, followed by a fully choral-backed solo, "Softly as in a Morning Sunrise," from Sigmund Romberg's *The New Moon*. Cary did himself proud and also helped us take a major step toward balancing our budget. The novelty was greeted warmly by the audience and I can't possibly state why we never tried it again.

In March 1993, one of my all-time finest friends died. William Smith, associate conductor of the great Philadelphia Orchestra, had not only conducted the premiere but actually prompted the writing of my *Herodotus Fragments* in 1970. Bill was one of the most brilliant, interesting, and articulate men I've ever known, and his great friendship and companionship will always occupy an immense, valued place in my life and heart. His widow, Debbie, paid me a tremendous compliment by asking me to be the sole speaker at his memorial service. And then, in a very touching way, she thanked me by presenting me with Bill's five bow ties! Every time he put one of them on, she said, he remarked that he wished that he could tie them as well as I. As one who does not even possess a four-in-hand tie, I chuckle every time I wear one of Bill's.

The next season began with a real home run! The auditions were over. The new men were accepted into the club. We had our customary wine and cheese party with the inspirational welcoming words of Greg Suss, president of the Glee Club Graduate Club, who always came in from New York for the occasion. We had a rehearsal for an hour and left that evening to sing our national anthem at a Phillies-Marlins baseball game at Veterans Stadium. This is called trial-by-fire and instant gratification. It's also referred to as Operation Snowjob, because it gets the freshmen into a public performance two hours after they joined the club. To an automatic standing ovation, yet!

So successful was our performance that we were invited for an encore at the National League playoff game between the Phils and the Atlanta Braves. Unfortunately, the Phillies' performance was not as successful as ours—or, as one wag in the club put it, our "pitching" was better than theirs. Had the Phillies won, it would have opened an exciting door for us. We had already accepted the invitation to perform at the World Series, an opportunity we were not to realize. It would have been fun.

The 132nd annual production was another student-written show. Dan Coelho, one of our two exceptional accompanists, was something of a masochist and, with the experience of one show already under his belt, he felt that he'd like to try again. What's more, it was the first Glee Club show that I didn't direct. Along with a few others, I staged and choreographed some of the musical numbers, but sophomore Todd Shotz directed all the dialogue scenes. He did a superb job and prepared himself for considerable directing of future campus shows and a sterling career in professional theater. In 2003 he went on tour as company manager with the national company of *Kiss Me Kate*, and now works for Bruce Willis's production company.

With another fifty-foot painting (of the Chicago El) as its backdrop, *Coda Nostra* turned out to be a bit more fun than the previous year's show. Though the Mafia theme was almost as dark as the last show's, it was treated with such bravado and lightness that it sped along joyously to the delight of audiences and performers. Todd as a feisty five-foot-five, hundred-and-thirty-pound boxer took on Peter Bine at six-foot-five, two-thirty! The very names of characters were funny: Paddy O'Furniture was an Irish cop; "La Familia" included such as Guido Testosteroni, Arturo "Art" Deco, Caesar Spalace, Velveeto Fromaggio, Viola Da Gamba, and Crusti Pannetoni.

The big tour for the spring of 1994 was announced for Ireland. Preparations were going along fine, we were told, and we had even learned the Irish national anthem (by far the most difficult, by the way, of any we had done), when the rug was pulled out from under us. It was about the only time in my long career that a student who had accepted a responsibility of major significance in any group totally dropped the ball and never let us know that it simply wasn't going to happen. In weekly business meetings and face-to-face conversations we had been assured that all was well and that bookings were proceeding according to schedule. Funds were even coming in from our loyal and helpful alumni. It was almost by accident that we discovered that all this was a lie, that nothing whatever had been done until it was too late to salvage the season.

Thanks to a tremendous effort (and a large telephone bill) by Brian Turnbaugh and Seth Bloom and the marvelous cooperation of officials in numerous offices, the bitter disappointment was tempered by an unbelievably hastily conceived tour to Florida that saved the day for the morale of the club.

We spent four days of fun and performing in Disney World. Whether it was the EPCOT Center, the Magic Kingdom, MGM, or Universal Studios, the club took the Florida resort by storm. Our major performances were at the theater in EPCOT's American Pavilion and on the New York Library set at Universal Studios, each to enthusiastic crowds.

Scott Romeika came up with "a tale of Tut Uncommon" for the 1995 show. His story was written into an actual libretto by Dan Coelho and me. And *Sing Tut* was jolly good fun. With Seth Bloom as Howard Carter and Erik Nordgren as Lord Carnarvon, we followed Monterey Jack, as played by Brian Turnbaugh (with more than a tip of the pith helmet to Indiana Jones), and Amol Dixit as his baseball-loving sidekick Mel, leading a 1922 trek through Egypt to find the tomb of King Tutankhamen.

Perhaps the most important development of 1995, however, was the official debut of Erik Nordgren as student conductor of the Glee Club—and we all know what *that* would mean to him a few years down the line! Erik was a graduate of Case Western Reserve in Cleveland and came to Penn for graduate study. Before he left Ohio, my friend Quentin Quereau, chairman of the music department at Case, told Erik to "look up Montgomery" at Penn. Not only did he look me up, he auditioned for the Glee Club. While he was taking graduate work at Penn, he also was working in our chemistry department. Therefore, his tenure in the club was considerably longer than that of the typical graduate student and we benefited greatly from it.

In 1992, Sharon Hudson was ceremoniously made the first female full member of the Penn Glee Club. Affectionately known as "Norm," she richly deserved making history with us. She was a fine clarinet player in our pit band and an all-round good sport and companion. Now in 1995 she was joined by some other history makers. The first woman to hold a position on a Glee Club board was Dawn Lanzalotti, who, in addition to being one of our best choreographers, was elected to the position of treasurer. And Annie Kaminski, our other superb pianist, was the first female to be awarded the coveted Penn Glee Club rosette, our highest student honor.

May and June 1995 found the Glee Club on a fascinating tour of the Czech and Slovak Republics—with Vienna thrown in for good measure at the end. I have always considered Vienna the most musical city in the world. Now I am forced to amend that evaluation to include, right along beside it, Prague. There must have been more than a dozen major concerts going on throughout the city every day. We attended as many as we could fit in. But we were also part of the roster. Wherever we sang, appreciative crowds clamored for more. Among our Prague performances, we sang a joint concert with a Czech youth choir in the ancient Saint Stephen's Church. In Bratislava, we sang in Klarisky Concert Hall and for a mass in Saint Martin's Cathedral, at the spot where Beethoven conducted the premiere of his *Missa Solemnis*. In Brno, we shared a concert with one of the world's great choruses.

After this performance, the marvelous chorus gave us a superb midnight supper, and they and we sang throughout. At one point, they wished to honor us by singing an American spiritual. They sang William L. Dawson's wonderful arrangement of "Soon Ah Will Be Done." I would have given almost anything to pick up the phone and call Bill. He would have chuckled, much amused by the way they rolled r's in the extreme: "Soon-ah will be done-a wid de tr-r-r-r-roubles uf de vorlt, tr-r-r-r-roubles uf de vorlt, tr-r-r-r-roubles uf de vorlt!" Unfortunately, Bill had died just a few months earlier.

In Uherské Brod, we charmed nearly a thousand school children at the Palace of Culture. We sang for children and everyone else at the drop of a hat. We sang beneath the fabulous clock overlooking the Old Town Square in Prague. We sang to the people gathered in Wenceslas Square around the statue of Good King Wenceslas. We sang on a boat as we cruised the Moldau River and thought of Smetana all through the journey. We sang on the Karluv Most, the famous Charles Bridge.

A very ancient structure, the Charles Bridge is closed to vehicles and is where all of Prague and all tourists walk and gather. As we were singing on the bridge to a large and happy crowd, a policeman shoved a paper in front of my eyes while I was conducting and spoke heatedly and rapidly. The paper was in several languages—including English—and there was no mistaking its message. One had to obtain a permit to perform on the bridge. Feigning total ignorance of what it was all about, I kept right on conducting, to the delight of the listening crowd. They were so vocal in their disapproval of what was being forced on us that they cheered loudly when I continued and even went immediately into another song in Czech. With his tail between his legs, the offending policeman finally slipped away and didn't bother us again. Perhaps this sort of action is not highly recommended on the official level, but it sure works on the popular level.

We had a free evening in Brno and went to the marvelous opera house to attend a superb performance of Wagner's *Tannhäuser*. Magnificently sung, this was grand opera at its best. And best of all, the finest seats in the house, when translated into American money, came to about ninety-eight cents! The club was jealous of the fine rendition of the great "Pilgrims' Chorus" which we had sung so often.

In Vienna, we sang again in Saint Stephen's Cathedral. As a few years earlier, it was a tremendously emotional experience to sing where Mozart had conducted, where he was married, and where his funeral took place. Naturally, we also sang outside the church in Stephensplatz with our customary hats in place and garnered enough contributions to underwrite our tour dinner. After dinner, we continued the tradition started in Budapest of singing to each man (and woman) as the bottle of champagne was passed around.

Brian Turnbaugh later wrote a fine assessment of the trip. "Wherever we sang (and danced) the club and the crowds had a wonderful time. . . . Whether it was the thrill of performing in numerous historic sites or just seeing places like the Schönbrunn Palace in Vienna, this tour provided every clubber with memories to last a lifetime. The Club also experienced a mysterious daily growth in the number of vegetarians, perhaps related to the generosity of our hosts with their fine local pork products." To which another sage added, "And everywhere, the beer was fine . . . and we were legal!" And one doesn't leave Vienna without sampling a Sacher Torte.

Amol Dixit, Annie Kaminski, and Brian Turnbaugh authored the 1996 show, our 134th, and *Killing Time* had one of the most off-the-wall, convoluted plots we ever put on the boards. Staged by Brian Turnbaugh and Eric Schinfeld, it ostensibly took place in my Maine summer home, Connemara, and Mike Manolas even played a mythical host of the house named Monty. (His vocabulary, speech patterns and other idiosyncrasies were close enough to home to make a certain aging director very self-conscious.) But the very complications—which involved such bizarre items as double identities, a gay movie director, cowboys, a caped superhero, a crazed one-armed fisherman, the Royal Canadian Mounted Police, a bowling team, and assorted ultra-vain actors—were hilarious. The solving of murders by any of your favorite sleuths was never like this.

Saturday, April 27, 1996, was a day I will never forget. Unlike the surprise party thrown for me in 1981, I knew there was going to be a celebration of my fortieth year as director of the University of Pennsylvania Glee Club. What I didn't know was what form it would take or who would be there. It took place in the Zellerbach Theatre, and I was told to wait upstairs in my office until someone came for me.

The celebration began with some of the songs I had composed for the club over the years, arranged into a medley by Dan Coelho. Greg Suss conducted. Then it was discovered that no one had remembered to get the guest of honor! My sister Liz Thomas rushed up to my office, hurried me down as Greg was explaining the oversight to the audience, and the whole thing began again. From then on, it was one performance and testimonial after another. Small groups from over the years performed; Rich Gusick did a devastating impersonation of me in a fast-food joint ponderously ordering a cheeseburger; Marc Platt came in from Universal Studios in California and was very touching in his tribute; Fran Walker, who professes to hate speaking in public, was marvelously comic in telling what it was like to be my boss; Brendan O'Brien knocked my socks off with "Empty Chairs at Empty Tables" and Nick Hunchak's "Anthem," and Jeff Coon's "Music of the Night" did the same; and David Vaughn, Don Leroy Morales, Brian Kardon, Carlo Nalin, George Pologeorgis, Jerry Berkowitz, Jim Baumgartner, Rick Cummings, and Jonas Wagner performed as brilliantly as they had when students. Nick Constan, who should have been a stand-up comic instead of a lawyer and professor, was hilarious at my expense; Liz spoke humorously and eloquently for the family; Doris Cochran-Fikes and Bob Blake were clever as ever with their musical tribute; Steve Goff, managing director of the Annenberg Center, was thoughtful and humorous as always; chaplain Stanley Johnson was his customary eloquent self. Stanley Chodorow, then provost of the University, spoke for the president and trustees and presented me with a handsome Steuben bowl engraved with the University seal and my hands logo; the Three Pennce and a Yen were typically professional; Jack Reardon, on behalf of the alumni, read a beautiful citation; and there were so many more that I simply don't recall at this writing. I was in shock, you know. The huge rear-projection screen up center was suddenly filled with a 1948 photograph of the PitchPipers, my old college quartet, smiling self-consciously from a sleek convertible, and, simultaneously, onto the stage walked LaRue Olson, our wondrous first tenor, in from Kansas for the occasion. He recounted our college experiences together as well as a happy reunion we had in Korea—both of us members of the 45th Infantry Division.

Edward Rendell—mayor of Philadelphia—walked onto the stage and charmingly told of the personal and official events we had shared. Ever gracious, always charming and good humored, Ed went on far beyond what was required and delighted everyone. He then read a much too laudatory but deeply appreciated citation from the city of Philadelphia. This was followed by the reading of a personal letter from Bill Clinton, president of the United States. The very last presentation was the most touching. The club had written to all known Glee Club graduates asking for letters. These had been transcribed and printed in a handsome hardback book, *Reminiscences—A History of Bruce Montgomery as Director of the University of Pennsylvania Glee Club.* I have a great many wonderful books in my library but none more cherished than this.

After all the presentations, I was asked to conduct the 1996 Glee Club. We went backward in time in repertoire. With each successive number, more and more alumni came down the aisles and joined the club. By the time we had reached songs we first performed in the 1950s, there were three hundred men onstage. I was told in advance how this would work and that the chorus would be larger with each song. I was *not* told in advance what songs had been chosen to highlight, and I must admit to considerable pride—and astonishment— that I was able to conduct each in turn entirely from memory.

I believe the happiest aspect of the entire evening was that they had chosen to honor my *fortieth* anniversary. My mother was still alive and beamed throughout the evening—even dancing and socializing until 4:00 A.M. at the party in the lobby! Even at ninety-six she was a perfectly beautiful lady, and it was wonderful to see her holding court with so many former students who constantly surrounded her with happy reminiscences of savored times in her presence and in her gracious home. It was a very special night for her, and I am grateful that she was there to enjoy it so.

The year 1996 also was my twenty-fifth anniversary of directing the Penn Singers and, once again, they elected to honor the occasion by presenting *Spindrift.* I was particularly happy with the choice because of my mother's delight in the work and the opportunity for her to see it once more. The demanding character of Patch was powerfully made his own by Dan Gorelick-Feldman, whose handsomeness, height, and intensity brought real stature to the part.

The year was a difficult one for me personally as I was uncharacteristically sick at a time that I absolutely had to be well. I had a painful prostate problem that forced me to miss my first tour in all my years with the Glee Club. The club took a five-day tour to Georgia, and I had to remain home. Angry as hell, I nevertheless felt genuine consolation in the fact that Erik Nordgren was my spectacular student conductor. Every night I received a phone call from one member or another to tell me how well everything was going and to reinforce my belief and trust in Erik.

During the production of *Spindrift*, I was so ill that—gross though it may sound in the telling—I conducted in the pit of the Zellerbach Theatre with a tall waste can beside me in full view of the twenty-six piece orchestra. Fortunately, all concerned were spared any gross indignities. The production went beautifully and I was grateful to all the students involved who made it come off so well. I've seldom known a greater team effort.

In accepting the Thanksgiving Day invitation from Macy's so frequently, we had sung and danced on Broadway a number of times. We had never performed on a Broadway stage, however, until 1996. Greg Suss, our stalwart in New York, contacted Glee Club grad David Vaughn, who was the house manager of the Minskoff Theatre when Betty Buckley was starring in Andrew Lloyd Webber's *Sunset Boulevard*. With financial assistance from the GCGC's Montgomery Fund, together they arranged for the entire Glee Club to obtain tickets to the show and have a special party onstage afterward with the cast. We gathered on the extraordinary living room set and, as soon as they were out of costume and makeup, the cast joined us there. Miss Buckley was a gracious hostess, and we pretty well blew them all away when we sang a number of toasts and songs to them and ended with my full choral arrangement of "As If We Never Said Goodbye" from their own show.

Also about this time, I was hired by the Women's Committee of the Philadelphia Orchestra to lecture on Benjamin Britten's *War Requiem*. For my lecture I wished to have several points illustrated, so I engaged a talented friend to sing a few of the soprano solo passages. Jody Karin Applebaum was not only an accomplished singer but a fine voice teacher and vocal coach as well. I had been sending voice students to her for some time. When we discussed the sections I wished her to sing at my lecture, she volunteered that her husband Marc would be home between concert tours at the time and she would be happy to have him accompany at the piano the passages she was to sing. He also would play any other segments I wished.

I was ignorant of the fact that "Marc"—the husband of whom we were speaking—was Marc-André Hamelin, one of the world's great piano virtuosos! Of course I met him on the day of my lecture and shook his hand. As yet, I could hardly call him a friend. That didn't happen until after Jody's students were working with her on their roles in *Spindrift*. In the first act of my show, the Priest sings an idealistic song about Patch, "I See a Boy." In the second act, Patch sings a bitter diatribe, "Where?" Cathleen reminds him of the Priest's hopes for him and, with Patch and Cathleen on opposite sides of the stage stating their estranged feelings, the two very different songs go together in ironic and unexpected counterpoint. Marc had been home when Jody was working on the two songs with their protagonists. Marc rushed into my office on campus one day with arms outstretched.

"I want to embrace a true master of counterpoint!" he said, grasping me in a bear hug. With that began a friendship that I value as highly as any I have ever had. "I heard both songs being rehearsed," he continued. "I never connected them harmonically. I swear I didn't see it coming! Congratulations!"

Ever since the days when we began each new season at the Inn at Buck Hill Falls, it had been a hope to have a "retreat" early in the season that included both the old and the new men. We finally put it into effect, and by September 1996, it was an established "tradition." Ever since, the Club has spent a long weekend at Camp Onas near Doylestown, Pennsylvania, where extraordinary bonding takes place in rehearsing, eating, softball and other games, absurd "confessional" games indoors at night, sitting around a huge campfire with marshmallows on sticks, and generally getting to know each other. It has been a valuable addition to the annual agenda.

Lost on the high seas, a magnificent cruise liner runs aground on an unknown island that has mysteriously risen from far beneath the ocean. Thus the Glee Club found the mythical Atlantis! Sound like a show plot? Well, it was exactly that as we launched our 135th annual production, *Treble in Paradise*. The 1997 show was the brainchild of Brett Lovins and Matt Seneca and was every bit as strange as their weird minds could make it, with the music ranging from Bach to Broadway and almost everything in between. I've put together eclectic scores before but with this one I outstripped them all! The entire travesty was directed by Eric Schinfeld. Over the years, we have often had our private little jokes when we have come up with names for characters, but none has been more off-the-wall than the names of three of the Greek natives of Atlantis: Play-do, Soccer-tees, and Eddy-pus.

It seems as if this volume is devoted almost exclusively to our Penn Glee Club tours and shows. This has simply been a convenient device to keep the narrative in a semblance of chronological order. Of course we had a full schedule of other events each year as well. For the university, we always sang at opening exercises, Baccalaureate chapel, untold numbers of banquets and fundraisers, frequently at Commencement, the inaugurations of two of Penn's presidents, and special convocations for visiting dignitaries from the Shah of Iran, President Lech Walesa, Princess Grace, and Lord Louis Mountbatten to Jimmy Carter, Gerald Ford, Ronald Reagan, and Bill Clinton. We sang our own concerts both on- and off-campus throughout every year. We performed countless television shows, both local and national. During my tenure, we did the Macy's Thanksgiving Day parade at least five times on NBC and the CBS parade in Philadelphia three times. We were hired for many corporate and industrial affairs as special entertainment at dinners and conventions. We were frequently hired for Christmas caroling. We were the entertainment at Mickey Mouse's official fiftieth birthday party. We sang services and concerts in churches, synagogues, and the National Cathedral. We taped radio commercials for Canada Dry and followed that with thirteen weeks on TV for them.

And, of course, we sang with superb women's choruses all over the country. Generally, on these occasions, we would sing one-third of a program and the women one-third, and then we would join ranks to perform a major work. Among the many, many works we performed this way were Franz Schubert's *Mass in G*, Johannes Brahms's *Liebeslieder Waltzes*, Ralph Vaughn Williams's *Five Mystical Songs*, J. S. Bach's *Magnificat*, Randall Thompson's *Frostiana*, Antonio Vivaldi's *Gloria*, Marc-Antoine Charpentier's *Magnificat in G*, Randall Thompson's *Ode to the Virginian Voyage*, Paul Hindemith's *Apparebit Repentina Dies*, Charles Ives's *They Are There!*, Gabriel Fauré's *Requiem*, and Carl Orff's *Carmina Burana*. We performed these with women's choirs of Wellesley, Vassar, Goucher, Pembroke, Smith, Hunter, Simmons, Connecticut, Mount Holyoke, Bennington, Bryn Mawr, Wheaton, and many others. We sang a number of times with the Orpheus Club of Philadelphia in the Academy of Music and with its counterpart the University Glee Club of New York in Avery Fisher Hall in Lincoln Center.

May 20, 1997, was the darkest day of my life. At 6:00 A.M. I went to my adored mother's apartment to say goodbye, knowing that it would be for the last time. I was about to leave with the Glee Club on a spectacular tour of Spain and Morocco. Two weeks earlier, Mother had celebrated her ninety-seventh birthday, and all of us—her children, grandchildren, and great-grandchildren—came in to spend quality time with her, to exchange happy reminiscences, and to say goodbye. Diagnosed with cancer, she had recently stopped riding her bicycle and doing her daily crossword puzzle. She was very alert and very beautiful as she raised her arm to me when I kissed her goodbye after a magical hour with her.

"Goodbye, darling," she said through her still radiant smile. "I love you so much. Have a safe and wonderful trip. And please, *please* don't grieve for me."

She went into a coma three hours later, surrounded by the rest of her family. Her final words to them were a characteristic misquote of Emerson.

"Farewell, proud world, I'm going home," she said with a magnificent smile. "Goodbye. I love you all very, very much."

I am absolutely convinced that she orchestrated her death. She was determined to see me off on my tour, and she refused to die on her great-granddaughter Krissy's fourteenth birthday. And her remarkable heart held on until 6:55 the next morning.

The Glee Club arrived in Barcelona, Spain. That evening's promenade on Las Ramblas was to continue the long-standing club tradition of singing on the streets for the benefit of the traditional tour dinner. I was on my way with the guys with this intent when I stopped in my tracks.

"Gentlemen," I said without explanation, "I'm sorry. I have to return to the hotel. Erik, please take over."

Except for Fair Lawn, New Jersey, in 1960, following an appendectomy, and the 1996 Georgia tour when I was too ill to travel, I had never done anything like that. I even performed the night my father died in 1955. But, somehow, this was very different. At the desk at our hotel I was handed a FAX from Connie and Liz. My wonderful mother had died that morning. Anyone who feels that it was unnatural for a seventy-year-old man to be so affected certainly didn't know my mother. She was the most supportive, most loyal, most sensitive, most gracious, and most wonderful person I have ever known. Hers was the most unconditional love I ever expect to witness. Whatever good I may possess as a man is the direct result of her example. I miss her dreadfully.

But the tour went on—and I with it. The next morning was spent seeing much of the city, including the famed Sagrada Familia cathedral by Antoni Gaudi. Although I had seen it on earlier trips to Spain, this was my first opportunity to go all through the fantastic church, climb its spires, and see close up the intricate details of its aberrant architecture.

Barcelona was a perfect way to begin a tour. Only two major performances had been planned, but we more than made up for the lack of formal bookings: we sang wherever we saw people gathered.

On our second afternoon, we had our first major concert, outdoors in a gazebo in the Parque del Retiro. The large crowd sat on folding chairs set up for the occasion. I even got to use my 1969 "Buenas tardes, damas y caballeros . . ." speech again. I've never written a speech from which I've derived more mileage!

Our night's performance was scheduled for a fine theater at one of the large universities. We spent our customary one hour setting up and with a vocal and physical warm-up. Our programs—we always took special programs with us on foreign tours—were in neat piles at the doors for the ushers. *Not one single person showed up!* This is something that never had happened before in all my years with the Glee Club. If only one or two people had shown up, we would have performed. As it was, our greatly embarrassed "promoters," who apparently had never publicized our engagement, took us all to a local establishment where they plied us with beer and tapas for hours. It was a thoughtful if minor consolation.

A couple of days later, we flew to Spain's interesting capital city, Madrid. Our first day was spent enjoying the sights. One of the first destinations was a return to the great Prado Museum, which I had loved so often before. Once again, Velásquez, Goya, El Greco, and so many others beckoned to me enticingly. This time I was able to share my admiration of these glorious masters with groups of delighted students for whom it was a brand-new introduction.

Without a planned performance that first night, we went to downtown Madrid's popular walking street and sang for a large and appreciative crowd. During our impromptu performance—with the ubiquitous hats placed for pesetas, naturally—we were singing "Du, Du, Liegst Mir im Herzen," a German song popular throughout the world, when a very inebriated spectator came up behind me and began aping my conducting. To the delight of all of us, the Glee Club wisely followed *him*. The crowd loved it. They also couldn't help but admire the choristers' ability to follow his wild and frequently unintelligible gyrations. Damn, they're well trained!

During the daytime, between museums and other tourist attractions, we also sang on the streets, particularly the broad avenues of the Puerta del Sol, and felt much like pied pipers as we gathered followers from one site to another. While most of the club made no special effort to learn the language other than the most basic phrases, one phrase they all learned rapidly was "Mas sangría, por favor."

From Madrid we made a one-day excursion to wonderful Toledo. A dramatic, fascinating cobblestoned town built on the top of a hill crowned by the majestic Alcázar, this is an ancient jewel. Unfortunately, it rained the entire day, but we still got to see and enjoy much of the city. We walked the quaint old twisting streets—some so narrow that you can reach out your arms and touch the houses on both sides—and visited, among other places, the exciting Casa El Greco. The artist's home and studio contains twelve marvelous paintings, one each of the twelve apostles. Unlike in the museums, you are right there with them, one even still on the easel, and feel as if El Greco has just stepped out for a minute and will return shortly.

As we boarded our plane for Spain, Connie had given me a farewell card that I was not to open until airborne. When I opened it over the Atlantic, I found a delightful note and a fifty-dollar bill. The note instructed me to spend the money "on a really fine meal in Spain." Well, there was no way that I was going to blow Connie's generous gift on a one-shot deal like a dinner. Everyone in the Glee Club was fascinated and enamored of the magnificent Toledo steel swords and daggers. I took them to a fine store where I had purchased some things on other trips to Toledo. I selected a wonderful sword that came to exactly fifty dollars. This would be Connie's gift to me. When I went to purchase it, the clerk called the owner over.

"You have brought many customers to me today," he said. "You will not go home with that sword. Come."

He insisted that I put back the sword I had selected and walked me to another area of truly magnificent swords costing a hundred dollars and more. In Spain, that's steep.

"Please. You will select one you want," he instructed.

"But this is a special gift of my sister," I protested and waved the fifty-dollar bill.

"Please select one you want from here," he insisted as he took the bill.

I selected a glorious sword—which, incidentally, I since have used dramatically in two productions of Gilbert & Sullivan's *Princess Ida*—and he wouldn't hear of my making up the difference. I thanked him in my most florid basic Spanish before he could change his mind.

Our concert that night was in a huge church. After a full day of steady downpour, the rain receded into a gorgeous sunset. The break in the weather brought out a large and enthusiastic crowd to our performance. Although it was held in a church, it was indeed a concert and not a religious service. The attendees were ecstatic that we were dancing in their sanctuary. I'm willing to wager that this had not happened before.

Our next stop was beautiful Seville. This was perhaps the most typically Spanish city of our tour, and it captivated the club. The wonderful little old Moorish tower Torre del Oro, the Plaza España, the Plaza de Toros, the old cigarette factory (now part of the university), supposedly where Carmen worked in Bizet's opera, the magnificent cathedral—the largest Gothic edifice in the world, built to butt up against a huge old Moorish minaret, an interesting juxtaposing of Moorish and Gothic—all these held us entranced.

That night, we were the special guests at El Patio Andaluz, where we witnessed the most astounding flamenco dancing I have ever seen. Their last show was over and the public had departed. We were told to come to the very front, and a spectacular show was performed just for us! It was a company of twenty-three dancers, guitarists, and musicians. The costumes were riots of color, the women mostly beautiful and lithe, and the men unbelievable in their tremendous power, variety, skill, and grace. And I hardly think it necessary to inform you that we sang with great enthusiasm for them after the performance.

The next day saw us aboard our ship crossing to Tangier, Morocco, and adding Africa to our list of continents. The three-hour ride was a pleasant bridge between two highly contrasting cultures. We had no scheduled performances in Morocco, but you can be certain that we gave a few unscheduled ones. The Moroccan desert stretches almost to the Mediterranean, and some of us even endured the rolling lope of the camels. The markets of Tangier were right out of all the bizarre bazaars you've ever seen in Hollywood movies: noisy confusion, pungent odors, brazen bargaining, stifling heat, fluttering banners, wretched animals, overpowering filth—all these hit you immediately with none of the subtlety of arriving in a European country for the first time. Erick Wollschlager summed it up very compactly for us. It was "a sinister mix between the twilight zone and a K-Mart blue light special!" The high-pressured Arabs tried to sell us "priceless Oriental carpets." We bought a few aromatic herbs instead.

When we returned to Spain, we spent a glorious day at Gibraltar. You see this massive Pillar of Hercules all the time in pictures and insurance logos, but they don't prepare you for the real thing. We climbed all over the massive rock and posed with the ever-present monkeys. To our great surprise, we found a gigantic cave in the center of the rock. The acoustics, as in most caves, were spectacular and, since they had built a concert hall there, complete with stage and seats, we couldn't let that venue go untried. I spoke with the head guard, had the canned music turned off, and on we went with yet another impromptu concert—to the delight of hundreds of tourists. "It is in moments like these," wrote Erick, "that you remember why you love this institution so much." On the busy shopping street on our way back to the bus, we stopped once more and "sang for our supper" for the crowd that quickly gathered whenever we did this.

Our final destination of the tour was the town of Málaga on the southern coast. Here we celebrated our tour dinner, for which we had been soliciting funds from passersby since the moment we arrived in Barcelona. As always, our final night was filled with fine food, many emotional toasts, tears, the traditional circle passing of the champagne bottle with song, and an inordinate amount of Sangria. It ended (I have it on unimpeachable authority) with a delightful midnight coed skinny-dip in the Mediterranean.

An early summer tour of this sort is always great fun, but it invariably ends sadly, as it is the last time that that particular group of friends ever will be together.

When we returned from Spain and Morocco, I had two days to do laundry, tie up a few loose strings pertinent to my mother's death, and assist in arranging for the emptying of her apartment. Then I was flying to the far west Pacific: to Guam. It seemed strange to be on such a flight without at least a few dozen companions. It seemed stranger still not to be something of a celebrity who could conjure up a choral song with the peep of a pitch pipe and the flick of a downbeat. However, this time I was alone, asked to deliver the keynote address for a newly established award in Guam.

Patrick Wolff had created an award some years earlier to be given each year to a high school senior who excelled in athletics and maintained a high academic average. It had become a much coveted and highly regarded award in Agana. Building on its success and acceptance, Pat next conceived of an award to be given annually to a high school senior who excelled in the arts. I'm sure that there were any number of people he could have contacted to inaugurate this award, but, as they say, timing is everything, and the *Wall Street Journal* had just published a front-page profile of me. So he had an "easy sell" to get everyone involved in the First Annual Performing Arts Scholar Award to approve my selection. The Hilton gave me free lodging and meals while I was on the island, Avis put a car at my disposal, Continental Airlines gave me free round-trip passage, and I'm sure there were other favors of which I wasn't aware.

My plane was delayed in Hawaii so long that I didn't have time even to change my shirt when I arrived in Guam. The banquet at which I was the featured speaker had already started when my plane set down in Agana. As we taxied to the terminal, there was an announcement on the plane's PA system for me to come to the front of the cabin at once. The instant the door was opened, I was whisked into the terminal, whizzed by passport control without stopping, relieved of my baggage claim tickets and told that all would be delivered to my hotel room, shoved into a limousine, and sped to the dinner. When I was led to the podium, I was my bow-tied but grimy self, exactly as I had traveled from Philadelphia almost a day earlier. Never underestimate the powers of the governor when red tape must be cut! All this was accomplished in the governor's name by his director of communications, Ginger Crunden Cruz, who had been one of my Penn Singers a few years before (as well as Miss Guam in the Miss America pageant).

For the next several days, I was shown every nook and cranny of this beautiful island and was fed marvelously by Pat and Vivian Wolff—parents of clubber Ken—at their wonderful home, dramatically poised on a hill that sweeps down to the ocean. From their porch I saw as breathtaking a sunset as I have ever seen. And I was honored everywhere. The Twenty-Fourth Guam Legislature presented me with a handsome resolution of "its commendation and gratitude . . . on behalf of the people of Guam." On June 6, I met with the governor, who officially named me "Honorary Ambassador-at-Large" for Guam and gave me an imposing certificate so stating. It seems almost indecent and dishonest to come to a place to honor others and receive such honors in return. However, the framed citations look so great on my wall so I shan't make too big a fuss about it.

On September 13, we held a "Celebration of the Life" of my wonderful mother at the Memorial Church of the Good Shepherd in Germantown—and the Episcopal church may never be the same again! It was filled with music and tears and laughter throughout the service. Three generations of Mother's family held forth with touching reminiscences. The church choir sang. The Penn Singers sang. The Glee Club sang. All were groups of which my mother was extremely fond. There was beautiful music of all sorts. Vic Zicardi was exceptional with his "Amazing Grace" solo with the Glee Club. "The Blessing of the Fleet" (Domine Jesu Christe) from *Spindrift* was movingly performed by the Penn Singers. "Panis Angelicus," one of my mother's favorites, was gloriously performed by the church choir and Matt Zarcufsky. Even the beautiful "Madrigal" from Gilbert & Sullivan's *Ruddigore* was part of the service. The hymns were Mother's favorites. Ernest Wells outdid himself at the organ. But the real kicker came at the end of the service. Perhaps the last exchange Mother had with her rector, Maurice Coombs, was to plan her service.

"May I have the University of Pennsylvania Glee Club sing at my memorial?" she asked, *almost* innocently.

"Whatever Connie Montgomery wants, Connie Montgomery gets!" he answered, with no notion of how devious she might be.

"May they sing 'Walk Him Up the Stairs'?"

"Whatever Connie Montgomery wants, Connie Montgomery gets!"

That September afternoon, following all the remarkable beauty of the service for my mother to a "packed house," the Glee Club performed "Walk Him Up the Stairs" from the Broadway show *Purlie*. And by "performed" I mean they came down the aisle in choir robes, led by graduate David Vaughn, while our full pit band played. I'm certain that our church had never before reverberated to piano, bass, drums, clarinet, trumpets, trombone, sax, and flute. And I am equally certain that Broadway dancing had never before had filled the transept. And only rarely has anyone applauded in our church. But all this transpired on September 13, 1997. Wow! What a send-off!

The Glee Club's 1998 production was a "quasi-revival." Our 1989 show *Is This for Reel?* told of the making of two movie musicals, with the second act depicting a group of bad actors making a musical version of Shakespeare's *Julius Caesar*. Immodestly I admit that it was the funniest show I ever wrote, and I thought it was too good a premise to have been given only a one-act shot nine years earlier. Our 1998 show was indeed a remake of that Act II epic. But *GO Forum!* was much more than its model: it was a full two-hour production with virtually all the '89 material intact plus lots, lots more fun and more wonderful music added. Besides, it gave Adam Sherr a chance to recreate his stellar performance as Gopher, and I appeared once again in my cameo of Cecil B. DeMillions. In addition, it boasted the phenomenal talent of one of the most versatile accompanists we ever had: Ron Isaacson. Now I ask you, who could fault an extravaganza like that?

GO Forum! (or *Roman in the Gloamin'*) was indicated on our posters and the program cover as our "CXXXVI Annval Prodvction"—the first time we had resorted to a gimmick like that. My cousin, Robert Montgomery Scott, who was then president of the Philadelphia Art Museum—the colossal neo-Roman edifice at the head of the Benjamin Franklin Parkway—gave us permission to appear in togas and take publicity photographs all over the museum with its gigantic pillars prominently featured. With such notable characters as Aaron Perlis as Julius Caesar, Ken Wolff as Brutus, Erik Nordgren as Cassius, and Eduardo Placer as Mark Antony, the show romped on as lively as the first time we told the story and equally irreverent with its puns and anachronisms. As before, the entire show was hilariously narrated by an absurd character, Explanus, skillfully played by Eric Schinfeld. (We had three Erics in the club at that time and each spelled his name differently! The Schinfeld Eric has gone on to found his own theatrical troupe in Seattle.) I seriously doubt that the Glee Club will present "revivals" very often—although they certainly have that capability as all my shows are spiral-bound full scores including all characters, music, set descriptions, and dialogue. (No, Erik Nordgren, that's not a hint!) But this one was a great hit.

Meanwhile, the Penn Singers continued with outstanding productions of Gilbert & Sullivan's *Iolanthe* in 1997 and *Princess Ida* in 1998. One of the delightful facets of directing college women in the G&S operas is the fun that they receive from observing how women were portrayed in plays of an earlier era. It is amusing for us to watch—and for them to play—the wide-eyed, wondering, utterly innocent ladies featured in some stage genres. We made every effort to recreate the genre with total accuracy. I always have been opposed to updating G&S to make it more "relevant" to today's audience. My feeling is that if you play them as straight period pieces—and permit the intelligence of the audience to enter the picture and draw its own parallels with today—the fun is greatly enhanced. And that holds true, I believe, with the performers as well. My students have derived genuine pleasure from this approach.

The lone exception to that rule was in 1977, when the Penn Singers did *Patience*. The parallels between the Pre-Raphaelite movement of Gilbert's day and the coffeehouse poets and "flower children" of ours were just too irresistible to ignore. Without changing a word of lyric or dialogue or a single note, the costuming and staging said it all. For example, instead of velvet Buster Brown-type costumes, the two poets in our version wore turtlenecks and matching jeans, sat on high stools, and held electric guitars. In the "transformation scene" at the end, the women's chorus entered in mini-skirts and high white boots and carried clear plastic umbrellas. It was a relevant success.

The tour of the Penn Glee Club in the summer of 1998 took us to Niagara Falls, Toronto, Detroit, Cleveland, Chicago, and Pittsburgh. Never let anyone try to persuade you that the foreign tours are the only great trips of the Club. We were able to derive great pleasure from one performance, a weekend, or an extended domestic tour. The reason, of course, is obvious. We simply enjoyed being together and performing. And nearly every trip of any length includes some part that is new to *someone* and often to many. While it's always tremendously exciting to see the Parthenon or the British Crown Jewels or the Panama Canal together with your friends, it is great fun as well to go to the CN Tower in Toronto, catch a baseball game at the Skydome, eat at the Hard Rock Café, or just sing on a street corner to surprised and delighted listeners. As a chorus, we *made* our fun, and the spot need not be exotic for it to be enjoyable.

We were in Toronto for two days and had no performance scheduled for the second night. It didn't take a lot of arm-twisting, therefore, for the club to drag me to the production of *Rent* that was currently playing there. It is not my all-time favorite musical—primarily because in my old-fashioned way I can't grasp the necessity to amplify music to such decibels that the human ear cannot bear the volume and not a syllable can be discerned—but I was struck by one song that made it into our next Glee Club show. "Seasons of Love" opened Act II of the 1999 show. In Cleveland, many of us visited the Rock and Roll Hall of Fame and Museum. An appropriate and stunning museum, it juts out into Lake Erie on newly built piers and, whether you appreciate the cult it is celebrating or not, the architecture and design concept are very exciting.

One of the true high points of the tour was the day we spent at Cedar Point Park in Sandusky, Ohio, home to the fastest and most exciting roller coasters in the world. I believe I rose in a few estimations when I rode every roller coaster in the park and did the 240-foot sheer drop in the Power Tower as well. The impression on the club was reminiscent of that of cliff-diving in Jamaica. It doesn't take a whole lot of guts for an old man to impress kids these days.

Our stop in Chicago was, as always, enjoyable. For several it was their first time atop the Sears Tower, at the Chicago Art Institute, in the shops along Michigan Avenue, and among the wide variety of things to do on the fabulous Navy Pier. Our major performance for the alumni club was at the famed Second City. And, even though we still had one city to cover, we decided to hold our tour dinner in Chicago and enjoy the Riva Café on the Navy Pier. There we enjoyed a beautiful view of Lake Michigan with all of Chicago as a dramatic background. The customary traditions applied, including "Here's to you . . ." as the champagne bottle made its rounds.

Our last stop was Pittsburgh, where we gave our final performance of the season for the Penn alumni. Again, the year came to a happy and successful close tinged with the sadness that comes with the end of any year—and particularly the four years of our seniors who had just graduated.

Opening exercises, auditions, the national anthem for the Phillies, the Camp Onas retreat, the Family Day brunch, and the Fall Show all occupied our time and efforts during the first semester as we were preparing our 1999 production.

Through the hard and persuasive work of our business manager, Jared Susko, we went to New York City in early December and performed in Rockefeller Center for the *Today Show*. While our performance was live and to a huge appreciative crowd, the actual telecast was on Christmas Day 1998. We're still getting reports about our singing of Christmas music but, even more, about our rendition of "Jingle Bells," when I asked the club and all the onlookers to take out their key chains and, on my cues, jangle them in time with the music. This was such a happy inspiration that, at the end of the program, the finale was a reprise of that segment.

The 1999 show, *The Twain Shall Meet*, retold the story—both factual and not-so-factual—of the completion of the transcontinental railroad in 1869. Two railroads worked feverishly to meet each other to join the U.S. from coast to coast. The Central Pacific headed east from California, while the Union Pacific worked its way west. When they met at Utah's Promontory Point and Leland Stanford drove in the final gold spike, two full-size engines came onstage from opposite sides of the stage. Adam and the stage crew hated me for the concept and the massive set pieces, but the audience loved it. Erik Nordgren made a fine Leland Stanford, and Fred Jauss was an ideal Mark Twain. Now we know that Stanford was there (even though his wide swing missed the spike), but my only excuse for adding Mark Twain to the cast was to accommodate the title! Don't even ask me how I worked Eduardo Placer's Jesse James or Chris Cyr's Frederic Remington into the plot. In a Glee Club show, I've never been hampered by authenticity or historical accuracy.

For years I had been indebted to Marc Mostovoy and his superb Concerto Soloists, once with the Glee Club and once with the Gilbert & Sullivan Players. The near disasters from which he twice had saved me had begun a very real friendship, and I was constantly seeking some way to repay him for his great kindnesses. At last a window opened when he asked me if I ever would consider writing something for string orchestra that he might introduce. It was just the sort of opening for which I had been searching, and I launched into my work with tremendous enthusiasm.

Roger de Montgomerie had come from Normandy with William the Conqueror in 1066 and had settled in Scotland after the Battle of Hastings. For a thousand years the family seat had been there, and I had visited the "auld sod" many times and felt thrust back into my genealogical past. Eglinton Castle (my middle name is Eglinton), the ancestral home of the family, today is a dark, brooding, imposing ruin of the magnificent edifice where the Montgomerys held forth for so many years. It has round turrets on each of its corners from which my ancestors could look over the moat and across the jousting field from their battlements. It has great Norman fireplaces with the Montgomery coat of arms carved in stone sloping up from their mantels. It is a dream castle right out of fairy tales, and I had many times climbed all through the ruin discovering the immense banquet hall, complete with minstrel gallery, and winding, secret staircases hidden within its massive walls.

Here, then, was marvelous inspiration for an extended work for Marc. Although titled "Eglinton—Elegy for Strings," it is not programmatic. No picture is painted, no story is told, but I intended it to convey a mood or two of the old castle. In this I believe that I was successful and it received its impressive premiere on October 31, 1999. At last I was able to say a meaningful "thank you" to Marc Mostovoy.

And while we're at the business of remembering those remarkable people who greatly assisted me and the students with whom I worked, I would be very remiss if I let this book pass over Penn's superb alumni magazine, the *Pennsylvania Gazette*. Frequently cited as one of the premier alumni magazines in the country, it was exceedingly generous to the club and me over the years. Robert "Dusty" Rhodes ran a cover story on the Glee Club's Gettysburg adventure, a large photo spread on the first production of *Spindrift*, and numerous other pieces. Anthony Lyle did many features on the club and on my paintings in the Burrison Gallery. And, while I wouldn't meet Samuel Hughes until the end of my career, his was the only magazine cover story ever lavished on me personally.

I like to think that much of what the Glee Club did was newsworthy. I was grateful when others felt that way as well. In a era when young people made headlines in amorality, destructiveness, and body bags, it's refreshing to note that newspapers and TV determined that the positive actions of the club merited local and national coverage, too. For at least the fifty years to which this volume speaks, the *Gazette* also recognized this and spread the word thoughtfully to its readership around the world.

I had already announced my retirement from the University of Pennsylvania for June 1, 2000, exactly fifty years to the day after I started there in the Cultural Olympics. Many plans were being made, many concerns addressed. One of the plans we talked about repeatedly was a grand final tour for 1999. Ronald Klein had been the club business manager in 1969 and now lived and taught in Japan. He and the current manager, Erick Wollschlager, dreamed up the ultimate trip. Called my "Sayonara Tour," it would take us to Guam and Japan. A pretty spectacular way to end my long and joyous tenure with the group with which I already had covered so much of the globe!

♦ N I N E ♦

A High and Positive Note

DURING THE KOREAN WAR, I had been sent to Japan for three weeks to illustrate and oversee the publication of a history of the 45th Infantry Division. I'll never know, I guess, just how the army figures out who can do what. Generally they assign you to a job for which you are totally untrained and unsuited. This time I couldn't complain—they got it right. In November 1952, I worked at the Toppan Printing Company in Tokyo and labored hard for a week. When my young interpreter, Shimizu, answered my office telephone for me all was fine. When she stepped out for a few minutes and I picked it up, I bravely parroted her technique "mushee, mushee" and then panicked as I was greeted by a stream of excited Japanese. Shimizu generally returned in time to salvage the conversation.

There would be another week before I could see the proofs of my labors. I took full advantage, therefore, of the unexpected spare time and saw a great deal of this fascinating and beautiful country. Some of my delightful experiences in music there made for an effective article in the *New York Times*. I had wanted ever since to return to Japan. In 2000 I was going to be given that chance.

There was constant correspondence between Erick Wollschlager and Ron Klein, a professor at Hiroshima Jogakuin University. They had let us know that they were actively working for a year, but we had little notion of how complete and involved their intricate plans had become. We also didn't know until much later how greatly talented they were in realizing their dreams and negotiating to make them happen. At this writing, several years later, I still marvel that they pulled it off so successfully.

The major tasks assigned to me were selecting the repertoires and ordering or arranging the music for the many concerts. We would do numerous performances of our own, I was told, but at least two concerts would be with the two top male choruses in Japan and one would be with a female chorus. This required considerable repertoire planning and sending music to the several choruses for whatever joint numbers I chose. I in turn asked Ron to send me music of several well-known Japanese songs so that I might choose a few and arrange them in a medley for our Glee Club to sing. He sent me eight, from which I selected three and arranged them as "Three Songs of Japan" for male chorus and piano. Ron knew what he was doing. Later I was to find that the three I used were among the best known and best loved songs of the country. I have to assume that the other five were as well. I would be hard pressed to select from among American songs were I put in a similar position by a Japanese chorus. Thanks, Ron.

I mentioned earlier that I had composed a setting of translations of three Japanese haiku and that this work was among the first to be published in my own series. Now the time came to turn them back into the original language. While this is not generally possible from language to language, it is with Japanese—at least in the case of haiku. In both tongues, a haiku consists of seventeen syllables—five, seven, five—for its three lines. What's more, Japanese has virtually no emphasis on any single syllable, so the prosody of the music for English would be identical for Japanese. This didn't start out to be a lesson in song writing, but I wanted to explain that it was possible to go back to the original poems without any adjustment to the music. "Three Haiku," therefore, became a part of our repertoire for the tour and was greeted with enthusiasm and surprise that an American composer would choose to set their language to music for chorus.

With every language we ever came across in our singing, at an institution such as the University of Pennsylvania one is surrounded at all times by such talent in so many disciplines that there always is someone to guide you in inflection and pronunciation. If there ever was a question, I sought expert advice. As expected, we were blessed with superb assistance in the several songs we sang in Japanese and were frequently complimented on the purity of our lyrics while in Asia. We had fine tutors here, and for the Guam anthem, of course, we had Ken and Matt Wolff.

Our 1999 show, *The Twain Shall Meet*, was not going to be understood in Japan, we felt, and besides, the full-size steam engines were a bit more cumbersome than what we intended to take with us. Therefore, we planned our repertoire for a more traditional stand-up presentation with our costume changes limited to blazer outfits, uniform polo shirts specially embroidered for the tour, and white tie and tails. Stand-up, however, did not limit us to choral formation. We staged our concerts carefully and imaginatively and, of course, included a great deal of dancing.

And off we flew to Guam.

In addition to our performances there, we were able to tour the beautiful island and see the many sights I had so enjoyed before. The one disappointment was that Kenon and Matt Wolff's wonderful parents—who had so beautifully entertained me in their home when I was in Guam two years earlier—were not at home but in New Jersey! Typical of their thoughtfulness, however, they had arranged for family members to be in their hillside house and entertain us with a lavish dinner, and Ken was a gracious host. (Matt wouldn't join the Glee Club until the following year.) Of course, even thoroughly gorged with spectacular local and Philippine dishes, we sang for our supper.

Our first concert was in a large private dining room in the Hilton Hotel, for a small "but choice" audience of perhaps sixty or so sitting at tables in front of our tiny stage. Our next performance was in a real theater and boasted a stage that could accommodate all of us and our athletic dancing.

Thanks to dear Ginger Cruz, we were received by the governor and, as his Honorary Ambassador-at-Large, I had the opportunity to return the favor as we sang for him in his office. I'm not certain how much territorial work was done that day, since all the employees of his office ceased whatever they were doing and joined the party. The Club members had wonderful opportunities to swim during the day, and that night we were treated to a delightful show of Guam's native dances and songs—including a not-so-native Brian Chirls who was "volunteered" from the Club to everyone's amusement.

We flew to Japan and took the subway downtown from Tokyo's airport. It was then that we were particularly grateful that we hadn't brought the steam engines with us as we negotiated the high-speed escalators. From the subway, a caravan of taxis took us to our little hotel, and it was here that we were introduced to Japanese bathrooms. Bathing takes some getting used to as you ladle water over yourself sitting on a little wooden stool beside the tub of water, soap down, ladle some more, and finally step into the tub for the final rinse. We knew we weren't at the Hilton anymore.

One of the first people to meet us was Aki Peritz's mother, Keiko Abe. We immediately fell in love with her. She is not only a fine violinist but also one of the most gracious of guides and, more important, a very real friend. One of my most vivid memories of the trip was her taking Aki and me to lunch at her club at the top of a tall building overlooking much of the city and, directly below us, the gardens and buildings of the magnificent Imperial Palace. When I worked in Tokyo in 1952, I passed by the moat surrounding it all every day but never saw the palace itself. Now here I was with a superb birds-eye view. Keiko also was generous in driving Aki and me to many interesting parts of her city that the rest of the Club unfortunately missed.

The wonderful and helpful coordinator for our Tokyo stay was Junko Hibiya, a professor at the Keiko Gijuku University. Having Junko with us was the perfect way to begin our tour. She was solicitous of our needs, helpful beyond measure in translating for us with hotel employees, students, cab drivers, restaurants—whatever needed doing. She also took me and a few of our board members one evening to the most fabulous sushi bar I've ever encountered.

Our first scheduled performance was at a school not far from where we were staying. We donned our blazer outfits and walked to the school. The students were quite naturally expecting a concert. That's what choruses do over there. When we interspersed dancing, they went wild! This was a reaction we would encounter everywhere thereafter.

Other than the Soviet Union in 1971, Japan was the only country we ever visited that specifically requested that we refrain from singing their national anthem. In 1999, the country was in a passionate debate over whether to retain its prewar anthem which, to many, belonged to an era gone by not to return, or to adopt a new anthem that more accurately reflected its present place in the world. Therefore, we were requested to show no leaning, one way or the other. As it turned out long after we departed the decision was to retain the old.

As we began our full and carefully planned performances, we became acutely aware of the herculean job Ron Klein had accomplished on our behalf. Our very handsome twenty-eight-page souvenir program itself was a major triumph, and displayed the detailed planning he and our own Erick Wollschlager had achieved for us. Erick had told me months before that I was requested to do a watercolor of Penn's campus for the program cover. I had no idea that it would be part of so special a project.

The program started off with photographs and personal letters of greetings from our U.S. ambassador, Thomas Foley; Yotaro Kobayashi, chairman of the board of Fuji Xerox Co., Ltd.; Yoshihiko Miyauchi, president of ORIX Co.; and Judith Rodin, president of the University of Pennsylvania. Their letters, and all the texts that followed, were in both English and Japanese.

Mr. Kobayashi and Mr. Miyauchi were responsible in large measure for making this fabulous tour happen. They and their companies underwrote much of the expense of the undertaking, and we are eternally grateful to them. What's more, they even showed up for some of our concerts and we were able to see their joy in our work and to thank them in person. Some of the other organizations that helped realize the trip were American Airlines, Coca Cola Japan, Cresco, Higa Industries, and Häagen-Dazs Japan. The Häagen-Dazs sponsorship particularly amused us: ice cream—not the very best throat-coating substance through which to sing—was backstage at each venue. We sang and *then* enjoyed our ice cream bars.

There was a history of the University of Pennsylvania and of the Penn Glee Club in the program. There was a photograph and biography of me and of each of the members of the club. There was a marvelous "scrapbook" of fourteen photos of the club in Russia, Israel, Peru, Denmark, Morocco, at the Grand Canyon, in New Orleans, at the Golden Gate Bridge, and much more. There were complete programs of each of our performances and, when it was to be a joint concert with a Japanese chorus, a photograph and history of each of these as well. It even contained lyrics of twenty-five of the songs we were to sing. In short, it was one of those publications that you don't just leave behind. We value ours as tangible souvenirs of a remarkable tour, wonderfully planned and superbly carried out.

Our initial major performance was in the ballroom of the Hotel Okura and was sponsored by the University of Pennsylvania Club of Japan and the Wharton Club of Japan. Talk about having a thoroughly biased audience! It was great fun to be halfway around the world and see our entire audience enthusiastically waving napkins while lustily singing "Hoorah! Hoorah! Pennsylvania . . . ." One of the numbers on our program was the exciting "Sanctus" from the *Missa Luba*, a Congo folk mass. This required a conga drum for its very important percussion underscoring. We didn't bring a drum with us, with the thought that we would be able to pick one up at virtually every location in which we would be singing. This was not the case, so Anthony Co was highly creative. In Guam, he played on an empty cardboard box. Here in Tokyo, he played squatted at the hollow podium—to the amusement of everyone. The two remarkable pianists we had brought with us were Grace Kim and Nicholas Doering-Dorival. Their sensitive playing was greatly admired and appreciated in this first concert and in all that followed. After the concert, we had a joyous reception with our audience, many of whom were graduates of Penn and wished to trade animated stories with us.

Our first joint concert was with one of the finest male choruses I have ever heard. The Keiko Gijuku Wagner Society Male Chorus was founded in 1901 as "the first music performing group by students who did not belong to music schools" in Japan. From the start, this chorus played a major role in popularizing Western choral music in Japan. After each chorus had performed separately, we joined forces and sang six songs from Brahms and Sibelius to Thompson and Dawson—all music I had chosen and sent over in December. After all performances in Japan, there were receptions at which we could interact with our fellow performers and sing informally back and forth.

Traveling by train—the trains are wonderful in Japan—we next sang in Kyoto. The rides from city to city are great opportunities to see the countryside and the more traditional ways in which people live, work, and dress. But the high point of the ride to Kyoto was the miles and miles of breathtaking views of snow-capped Fujiyama, the picture-perfect sacred mountain. The excitement was palpable. You can't be blasé about Mount Fuji. It surpasses every textbook picture you've ever seen.

Throughout much of our tour of Japan, we were accompanied by two delightful young women, Yuki Sugiyama and Miho Yoshimoto, who endeared themselves to us immediately. Ron Klein would also show up frequently, and Joseph De Chicchis went with us on many of our excursions. I had known Joe back at Penn some years before and ours was a happy reunion. A professor at Kwansei Gakuin University where we would be going in a few days, he was also a tower of strength to us wherever we traveled in his adopted country.

In Kyoto, we sang at the Kyoto International Community House in their Event Hall to a wildly enthusiastic audience. The last number before the intermission was the lively spiritual "Rock-a My Soul" with Eduardo Placer on the rousing solo. Anyone who has ever seen us perform it knows that we spill out into the audience for the last half and get everyone clapping rhythmically with us. This bowled them over in Kyoto, and the Japanese looked for all the world like a Southern Baptist revival meeting.

From Kyoto, we went to Kobe and sang a fabulous joint concert with the men of the Kwansei Gakuin Glee Club. Celebrating their hundredth anniversary, the marvelous chorus sang two groups of songs and we sang two. We joined forces for two rousing songs to end the program. One of my arrangements that I had sent them in December that particularly appealed to them was of Carly Simon's "Let the River Run." We sang it to end the concert. We sang it again together informally in a garden where students who had not been to the concert were gathered. And then their conductor had the chutzpah to hand me a brand-new CD of their fine chorus, which included—with no permission sought or given, I might add—my arrangement of the song! What's more, they recorded it with great gusto, and it is a fine memento of their fabulous sound.

We made too many side trips in Japan to cite them all here, but three of my favorites were the Golden Pagoda, to which Joe took us and which was breathtaking, shimmering in gold and reflected in still water; the Kiyomizu Temple in Kyoto (strangely, the only place where we took a full group photograph on the tour); and sailing out to Miya Jima. This last is the sacred enclave seen so often in posters of Japan, with its magnificent torii standing out in the water as you approach the island. The island is entirely a series of religious sanctuaries and, with tiny wild deer running free, one of the most peaceful spots in the entire country.

The last totally solo concert we sang in Japan was in the Crystal Hall at the Rihga Royal Hotel. Once again we were wonderfully received and had a delightful reception afterward in which we had an opportunity to meet and chat with our audience and, of course, did considerable additional informal singing. When we first arrived at this hall, I asked of the availability of a conga drum for our rendition of the Congolese "Sanctus." Once again we were stymied. Anthony Co was challenged but came through with a fine performance on the huge inverted ice-bucket the hotel supplied. The rhythm was a bit more metallic this time than usual—or desired.

Our wonderful tour ended with several very special days in Hiroshima. I was eighteen years old in 1945, when the world's first atomic bomb was dropped on Hiroshima. The hideous pictures were emblazoned in my memory and I was deeply moved to be in this city at tour's end. The destroyed area of the busy city is now the level, green Peace Memorial Park. A ghastly reminder at the far end is the ruin of a bomb-scarred building with the skeletal, rusty remains of a dome as a grim monument.

Ron had arranged for us to meet with a survivor of the bombing. We sat in a classroom and were transfixed by the recounting of her terrifying experiences as a schoolgirl witnessing three planes fly over, actually seeing the bomb released from one of them, and diving instinctively into a gully face down. Her actions saved her life, but the scars disfiguring all of her skin are as vivid as those of her memory. It was an intensely moving afternoon talking with this generous lady who so willingly shared her memories with us. We also visited the harrowing museum filled with photographs and heartbreaking objects of the conflagration. Twisted toys, calcinated stone, pretzeled water pipes, mangled tricycles, melted dinnerware, corkscrewed household utensils, Daliesque watches, virtually unrecognizable everyday items—all tangible reminders of one of the worst days in history.

Ron Klein was not only the marvelous instigator and organizer of this spectacular tour but he was a most thoughtful host during our stay in Hiroshima. We sang informally for the students at his school and then had an excellent lunch with the president of Jogakuin University. The planners of our stay in Hiroshima, Toshiko Miyazaki and Emi Sugita, had originally planned for an average size theater for our last concert in Japan but, realizing that we had already obtained considerable fame and success, changed our venue to a very large one.

Once again, the music I had sent in December had been thoroughly learned by the resident chorus—this time an all-female choir. Over the years, we had sung with many a chorus that really hadn't spent much time preparing the works we would perform together. Such was not the case in Japan. Every chorus had done its homework before our arrival and made what could have been difficult rehearsals sheer joy. The only things that they could not have known ahead of time were my tempos and dynamics. These they caught onto readily in limited rehearsals. This had been true of the fine male choruses with which we already had sung. This was equally true of the young women we encountered in Hiroshima.

The Penn Glee Club sang two-thirds of the concert, and one group of four songs immediately after the intermission was sung by the combined groups. Then they joined us again for the final two songs.

During the performance, as in each of our previous concerts in Tokyo, Kyoto, and Kobe, we sang my "Three Haiku" and "Three Songs of Japan" in Japanese to considerable positive reaction. At the end of this last concert, the manager of the theater asked me to perform as an encore a repeat of the "Three Songs of Japan" and, with the house lights turned on, to face the audience and conduct the entire theater in the singing of these well-known songs. With all my memories of the war, with the highly charged experiences since we had arrived in Hiroshima, this was an emotional occurrence for me that I cannot describe in words. I conducted twelve hundred people unashamedly with tears literally pouring down my cheeks.

After farewell hugs, fervid, poignant wishes, and exchanges of gifts and addresses, we boarded the train to Tokyo and finally the plane for home. There was no way possible to convey to Ronald Klein and his cohorts how deeply we appreciated all that it took to make this tour the absolute triumph that it was.

Sayonara, Ronnie-san, to domo arrigato gozaimashita.

While Ron was the brains behind our tour and our-man-in-Asia, additional real gratitude must be recorded for the unbelievable enterprise of our student business manager Erick Wollschlager. How he succeeded in his immense task and still kept up his good nature and schoolwork is a tribute to his organizational skills and humor. As I reflect on our many travels, I have to conclude that this fabulous tour of 1999 was the best conceived, best executed tour of my forty-four years with the Penn Glee Club. For this, it is certain that a great share of the encomiums should be placed right in the lap of Erick Wollschlager. To our horror, Erick died suddenly on Walnut Street a year later.

We returned to our respective homes and, as rapidly as I could tie up accumulated strings, I left for my beloved Maine. Here, among other divertissements, I launched into my summer regimen of painting watercolors of the rugged Maine coast.

I haven't yet mentioned it, but my paintings have brought me a great deal of joy, even some pretty good income, and, most important of all, a coterie of very special friends. Maurice Burrison, a retired member of the university staff, used to say that he was a real collector—not of things but of interesting people. His table in the Faculty Club always was filled with fascinating men and women from across the disciplines of the university. Maury also championed the cause of artists, and when he found empty walls in the main dining room of the club he sought—and received—permission to fill them. Soon it was informally referred to as the Burrison Gallery. Soon after, in a formal ceremony, it was officially named the Maurice S. Burrison Gallery, and a bronze plaque was struck to commemorate the occasion. When the Faculty Club moved to a new location across Walnut Street, an area was purposefully put aside to perpetuate the gallery.

Soon after starting his gallery, Maury asked Charles Lee and me to share a show of our works. Over the years, Charles and I—or I alone—had many a show there. When the Faculty Club and gallery moved across the street, Maury honored us, as his most frequently exhibited artists, requesting each of us to donate a painting as a permanent greeting to everyone who enters the dining room and his gallery.

Whenever I had a new showing of my watercolors, an important and delightful feature of the festive opening wine and cheese reception was the appearance of the Glee Club, led during the past decade by student director Erik Nordgren. My wonderful young men were loyal to me at every turn, and I fairly burst with pride when they showed up at such a nonmusical affair as a gallery opening. Of course, when we knew they were coming, an extra few gallons of punch were provided, along with another wheel or two of brie and more crudités.

Among the fascinating people that Maury Burrison gathered around him, several became very special buddies of mine, and we ate lunch together nearly every day. Steve Shatz, eminent mathematician; Un-Jin Zimmerman, biochemist; Misha Lewyn, Russian historian, Charles Lee, author and critic; Maury himself, of course; and several others a bit less regular all contributed to lively discussion and sparkling conversation. Maury died in December 2001, at the age of ninety-three.

In addition to painting and running a virtual hotel in Maine in the summer of 1999, I wrote the next season's Glee Club show—my last. In the retelling it sounds frightfully self-serving, but it seemed appropriate for the show to relate the very high highlights of my fifty years at Penn. The British movie *The Full Monty* was hot at the time so I simply called ours *The Fool Monty*. It hit all the peaks that made the Penn Glee Club different from all the others.

The Fool Monty was a remarkable retrospective, containing such milestones as "Lachrymosa" from Mozart's *Requiem*; Randall Thompson's phenomenal "Tarantella"; a chance for American audiences to hear the "Three Songs of Japan" that had been so successful on our tour; our ever popular "Let the River Run"; my setting of "Lincoln's Gettysburg Address"; one of the most successful counterpoint stagings we ever did, of "By the Beautiful Sea / Salt Water Taffy," where visual counterpoint was as important as audible; "Arrirang" with full audience participation as a Korean orchestra (!) as first performed by us in the 1960s; and, of course, "Walk Him Up the Stairs"—virtually our signature production number. The show ended with our full tap dance finale "That's Entertainment" and contained some twenty-one other numbers that had defined us over the years. Sometimes retrospectives don't work. This one certainly did.

Early in the spring, as I was driving to work, I had the good music station on my car radio. One of the lighter numbers they played was Risë Stevens singing "My Hero" from *The Chocolate Soldier*. Oh, what pleasant memories it brought back to me of the several times that she and the Penn Glee Club had performed it together. As soon as I reached my office, I wrote to Miss Stevens and reminisced a bit with her. In my letter, I happened to mention that my very favorite role that I ever had seen her perform was her marvelous Octavian in Richard Strauss's *Der Rosenkavalier*. Almost by return mail, I received a gorgeous 8 x 10 photograph of her in that role, generously inscribed to me.

I can't explain it, but throughout my life I have had an uncanny knack of running unexpectedly into celebrities. Miss Stevens, of course, was not one of those, as each of our meetings was carefully planned. In these chapters I have mentioned numerous people of fame and stature whose paths I have been fortunate to cross. I now refer only to some of those individuals with whom I have spent varying amounts of time over the years and with whom conversations were spontaneous and decidedly unplanned.

The delightful morning spent with Pablo Casals was one of those. Broderick Crawford sipping orange juice with me at a sidewalk table in Belgrade, Yugoslavia, when he was making a movie there is another. Waiting for a young lady in the lobby of a Paris hotel before a planned date and chatting for half an hour with Henry Fonda was typical of my chance encounters. Then there was the time I ran into Robert Mitchum in the Hotel Grande Bretagne in Athens and we chatted about how enervating the heat was for running through back streets, as required in his latest movie there. Once, at another time in Athens, I told the great conductor Christophe von Dohnanyi that it seemed like a mini UN the night before to be an American sitting in the Roman theater of Herodes Atticus, built into the side of the Greek Acropolis, listening to German Beethoven conducted by a Hungarian! It was just dumb luck that I flew north from Boston one day and talked with Senator Edmund Muskie about music and lobster. I sat beside Secretary of State Dean Rusk on a flight from North Carolina but I have no recollection of what we talked about. At lunch with Yo-Yo Ma, I found him as charming and down-to-earth as he appears to be on stage. At a party in New York, no one seemed interested in joining him making a jigsaw puzzle, so, rather than see him at a table alone, I sat down and helped Leonard Bernstein find the interlocking bits of the picture. I told James Michener once that, of all his marvelous books, I felt my favorite was his superb reporting of the 1956 Hungarian uprising in *The Bridge at Andau.* Robert Frost told me he liked a watercolor I had done to illustrate his poem "Birches." And Stephen Vincent Benét discussed his *The Devil and Daniel Webster* with me over a black-and-white milkshake.

But I guess my favorite chance encounter occurred in London. I had been to the theater on Shaftsbury Avenue. When I arrived, it was a balmy, sunny day. When the play was over, it was a torrential rain storm. The British, naturally, all had their neatly furled umbrellas. I did not. I ran toward Piccadilly Circus to catch the Underground, darting into shop entrances to catch my breath for the next mad dash. After dozens of these repetitions, I almost had reached my destination when I slammed into a gentleman performing the same maneuvers from the opposite direction. When I gained control of my senses and looked into the face of my opponent, I exclaimed "Oh, Mr. Coward! I've just come from your play!" I had *literally* run into Noël Coward, and he invited me to join him at the Criterion Bar for a glass of stout to discuss his latest opus.

One of the things that I miss in my retirement is the joint concerts the Glee Club had with some of the most wonderful female college choruses in America, starting years ago with the inimitable Iva Dee Hiatt at Smith College. I looked forward to those weekends, when we would arrive at a campus on Saturday afternoon, have a grueling rehearsal of the joint work or works we had learned independently of each other, break for a delightful dinner with the women, dress formally, and put on our concert. This invariably was followed by a post-concert bash where the formality was abolished completely and where good times, an occasional beer, and a lot of singing took place. We would then spend the night and sometimes sing a chapel service on Sunday morning before heading back to Penn after lunch. From the very beginning it was understood that I would never be a chaperone at home or abroad, but that I expected gentlemanly behavior from everyone. Very, very rarely was I disappointed.

This last semester with the club, we made my last such journey. It was back to wonderful Smith College. We each sang a third of a concert, then we ended with Gabriel Fauré's glorious *Requiem* with full chamber orchestra and a hired baritone soloist. It was a great way to end my yearly club visits to women's colleges, where I also greatly enjoyed getting to know my conductor counterparts over the years. The hiring of a soloist was my only disappointment as our own Chris Neuhaus could have done every bit as fine a job.

My final tour with the Penn Glee Club took us once again to California. While not quite of the scope of the year before, it was a glorious way to end my tenure. We performed in many places, but the two high points of the trip were thanks to former clubber Marc Platt. As head of Universal Studios, he had arranged VIP passes for everyone in the club for the always fabulous tour of the studio's vast lot. With his connivance, we bucked every line and entered each attraction and each ride at the special VIP entrances. Shortly after noon, we had a scheduled performance in the center of all the activity and were delighted to see, standing out in the crowded audience, several former Glee Club members who had learned of our advertised appearance there.

But the greatest joy came that night when Marc and his wonderful wife Julie—as well as their gaggle of delightful kids—had all of us to their lovely home for a sumptuous dinner. They had even invited my California niece, Melinda Thomas, to join us. Afterward, we all sat around their living room singing and exchanging happy memories and jokes about our experiences together—including a goodly number from Marc, who related stories of his days at Penn. It always pleases me tremendously when alumni who have become highly successful in their professions can relive their experiences with today's students and make it seem as if no time at all has passed and as if all are of the same age and time. Marc and Julie definitely fit that description.

Jared Susco, our business manager, had planned for some time to produce a new CD of mostly serious music during my last year. To that end, we recorded almost everything we did. We had a long recording session in the Harold Prince Theatre; we had a recording session and live taping with the hundreds of alumni who came back for my retirement party; we recorded live at the Academy of Music when we performed as the guests of the Orpheus Club; and we recorded the combined forces of the Penn Glee Club and Orpheus Club at the same concert, all of which I was privileged to conduct. Jared turned out a stunning CD called *Echoes & Tradition*, handsomely boxed with an informative booklet that began, "This recording represents the end of a dynasty." I'm not certain that my time with the Penn Glee Club can accurately be termed dynastic, but it did represent one-third of the long life of the club.

Before I run out of chapters for this book of reminiscences, I really must mention one unique facet of my decades at Penn that doesn't appear on any job description or fit in any single time slot. I count it one of the most gratifying parts of my days there that the young men and women with whom I worked each day in one group or another—but mostly the Glee Club—always felt welcome and at home in my office. Many brought box lunches from the ubiquitous trucks that lined Walnut Street and sat on my piano bench or the carpeted floor. They were free, they knew, to discuss any subject, academic or personal, roommate or family, with me. I never have been a trained counselor, but I listen well and every now and then can give a useful piece of advice off the cuff or, more frequently, from the heart. I felt greatly privileged to be considered a person and my office a place where they could come for advice, to get something off their chests or even just to cry. You'd be surprised how many rugged, feet-firmly-on-the-ground guys feel the need for such an outlet and can't bring themselves to let down their macho images before their friends or roommates or fraternity brothers.

One touching example of this happened some years ago. I was working at my desk when there was a knock at the door.

"Mr. Montgomery? . . . Monty?"

A star Penn athlete, whom we all had seen play but with whom I never had exchanged even a word before, stood in the doorway.

"Come in," I said. "What can I do for you?"

"I understand you have an open door," he said self-consciously. "May I close it?"

"Of course."

He closed the door slowly and came to the chair in front of my desk, sat almost tentatively, as if searching for the next words to explain his visit, and quietly began crying. If he didn't need a syllable of advice but only to let his emotions out I couldn't have been more flattered and grateful. Actually, we talked for almost an hour. I have no idea if I imparted any words of wisdom or comfort, but he seemed considerably more at peace with himself when he left than when he arrived. And I fairly glowed that the word had gotten out that such a thing was possible in at least one office of this vast university. That scenario played more often than you would imagine. I miss that sort of unexpected exchange. I valued that trust.

The winter found us—alas, for the last time there together—in the wonderful Academy of Music before a capacity audience. I was conducting the Orpheus Club concert and, since it was my final year at Penn, the Penn Glee Club had been invited to be the special guest performers. Each chorus did its own groups of songs and then we put them together in one glorious-sounding male chorus for the final group. Among the stellar moments of the concert were "An Orpheus Triptych"—a major work which I had composed for the hundredth anniversary of the Orpheus Club in 1972; our Glee Club singing "Three Songs of Japan"; and our grand finale of the two Clubs singing a medley of songs from *Les Misérables*. Since I was a kid I've imagined that immense crystal chandelier falling. It's up there to stay, but if anything could loosen it, it would have been our rendition of "One Day More" from *Les Miz*.

As my fifty years at the University of Pennsylvania were winding down, I was the happy recipient throughout the spring of many honors and delightful celebrations. One of the most joyous was a surprise lunch in the lobby of the Annenberg Center. I thought I was going to a Penn Singers board meeting at the Inn at Penn. The president met me there and informed me that it was rescheduled for the Annenberg Center. We crossed the street and went in a side entrance. As we came out of the elevator on the lobby floor, there was a burst of song and laughter. The Penn Singers, my family, alumni, and friends had come in from all over the east and surprised me with a luncheon filled with singing and reminiscences by former students and G&S choruses throughout the day. One very special surprise was the appearance of Jody Applebaum and Marc-André Hamelin, who performed my 1949 "Christopher Robin: A Song Cycle." They later recorded it, and the CD began a whole renewed friendship with Californian Gloria Soice (now Hill), for whom I had written it so long ago.

The ultimate climax of the year 2000—and of almost any year—came on April 29, when the Glee Club celebrated finally getting rid of me. Wow, did they do it in style! Glee Club alumni met at the Annenberg Center at 10:00 A.M. and began a long and intensive rehearsal. Each man was given a spiral-bound score of all the music that would be performed at the big concert that night. The stage of the Zellerbach Theatre was set with a many-tiered set of risers that would accommodate the hundreds of men who were returning. The current Glee Club men were wonderful hosts and handled name tags and score disbursements as efficiently as if they were running a national convention.

At 12:30, we broke for lunch and repaired to the Inn at Penn across Walnut Street, where we had a huge private room engaged. To my delight, one man who had never sung with the Glee Club, but who had been made an honorary member in 1983, had asked weeks before if he might join us onstage. There was absolutely no way I would refuse such a request from Michel Huber, the much loved and admired former head of Penn's General Alumni Society. Mike claimed that he leaned on Jack Reardon for musical support. In fact he added greatly to the chorus and all the day's festivities. Actually, I doubt if Mike did a whole lot of leaning. He had heard us and sponsored us so frequently over the years that he probably knew most of our repertoire as well as we did.

During the afternoon portion of the rehearsal, Joe Hannigan of Weston Sound had set up his recording equipment, and we recorded several songs especially for a new commemorative CD. We did those same songs in the concert that night—also fully recorded—but we wanted several of them to be perfectly controlled in a way that we could not be certain of at a live performance.

Following a dinner break, we all reconvened at the Annenberg Center for the eight o'clock performance in a packed Zellerbach Theatre. The massed chorus was superb and sounded as if it had been singing together for weeks. A great time was had by all.

At one spot in the program—not even announced to the singers ahead of time—I mentioned to everyone that I had been blessed for some years with a truly outstanding student conductor, and I called on Erik Nordgren to conduct "Ride the Chariot" while I stood in the chorus and sang. He did his customary fine job and bowed appreciatively to the enthusiastic applause. Then I put my arm around his shoulders, walked him down to the front of the stage, and said, "And ladies and gentlemen, now that you've seen Erik do what he does so well, let me re-introduce him as my successor: the next director of the University of Pennsylvania Glee Club." The place went wild! Even the current club of which he was a member had not been told in advance. The spontaneous eruption of applause and shouts left no doubt that this was the happiest of choices and I'm certain let Erik know that he was being welcomed to the post on a high and positive note.

The concert ended with "Afterglow," and everyone went up to the lobby. Here speeches and presentations were made at a lavish reception catered by Culinary Concepts, the company of which my niece, Vicki Pohl, was director of sales. I have a feeling that extra special attention and care went into this job. My boss, Francine Walker, spoke from the heart and presented me with a handsome gold watch with the university seal on its face. Penn's president, Judith Rodin, even wrote and delivered a witty poem.

Several days later, I was asked to attend a trustees' meeting at which Judy read an extremely flattering special minute of the board concerning my service to the University and my impending retirement. And still later, the *Pennsylvania Gazette*, Penn's distinguished alumni magazine, made my retirement the subject of a cover story for the May–June issue. It also began a wonderful friendship with Sam Hughes, senior editor, who wrote the fine article.

I was selected to be the Grand Marshal of the 2000 Alumni Day Parade of the Classes, and it was highly gratifying to "review the troops" including so many wonderful former students with whom I had worked so closely over so many years.

Everyone made my final concert and my final days very, very special. I always have declared that my least favorite day of any year is Commencement. Contrary to the meaning of the word, it invariably has meant the end of daily contact with dear student friends. My "commencement" was the hardest of all because not only did it end such contact but there wouldn't be a "new man class" coming in to me in September.

As Chuck says at the end of *Basses Loaded*, "Well, that's about all there is to tell." Of course there's a great deal more that could be told. I could fill whole chapters with anecdotal descriptions of our rehearsals and rehearsal techniques. I could regale you with the intricacies of our choreographic sessions and how some of our more flamboyant inspirations came to us and eventually to fruition. I could explain in some detail the choices of our repertoire and the steps in arranging or composing huge amounts of music for our specific style or sound. I could write accounts of literally hundreds and hundreds of public performances that have not even been alluded to here.

Throughout this retelling, however, I have attempted to keep to the story in a fairly direct line. My several tangents have been largely to amplify the spirit of what the Penn Glee Club was doing during all those years and the outside influences that played important roles in determining its many enterprises.

Sometimes it seemed wise to let you in on some of my personal activities in order for you to understand more fully my role in shaping the nature and even future directions for the Club.

My job became so complete a life, and my students became "my kids" so thoroughly, that I grew more selfish as each year passed and realized that I could not give up any of it to lead the more accepted life of husband and father. This has given rise, naturally, to a few regrets—but really only a few. I'm as busy as ever. Vicki even asked me last year, "Uncle Bruce, when are you going to retire from retirement?"

I don't intend to. But I'll forever wish that I had a certain chorus with me when I greet someone.

"Oh, here's to . . . fill up the tankard."

And I would like to have a bottle of champagne with a circle of dear friends.

"Here's to you . . . Here's to you my jovial friend."

And I never will be with a group of students that I won't wish that I could extend my arms around their shoulders and sing with unabashed sentimentality and love the song I wrote for them so many years ago.

> Shadows grow long on the campus.
> Twilight has come again.
> Warm copper rays
> Streak the golden haze
> As peace settles down on Penn.
> And soft and low
> In the pale afterglow
> The voices of students ring
> With the songs and cheers
> Of their fair college years,
> The songs they love to sing:
> "Post jucundam,
> Juventutem,
> Vivat academia."
> Sing the praise
> Of college days,
> Sing of Pennsylvania.

Full to the Brim

MANY THRILLING THINGS were still in store for me after I celebrated my departure from Penn. The year 2000 was already so spectacular that it seemed impossible to keep topping itself, but joy built on joy and the months kept crowding themselves to fit in all the excitement.

A year earlier, Dr. Christopher Thomford, president of Bethany College, had invited me to deliver the Commencement Address at my alma mater in May 2000. So out I flew to Kansas. My old roommate and second tenor in the PitchPipers, Wayne Holmstrom, met my plane in Wichita and drove me to Lindsborg. It was Alumni Weekend, so it was filled with great reunions with former classmates and friends and professors of so many years ago. But the most eagerly anticipated reunions were those with Wayne and our first tenor LaRue Olson. As Carol Anderson had died in 1994, we were cheated of the chance to burst into four-part harmony. LaRue and Beverly had asked Wayne and Inez and me to a wonderful dinner party at their home in Marquette, and there we had further good times and memories with Andy's widow, Faye Ellen, and several other old friends of the 1940s. All these reunions fully lived up to my most enthusiastic expectations.

The commencement was as exciting as I knew it would be. The academic processional, wonderfully played on the marvelous organ in Presser Hall, was "Bethania," a work I had been commissioned to compose for the hundredth anniversary commencement in 1981. It was with a very special feeling of pride that I marched to my own academic processional. And it was immensely gratifying to be given the Honorary Doctor of Fine Arts degree in the place where so much of the training took place for the supremely happy professional life I was to lead.

When I returned home, I plunged immediately into another satisfying project of rehearsals for an August presentation. Talk about "coals to Newcastle"! I had been requested to bring a full production of my reconstruction of *Thespis* to the International Gilbert & Sullivan Festival in Buxton, England. That year the festival, to which G&S companies and aficionados came from all over the world, was to highlight this opera, and people came from as far away as Australia, South Africa, and New Zealand to see the one opera they never had seen before.

For it, I had reinstituted the Gilbert & Sullivan Players of Philadelphia and made no pretenses of being democratic about it. I held no auditions but carefully hand-selected my company—principals and chorus alike. Along with other fine stalwarts, I cast six former students in lead roles. Jeff Coon, fortunately, would finish his current show two weeks before we would leave for England and wouldn't begin his next until a week after we returned. Therefore, as he had done it so beautifully for me in 1989, I cast him in the tenor lead of Sparkeion. Jen Roussell was available to play Nicemiss, Rob Biron to play Mars, Erik Hanson to play Jupiter, and Ed Nealley to play Apollo. Brendan O'Brien, who had done a superb Mercury for me in the 1989 production, repeated his stellar role in England. My sister Liz came along as the "aging Venus," and her husband Nick did what I believe was his first speaking role ever, Tipseion. John Dennison played the title role of Thespis.

After music rehearsals in May and early June, we parted to learn the roles thoroughly and reconvened in July for intense action rehearsals. Meanwhile, I had sent all the necessary requirements for sets and costumes, as well as the orchestra parts, to England. All was in readiness when we arrived the first week of August.

Two days prior to our opening, I gave a lively lecture on the reconstruction of the opera, illustrated by several of the cast performing teaser renditions of some of the songs. This created considerable additional interest in the work, and the opera became the talk of the festival. The production, I am happy to report, was an unqualified success and has generated interest worldwide. Brendan even walked away with the award of Best Supporting Actor for the entire festival. One of these days, I hope, *Thespis* will become a standard in the repertoire of G&S companies everywhere.

In London, I went, as is my custom, to see the autographs at the British Museum—including the Emily Brontë workbook I had earlier handled. The entire collection had been moved to a new building farther up the Thames. But, parading right past the Magna Carta, I saw my treasured volume again.

While my long active tenure with the University of Pennsylvania Glee Club terminated on June 1, 2000, I have kept my fingers in the Penn pie.

Following my "graduation," I have returned to campus to direct the Penn Singers in Gilbert & Sullivan's *The Mikado* in 2001, *Ruddigore* in 2002, *Utopia, Limited* in 2003, and *The Gondoliers* in 2004. The *Ruddigore* production, incidentally, contained a first for me. While I had directed numerous fathers and sons, mothers and daughters, brothers, sisters, cousins, and aunts over the years, and had had several sets of brothers in the Glee Club at the same time, I had never had two brothers play opposite each other *as brothers* in any show. In the Penn Singers' *Ruddigore*, Gary Kurnov played Dick Dauntless while his brother David played Dick's foster brother Robin Oakapple. I had a worthy successor for the Glee Club in Erik Nordgren. It has not been quite so easy to come up with a replacement for G&S. I have no idea how many future productions are in the offing, but, since they have enthusiastically decided to continue with these timeless works, I told them that I would continue while we searched.

Erik Nordgren has been uncommonly generous to me after assuming the directorship of the Glee Club. I have felt warmly welcomed back time and again. He and the officers of the club have invited me to their concerts and parties and have even included me in the Parents' Weekend Brunch each autumn. And to make it even more special, each time Erik has called on me to conduct a number. In addition, I have been accorded the pleasure of staging some of the current energetic production numbers and even wrote the tap-dance finale for the 2004 show. I can't describe what all this has meant to me.

I believe it is a measure of both Erik's maturity and his security that he has continued to perform my compositions and arrangements and has invited me back to stage and choreograph a number or two, without it seeming in any way to be in competition with his new authority or condescending to me. It's his Glee Club now, and he has taken over with great self-assurance and grace.

Abe Lo—a recent past president—instituted a new "tradition" that each New Man Class come out to my apartment in Chestnut Hill to ask questions about the snippets of club history and anecdotes that they have heard alluded to since joining. Sitting around my living room enjoying pizza or hoagies and sodas, we have had lively conversations, and I have learned to know the new men who have come in since my time. This has become one of the happiest and most cherished annual moments of my retirement.

My retirement has been characteristically full to the brim. That's one of the reasons I retired in the first place. I have started a new company—Monty,

Inc.—turning some of my watercolors into unusual, distinctive notecards. I have been directing G&S on a regular basis both at Penn and in West Chester. I'm doing a great deal of composing and am enjoying performances fairly regularly. I'm writing my first string quartet—and it scares the hell out of me. I've written for full orchestra, for band, for string orchestra, and almost endless combinations of instruments and voices. But with a string quartet you can't hide behind a clarinet or a trumpet or anything else. You're absolutely naked. Every note must count at all times for each of the four instruments.

I even get to do a guest shot at conducting every now and then. I'm writing several books, of which this is only one. I make it back to the Faculty Club at Penn on occasion to meet my old cronies for lunch and to catch each other up with our latest doings. I'm also happily serving on a committee of the Faculty Club to determine the running and the future of the Burrison Art Gallery, which was so supportive of me and my painting over so many years. And, as if I didn't travel enough with the Glee Club, I have been seeing a good bit of the world.

In September 2001, I realized a lifelong dream of visiting China. I walked for miles on the Great Wall. "Walked" is not really the proper word here. I'm reasonably certain that there are, indeed, places on the Great Wall where one can walk. Not where I was taken, however. I'm one of those strange people who counts steps! The area of the Wall that I tackled was nothing *but* steps. I stopped counting after the first two thousand—and there were still thousands to go. To make it an even greater challenge, the steps are timeworn and range in height from three inches to two feet, so it is as difficult coming down as going up. For nearly four hours I climbed from one mountaintop watchtower to another. When I finally arrived back at my starting point I collapsed on the pavement for nearly half an hour with legs that declined to go one more pace before returning to my car and guide—who, incidentally, did not accompany me on my journey. He obviously had been there before!

I went through the Forbidden City in Beijing and was stunned by the immensity and opulence of everything I saw. I visited the exquisitely peaceful Summer Palace on Lake Kunming and walked the length of the Long Promenade, marveling at the beautiful paintings all along its ceiling and the four pavilions representing the seasons. At the far end of the promenade, I saw the fantastic solid stone Boat of Purity and Ease, a monument to royal excess if ever there was one. I visited the vast Tiananmen Square (the world's largest) and all I could think of was the ghastly, deadly student riots of 1989. One of my favorite spots of all that I saw in China was the very beautiful three-tiered, circular Hall of Prayer for Good Harvests. All the glorious photos I had seen over the years did not prepare me for its majestic beauty.

I was fascinated by the ten thousand life-size terra cotta warriors in Xi'an and even met the old farmer who found them when he was digging a well in 1974. More than two thousand years old, each one different, and already labeled the "Eighth Wonder of the World," they simply have to be one of the handful of the greatest archeological finds of the twentieth century. And I can say that with some degree of authority, having been through King Tutankhamen's tomb in Egypt and seen the Dead Sea Scrolls and the cave where they were found, Machu Picchu in Peru, the solar boats at the base of the Great Pyramid at Giza, the ruins of Knossos on Crete, the temple of Artemis in Ephesus, and so many other exciting discoveries of the century.

I sailed through the Three Gorges in a large boat and through the Three Lesser Gorges in sampans, in time to see sights and villages and whole cities that will never be seen again after the flooding created by the completion of the Gezhou Dam, the world's largest hydroelectric plant. I strolled through the sights and seemingly unending "streets" of ancient flights of steps in unbelievably crowded Chongqing.

I was drifting insouciantly down the Yangtze River on my way to breakfast with some new English friends on the fateful September 11, 2001. I was first informed by a German woman on my boat that "the United States was bombed last night." A tiny television set on board showed the ghastly pictures over and over, but the commentary was all in Chinese. Even when George Bush came on the screen, it was voiceover in Chinese; it was three days before I could be in Shanghai and get CNN in English to determine the details of what had happened. I walked along the Bund in Shanghai and total strangers came up to me and embraced me in sympathy for what had just happened to my country.

It was an immense irony that all my family was worried about my being halfway around the world in troubled times when it was they who were in harm's way. It was also eerie in the extreme to fly home on a Boeing 747 as one of only eleven passengers.

The world was forever changed in a single day while I was in China. And even there the impact was instantly recognized. The inevitable global consequences of the monstrous assault stunned every individual. You could read it on every face; you could discern it in tiny acts of compassion and sympathy from a people who had known decades of terror. It was acutely felt and deeply moving.

Everlastingly grateful that my family was spared the physical horrors of that infamous day, now I am back at my customary directing, painting, writing, composing and the like. So much for "retirement!" With all of the touring I did with the Penn Glee Club, you'd think I had had my fill of travel. However, one of the reasons for my retirement was to go to places I had only dreamed of seeing and to make some of those dreams a reality.

When I was eight years old, my father introduced me to the wonderful trilogy by Charles Nordhoff and James Norman Hall, *Mutiny on the Bounty*, *Men Against the Sea*, and *Pitcairn's Island*. This young boy's fascination grew each year into almost an obsession to retrace the wake of the *Bounty*. Not many of us are able to capture a dream and live it through. Nearly seven decades passed, but in March and April 2003 I did, indeed, fulfill my dream—and then some! Highlights included four days on fascinating Easter Island, climbing its volcanoes and wandering among its enigmatic moai—the huge carved heads and torsos that are scattered throughout the island.

Bora Bora was all I had heard it would be as one of the most beautiful spots on the globe. But in my mind, at least, it was eclipsed by Fatu Hiva and Ua Pou—each of which caused me to write in my daily journal that I might have "died and gone to earth's most glorious Paradise." Both are magnificent volcanic islands that jut thousands of feet straight out of the Pacific and reach for the clouds in breathtaking spires of rock. Ua Pou (which means "The Pillars") lives up to its name and was the inspiration for Jacques Brel's song "La Cathédrale." On Hiva Oa, incidentally, I visited the graves of both Jacques Brel and Paul Gauguin.

The coral atolls Ducie, Henderson, Puka Rua, Puka Puka, Takapoto, Mataiva, and the like were precisely what I had expected them to be—large, low coral reefs surrounding sleepy deep azure lagoons with coconut palms and hibiscus in profusion against breathtaking cumulus skies.

Tahiti was exquisite, and I spent many a contented day there in spite of the overpowering surges of tourism. On one day alone, a huge cruise ship disgorged more than three thousand passengers onto this once glorious island.

But the raison d'être for my trip was everything that I had hoped it would be. When the *Bounty* mutineers left Tahiti in 1789 and Fletcher Christian led the most famous mutiny in naval history, their search for isolated Pitcairn Island—misplaced on the charts of the day—took them away from any islands known to those men who did not follow Christian. It also took them to one of the most isolated spots on earth. In a little Zodiac rubber boat, I crashed through the huge boulders while the sea broke violently around us. We waited just beyond the crashing surf, poised on the crest of a long, furious wave, and, with hearts in throats, seized the chance to ride it in, roiling, to the tiny pebbled beach. At least one person was seriously injured in the process. But I, at last, was standing on Pitcairn Island—a dream come true after sixty-eight years!

After ascending the "Hill of Difficulties," I saw almost every inch of the fabled land. I met many of the forty-two residents, virtually all of whom are descended from the original nine mutineers and the Polynesian women they had brought with them from Tahiti, and I saw the modest homes in which they live—many with a corrugated iron roof to catch the rainwater. I visited the one-room schoolhouse Up Pulau and chatted with the schoolmaster. At one end of the room there was an old upright piano. I raised the keyboard lid and firmly believe that its last tuning was somewhere around 1923! I saw the anchor of the destroyed H.M.S. *Bounty* (more accurately: "His Majesty's Armed Vessel *Bounty*") and a cannon saved from the sea as well as the ship's Bible. All are in the lone village, tiny Adamstown, along with the post office (the sale of Pitcairn Island postage stamps to philatelists worldwide is one of the chief sources of income for the island), the chapel, the meeting hall, the small museum, and the even smaller library. I talked at length with Shirley Young, the librarian, and promised to send her some books. I've kept my promise.

One of the great delights, however, was talking with Dennis Christian—great, great, great, great-grandson of Fletcher Christian and a talented wood-carver. I purchased a stunning carving of a shark that he made of miro wood from Henderson Island. It now hangs in a prominent place on a wall of my house in Maine.

When we departed, all the Pitcairners very touchingly sang their traditional parting song which they sing to any of the rare visitors to their island:

> Now one last song we'll sing
> Goodbye, goodbye.
> Time moves on rapid wings,
> Goodbye, goodbye, goodbye.

As *Brothers, Sing On!* goes to press, other exciting things are in store for me and I have every intention of being around to see them through.

By the time this book comes out, I will have directed my favorite of all the Gilbert and Sullivan operas, *The Yeoman of the Guard*. This will be with the fine company I've been directing for fourteen years in West Chester, Pennsylvania. The following April will have seen the Penn Singers treading the decks of the ever popular *H.M.S. Pinafore.*

In between these delightful productions, I have planned another of my exciting foreign trips. At the Glee Club Graduate Club reception in May 2004, when the club president of the 1970s, Jay Scarborough, asked me what my next big journey would be, I divulged my plan to spend two weeks in Cambodia in December. I told him that I wished to climb all over the ruins of Angkor Wat while I can still climb! In a most off-hand manner, I impulsively said, "Want to come along?" Then and there we decided to tour together. This will bring my foreign travels to a total of sixty-four lands—so far. And as with nearly all my earlier foreign tours, it will be with wonderful companionship. I've been really blessed.

In August 2005, I'll be taking another production by Gilbert and Sullivan Players of Philadelphia to the International G&S Festival in England, where I hope to wow them again.

Retire? Not when there are still bountiful dreams out there to be lived.

If a man is truly lucky in this world, he is fortunate to have a champion—in the historical sense—who is a strong advocate for his career, his interests, his strengths, his successes. I have been blessed with many such champions. My entire family has supported me in everything I have done since my earliest days. Friends, professors, colleagues, students—all have encouraged me in virtually my every endeavor.

At the University of Pennsylvania so many advanced my life, loves, enterprises, and causes that I hesitate to mention any by name because it is so terribly unfair in the omissions. But, if really pressed, I would have to single out six without whom my fifty-plus years at that wonderful institution would have been very different, very much more "ordinary" as opposed to the "extraordinary" that they helped make them be. Steve Goff, Craig Sweeten, Ed Lane, Alice Emerson, Don Sheehan, and Mike Huber made my life truly extraordinary; supported me in ways of which perhaps even they are not aware; encouraged my wildest flights of fancy and helped me to realize their potential.

Love is a horribly overused word. But it is the only one strong enough to convey the devotion, appreciation, and admiration that I feel looking back from my new detached viewpoint. And it applies to each of them.

My "retirement" is busy and wonderful. But more than anything else, I miss the joy of going to campus every day to contemplate the young, inquiring minds of my marvelous, talented students.

They were my life.

In 1989 Jeffrey Coon, as Jack, climbed his beanstalk to prepare for
his role in *Is This for Reel?* Botanists: don't look too carefully,
it's really a tree over by the Bio Pond.

The Glee Club visited the Grand Canyon in Arizona for the first time in 1981.

In 1990, for the 250th anniversary of the University of Pennsylvania, the club shared the stage of Convention Hall with Kenny Rogers, Dolly Parton, and Bill Cosby. The lucky few men who were off-stage-right at the right time posed for a quick photo with Bill. To the left is casino owner Steve Wynn. Kelly & Massa Photography.

Rob Biron would even tempt personal injury to make it into a publicity shot for *Basses Loaded!* in 1990. He spent the next three days getting gravel out of his palms.

Mike Handler, as TV personality "Chuck" Roast, looks on approvingly as the team hoists Jeff Coon, as pitcher Joe Yoder, after a victory by the Juniata Junction Jets in *Basses Loaded!*

The 1990 Glee Club posed at the top of a hill above the Danube in Budapest.
Photos such as this make me realize what a motley crew we were on our travels.

On our 1992 trip to Israel, we swam in the Med, the Red and the Dead.
You can't really swim in the Dead Sea; you can't sink, either.

One of the most inspiring places the Glee Club has visited over the years was Masada in the
Israel wilderness. Here we posed in 1992 at the very top of the massive clifftop fortress.

The Penn Glee Club has won considerable praise for its rendition of our National Anthem before games by the Phillies, Eagles, and '76ers. Here we perform at the National League Playoffs in 1995. Photograph by Heddy Bergsman.

Halfway through our 1997 tour to Spain, we sailed across the Strait of Gibraltar to Morocco.
Even with fezzes and camels, you still look like Americans, guys.

On the 1997 tour, Amol Dixit, Brett Lovins, Dan Weinstein, Derek Smith, and Dan Pincus posed on the Rock of Gibraltar before joining the club to sing in the theater in the huge cave in the very center of the Rock.

The club appeared on the *Today* show in Rockefeller Center in 1998. We taped the show of holiday music early in December, so we were home to see it with our families when it was aired on Christmas.

One of our many stops in Japan in 1999 was at the beautiful Kiyomizu Temple in Kyoto. My "Sayonara Tour," Japan proved to be one of the most spectacular tours of my forty-four years with the Penn Glee Club.

THE UNIVERSITY OF PENNSYLVANIA GLEE CLUB TOUR OF JAPAN, 1999

The Penn Glee Club works and lives on a beautiful campus in Philadelphia, Pennsylvania, USA.

アメリカ
ペンシルベニア州
フィラデルフィアの
美しいキャンパスに
ペンシルベニア
グリークラブは
生きづいています。

At the request of the sponsors in Japan, I did Penn scene watercolors for the cover of the program given to all the audiences for the 1999 tour. (They looked a bit more impressive in color.)

One of the best loved spots in Japan is the glorious island of Mia Jima. With perhaps the exception of Mount Fuji, no Japanese scene is more universally known than the huge red torii rising up out of the bay and greeting boats that near the sacred island. The T-shirted club members, Grace Kim (accompanist), Eduardo Placer, and Ken Wolff (front row) and Anthony Co, Eddie Mercato, and Erick Wollschlager (back row) were accompanied in this photo by a deer and three young Japanese women.

The movie *The Full Monty* was out and a hit during my last year with the Glee Club. Needless to say, the term was applied to me with annoying frequency. Therefore, it seemed only natural for me to title my last Club show *The Fool Monty*. I even did my own caricature for the 2000 poster and program.

"Retirement" has meant that I could fulfill a few of the dreams that had occupied my thoughts for my entire life. Without question, the two greatest dreams-come-true were walking on the Great Wall of China in 2001 and climbing all over Pitcairn Island in the wake of the *Bounty* in the South Pacific in 2003. Unlike many long dreams, both surpassed my wildest fancies. Here I am atop the Great Wall forty-five miles northwest of Beijing . . .

. . . And standing on Pitcairn Island with a peek at Bounty Bay in the distance.

(If you look very closely, you'll discover that they're not the same shirt.)

The next several images show a few of the world renowned musicians who have come to our campus to receive the University of Pennsylvania Glee Club Award of Merit. Here Peter Kurzina and I greet the great choral conductor Robert Shaw in 1965. Jules Schick Photography.

Leopold Stokowski chats with me and Wayne Baruch in 1968. Jules Schick Photography.

Steve Grebe and I share a laugh with composer William L. Dawson and his wife Cecile in 1967. Jules Schick Photography.

Bob Hallock and I greatly enjoyed meeting the dean of twentieth-century American composers, Aaron Copland, in 1970. Jules Schick Photography.

Jay Scarborough (né Skarzenski) charms Eugene and Gretel Ormandy in 1972.

Jules Schick Photography.

Marian Anderson, shown here in 1973, was one of the truly
great ladies of the world. Jules Schick Photography.

Samuel Barber with Alice Emerson and me in 1974. Jules Schick Photography.

A WINNING SHOW FOR THE ENTIRE FAMILY!

A BLUE CHIP SONG-AND-DANCE-JACKPOT!

On two occasions during my forty-four years with the Penn Glee Club, I did posters and program covers that contained caricatures of all the men in the club. Each man would come to my office, sit for me for five minutes, and end up immortalized. The first was for *Casino* in 1982.

The second program cover was for *Time In—Time Out* in 1987.

APPENDIX I

University of Pennsylvania Glee Club Season, 1966–1967

Current and new Penn Glee Club members often are skeptical when older club men or I refer to the large quantity of performances "we used to have" every year and say that the glee club truly had to be your only major extracurricular activity because it occupied all your spare time. While putting this book together, I came across the following schedule of events for the club's 1966–1967 season. I'm certain that there were numerous additional demands on our time, but this gives a sample.

September	4	Annual Buck Hill Falls concert, Buck Hill, Pennsylvania
	5	Freshman Boys' Camp, Green Lane, Pennsylvania
	5	Freshman Girls' Camp, Green Lane, Pennsylvania
	9	Performing Arts Night Variety Show, Irvine Auditorium
October	7	Joint Concert, Columbia University Glee Club, New York
	15	President's Day, Van Pelt Library
	20	University Alumni Dinner, Mask &Wig Clubhouse
	21	Key Alumni Banquet, University Museum
	28	Moore College of Art, Philadelphia
November	4	Parents' Day Concert, Auditorium, University Museum
	14	National Bottlers Convention, Haddon Hall, Atlantic City, New Jersey
	18	Germantown Academy Concert, Fort Washington, Pennsylvania
	21	University Arts League, Annenberg Auditorium
	22	Alumni Annual Giving Dinner, Warwick Hotel, Philadelphia
	23	Macy's Thanksgiving Day Parade, NBC, New York
December	6	IBM Christmas Dinner, Mariott Motor Inn, Philadelphia
	7	Wharton Graduate Wives Dinner, Dietrich Hall
	9	Annual December Campus Concert, Irvine Auditorium

	12	Deans' Christmas Tea, Annenberg School
	18	Christmas Caroling, City Hall Courtyard, Philadelphia, noon
	18	Annual Christmas Caroling in West Philadelphia, 9 p.m.
	19	Christmas Caroling, Stock Exchange, Philadelphia, 4 p.m.
	19	Annual Christmas Caroling in University Hospital, 7 p.m.
January	15	Philadelphia Orchestra Rehearsal, Academy of Music
	16	Philadelphia Orchestra Concert, Academy of Music
February	10	Fairfield County Concert, Westport, Connecticut
	12	Smith College Joint Concert, Northampton, Massachusetts
	16	Inter-Fraternity Banquet, Barclay Hotel, Philadelphia
	25	Award of Merit Banquet, William L. Dawson, University Museum
March	4	DuPont Country Club, Wilmington, Delaware
	16	Harrisburg Alumni Club, Harrisburg, Pennsylvania
	31	Annual Winter Concert, Annenberg Auditorium
April	1	Alumni Dinner, Salisbury Inn, Long Island, New York
	7	Alumni Dinner, Westchester Country Club, Rye, New York
	14	Musical Activities Night, Irvine Auditorium
	20	Women's Hey Day, Irvine Auditorium, 2 p.m.
	20	Men's Hey Day, Irvine Auditorium, 3 p.m.
	29	Recording Session, RCA, Camden, New Jersey
May	13	Annual Glee Club Outing, Chestnut Hill, Philadelphia
	19	Alumni Dinner, Reunion Tent, Franklin Field
	19	50-Year Class Reunion Dinner, Union League, Philadelphia
	20	Performing Arts Tent, 4 shows, Franklin Field
	21	Baccalaureate Chapel, Irvine Auditorium

APPENDIX II

Some Comments from the Press About the University of Pennsylvania Glee Club

"Through universal music the Penn Glee Club helped to build new grass-roots bridges of understanding . . . and the inherent dangers and differences in a volatile land were forgotten for a while in rich and joyous harmonies."
—Jerusalem Post

"The young men fascinated the audience with their humor, singing and dancing, giving a fantastic show . . . a universe full of music and smiles."
—Apogevmatini, Athens

"An American Show Completely in the Top Class [headline]. . . .Thoroughly professional, very clever and well developed...It was a sensational tempo."
—Jydske Tidende, Aabenraa, Denmark

"This concert was a real Theatre Party with music to delight everyone no matter what his tastes. . . . If this is what glee clubs are doing today then here's one reviewer who hopes that more will find their way to our city."
—Kansas City Star

"The University of Pennsylvania Glee Club dazzled the hundreds of Cuencanos who came to the Teatra Cuenca to attend the presentation of this formidable musical group. . . . An unforgettable fiesta, it is one that the people of Cuenca, lovers of the arts, ought not to miss!"
—El Mercurio, Cuenca, Ecuador

"We expected to have to review this concert with the patronizing tone of an account of a pleasant amateur chorus out to entertain its prejudiced alumni. What we found was a slick, professional performance that holds its own with any show in town."
—Boston Herald

"Bruce Montgomery conjures up from his singers exquisite pianissimo sounds, organ-like basso, equally effective as cleverly accomplished nuance variations."
—Helsingin Sanomat, Helsinki

"The Penn Glee Club has created greater understanding between the United States and the people of South America than could be possible at this time on higher diplomatic planes."

—*New York Times*

"This magnificent musical group . . . blends its presentations alternating serious music with interpretations of modern music, unfolding different scenes and dance numbers."

—*El Commercio*, Lima

"Three thousand mostly young people crowded into the open-air theatre at Primorsko and stamped and shouted their approval with rhythmic clapping after every song."

—Voice of America, Sofia, Bulgaria

"Probably no other college ensemble puts on a show such as this one, but then, no other college is fortunate enough to have Bruce Montgomery."

—*Philadelphia Inquirer*

"The audience was moved by the delicate harmony and smoothness of the voices . . . For an encore, they sang 'Sakura Sakura' and 'Oborozukiyo' together with the audience to great applause."

—*Chugoku Shimbun*, Hiroshima

APPENDIX III

The Titled Penn Glee Club Shows, 1970–2000

Prior to 1970, the Glee Club presented concerts without titles. From the very first of the Montgomery era performances in 1956, however, staging and dancing became integral ingredients of those concerts and the logic of adding titles was apparent. The only surprising thing was that it took fourteen years to recognize it!

1970   Handel with Hair

1971   See Hear!

1972   Paint the Яed Town

1973   It's About Time

1974   Americ-O-Round

1975   Score!

1976   Opus 76: A Bass 'n' Tenoral Celebration

1977   Extravagancelot

1978   Next Stop: Manhattan

1979   The Magus

1980   Hit High Sea

1981   Double Take

1982   Casino!

1983   Saddle Up!

1984   Ye Merrie Adventures of Robbin' Hoods

1985   Where'm I Goin'?

1986   Holmes Sweet Holmes or Watson a Name?

1987   Time In—Time Out

1988   Heaven Help Us

1989   Is This for Reel?

1990   Basses Loaded!

1991   Step Right Up! (The Great Carny Caper)

1992   Cross Chris, Cross

1993   The Canterbury Scales

1994   Coda Nostra

1995   Sing Tut

1996   Killing Time

1997   Treble in Paradise

1998   GO Forum! or Roman in the Gloamin'

1999   The Twain Shall Meet

2000   The Fool Monty (A Wrap-Up)

APPENDIX IV

University of Pennsylvania Glee Club Honorary Members

Honorary Membership is something that the Glee Club does not give capriciously. In my many years with the Club, only fifteen such honors were awarded—and I don't believe any existed before that. An Honorary Membership represents extraordinary devotion to and exceptional deeds in behalf of the University of Pennsylvania Glee Club.

1968	E. Brooks Lilly
1968	Charles H. Cox, III
1969	Santiago Friele
1976	Edward F. Lane
1978	Stephen Goff
1983	Michel T. Huber
1987	William Kelley
1987	Steven Aurand
1990	Nicholas Constan
1990	E. Craig Sweeten
1990	Claude White
1991	Ray Evans
1991	Jay Livingston
1995	Stanley E. Johnson
1995	Timothy J. Alston

APPENDIX V

Discography

Over the years, the University of Pennsylvania Glee Club performed on many records, both alone and with other ensembles, most importantly with the Philadelphia Orchestra. The following list is limited exclusively to the sessions during the "Montgomery Era"—the years covered in this volume. The year before I took over the direction of the University of Pennsylvania Glee Club, when I was still working in the Public Relations Office, I designed a record jacket for a ten-inch lp for the Glee Club—never dreaming that in one more year I would be the club's director. In my years with the Club, we went on to release eleven more recordings: six twelve-inch lp records and five CDs. Ours was the first CD issued by any Penn group.

1957	"The University of Pennsylvania Glee Club"
1960	"Whole World"
1964	"Afterglow"
1966	"A Declaration of Peace" with Goucher College Choir
1977	"Extravagancelot"
1978	"Next Stop: Manhattan!"
1988	"Brothers, Sing On!"
1991	"Hail Pennsylvania"
1995	"The Penn Glee Club—In Song, of Course"
1998	"Joint Choral Concert" with Smith College Choirs
2000	"Echoes & Tradition"
2000	"Gabriel Fauré: *Requiem*" with Smith College Choirs

APPENDIX VI

Comments from the Press About the
Gilbert & Sullivan Players of Philadelphia

"To laud this company for singing, acting, décor and stage 'business' is merely to continue the string of encomiums."

—*Philadelphia Inquirer*

Thespis: "A most creditable job . . . the production, in singing, acting and bright costuming is fully up to this troupe's standards."

—*Philadelphia Inquirer*

Trial by Jury: "All trials should be as eye-filling, happy, colorful and excellent."

—*Philadelphia Inquirer*

The Sorcerer: "There is only one thing wrong: the lively production is so well sung and acted, so authentically staged, so brightly costumed, that it is a shame it runs for only one weekend."

—*Philadelphia Inquirer*

H.M.S. Pinafore: "As always, this is a superlative production, enacted in stylized fashion, which is all to the good."

—*Philadelphia Inquirer*

Pirates of Penzance: "This fine local company radiated talent and good spirits that came trippingly over the footlights."

—*Philadelphia Evening Bulletin*

Patience: A superb production of unerring taste. . .a visual joy as well as brightened by excellent singing."

—*Philadelphia Inquirer*

Iolanthe: "One of the chief strongholds of G&S traditions in this country and the audience last night had a fine time."

—*Philadelphia Evening Bulletin*

Princess Ida: "A production that is a treat to both eye and ear . . . skillful, handsome, imaginative and tasteful."

—*Philadelphia Inquirer*

The Mikado: "A superlative production that is a gem on all counts."
—*Philadelphia Inquirer*

Ruddigore: "Whether in one of the favorites or, as in this case, one of the lesser known works, this company is first-rate in every respect."

—*Philadelphia Inquirer*

Yeomen of the Guard: "Rousing and beautiful, rich in comedy and subtle balance put over with real finesse."

—*Philadelphia Evening Bulletin*

The Gondoliers: "An evening that was so absorbing it went by almost too quickly."

—*Philadelphia Evening Bulletin*

Utopia Ltd.: "As is true of this company, it made this gentle parade of wit seem better than it may be. It has the fine tone of absurdity which this production catches and holds."

—*Philadelphia Inquirer*

The Grand Duke: "A true rarity, some say justifiably, but this show belies that assessment. The Gilbert & Sullivan Players give it their all in singing and acting, and in beauty and good taste."

—*Philadelphia Inquirer*

"Bruce Montgomery's direction of a Gilbert and Sullivan production carries just about the same sterling assurance as does Music from Marlboro for chamber concerts."

—*Philadelphia Inquirer*

Acknowledgments

It is very difficult to come up with a list of acknowledgments for a volume such as this. Every paragraph on every page is there because of the special deeds or experiences of the many, many people who made the entire narrative happen in the first place. Consequently, every page actually is a litany of acknowledgments and each person or organization should so consider himself, herself, itself. (English, however wonderful, is an awkward language when one writes a sentence such as that.)

But in addition to the mentions in the body of the text, some individuals deserve special recognition here for those extra tasks performed and that special support shown to make this project actually happen.

I'd like to single out, therefore, eight individuals who did me Herculean service by reading the text before it was submitted to the publisher. Their wise counsel was deeply appreciated even though I did not always incorporate their every suggestion into the final draft. Deep thanks for this special service are extended to Constance Cook, Stephen Goff, Michel Huber, Samuel Hughes, Erik Nordgren, Brendan O'Brien, Gregory Suss, and Elizabeth Thomas. It's a better book because of them.

Thank you Christopher Pohl, Graeme Frazier, and Nicholas Thomas, Jr., for saving my sanity when my computer raced on beyond my ken and capabilities to control it.

Thank you Erik Nordgren for lending me continuing support as well as several of the photographs that illustrate these chapters.

Thank you Marguerite Miller, Samuel Hughes, Stuart Wilson, and Vic Perleman for helping me with some dates and the seeking of photo release permissions about which I had a question or two.

Thank you Pamelyn Jones for checking some information for me in the records of the Curtis Institute of Music.

Thank you Ty Furman for making it possible for me to peruse material in several of your filing cabinets to verify some titles and dates.

Thank you Ronald Shapiro and your fine Campus Copy Service for so generously making the copies that were submitted to the necessary people prior to publication.

Thank you to the University of Pennsylvania Press for believing in this rambling labor of love, and for your expertise, care, and tireless effort to see it happen.

But—and the thanks and devotion are manifest throughout the book—the University of Pennsylvania Glee Club deserves more thanks than a dozen volumes could state. You often have said publicly "We love the Big Lug!" The Big Lug loves you back more than he is capable of expressing.

And this is my attempt at proving it.

A good number of the photographs that appear in this book are by the author, members of the Penn Glee Club, or unknown photographers, taken informally with no thought at the time of their appearing in a book. The anonymity of these photographers has made it impossible to credit many pictures to their individual takers. Each of these is deeply appreciated, however, and it is my hope that those who recognize their own work will take satisfaction in the fact that they have added substantially to the interest of the book and will accept my gratitude for being an important part of it.

To those photographers who can be identified by information on the backs of their images, I express my very deep appreciation not only for granting permission to reprint their work in these pages but, in each instance, for having done so gratuitously with only the printed credit being required.